# Better Together

Blending the Science of Reading and
Professional Learning Communities at Work®

George Georgiou     Greg Kushnir

*Foreword By Mike Mattos*

Solution Tree | Press

Copyright © 2025 by Solution Tree Press

Materials appearing here are copyrighted. With one exception, all rights are reserved. Readers may reproduce only those pages marked "Reproducible." Otherwise, no part of this book may be reproduced or transmitted in any form or by any means (electronic, photocopying, recording, or otherwise) without prior written permission of the publisher.

555 North Morton Street
Bloomington, IN 47404
800.733.6786 (toll free) / 812.336.7700
FAX: 812.336.7790

email: info@SolutionTree.com
SolutionTree.com

Visit **go.SolutionTree.com/literacy** to download the free reproducibles in this book.

Printed in the United States of America

Library of Congress Cataloging-in-Publication Data

Names: Georgiou, George (Professor of educational psychology), author. | Kushnir, Greg, author.
Title: Better together : blending the science of reading and professional learning communities at work / George Georgiou and Greg Kushnir.
Description: Bloomington, IN : Solution Tree Press, 2025. | Includes bibliographical references and index.
Identifiers: LCCN 2024043289 (print) | LCCN 2024043290 (ebook) | ISBN 9781958590751 (paperback) | ISBN 9781958590768 (ebook)
Subjects: LCSH: Reading (Elementary)--Canada. | Professional learning communities--Canada. | Reading, Psychology of.
Classification: LCC LB1573 .G398 2025  (print) | LCC LB1573  (ebook) | DDC 372.40971--dc23/eng/20250117
LC record available at https://lccn.loc.gov/2024043289
LC ebook record available at https://lccn.loc.gov/2024043290

---

**Solution Tree**
Jeffrey C. Jones, CEO
Edmund M. Ackerman, President

**Solution Tree Press**
*Publisher:* Kendra Slayton
*Associate Publisher:* Todd Brakke
*Acquisitions Director:* Hilary Goff
*Editorial Director:* Laurel Hecker
*Art Director:* Rian Anderson
*Managing Editor:* Sarah Ludwig
*Copy Chief:* Jessi Finn
*Production Editor:* Gabriella Jones-Monserrate
*Proofreader:* Elijah Oates
*Text and Cover Designer:* Laura Cox
*Content Development Specialist:* Amy Rubenstein
*Associate Editor:* Elijah Oates
*Editorial Assistant:* Madison Chartier

# Acknowledgments

We would like to thank Ms. Tara Kushnir for her comments on earlier drafts of this book and Dr. Kristy Dunn for her suggestions on the activities included in our lesson plans. Finally, we are indebted to the many teachers and principals who have worked closely with us to change the culture and reading practices of their schools for the benefit of their students.

Solution Tree Press would like to thank the following reviewers:

Becca Bouchard
    Educator
    Calgary, Alberta, Canada

Courtney Burdick
    Apprenticeship Mentor Teacher
    Spradling Elementary, Fort Smith
      Public Schools
    Fort Smith, Arkansas

Gina Cherkowski
    Education Researcher
    Headwater Learning
    Calgary, Alberta, Canada

Doug Crowley
    Assistant Principal
    DeForest Area High School
    DeForest, Wisconsin

John D. Ewald
    Educator, Consultant, Presenter,
      Coach, Retired Superintendent,
      Principal, Teacher
    Frederick, Maryland

Laurie Warner
    PLC Trainer
    Deer Valley Unified School District
    Phoenix, Arizona

Visit **go.SolutionTree.com/literacy** to download
the free reproducibles in this book.

# Table of Contents

*Reproducibles are in italics.*

About the Authors. . . . . . . . . . . . . . . . . . . . . . . . . . . . . . . . ix
Foreword. . . . . . . . . . . . . . . . . . . . . . . . . . . . . . . . . . . . . . xi
Introduction. . . . . . . . . . . . . . . . . . . . . . . . . . . . . . . . . . . . 1
    How We Came Together . . . . . . . . . . . . . . . . . . . . . . . . . 2
    The Purpose of This Book . . . . . . . . . . . . . . . . . . . . . . . . 2
    About This Book. . . . . . . . . . . . . . . . . . . . . . . . . . . . . . . 3

## Part 1: Literacy Instruction at the Leadership and Teams Level. . . . . . . . . . . . . . . . . . . . . . . . . . . . . . 7

    For Teachers: Understanding How Leadership Decisions Shape
        Literacy Instruction . . . . . . . . . . . . . . . . . . . . . . . . . . . 8
    For Leaders: Creating Systems That Support Effective Literacy Instruction. . 8

### 1 The Case for Change . . . . . . . . . . . . . . . . . . . . . . . . . . 9
    The Reading Wars . . . . . . . . . . . . . . . . . . . . . . . . . . . . . 11
    The Science of Reading . . . . . . . . . . . . . . . . . . . . . . . . . 13
    School-Based Solutions . . . . . . . . . . . . . . . . . . . . . . . . . 16
    Conclusion . . . . . . . . . . . . . . . . . . . . . . . . . . . . . . . . . 19

### 2 Successful Schoolwide Implementation of the Science of Reading . . . . . . . . . . . . . . . . . . . . . . . . . . . . . . . . . 21
    Teacher Isolation and Learning Loss . . . . . . . . . . . . . . . . . 22
    Scripted Versus Adaptive Instruction . . . . . . . . . . . . . . . . . 24
    Motivation for Change . . . . . . . . . . . . . . . . . . . . . . . . . . 26
    A Professional Learning Community . . . . . . . . . . . . . . . . . 27
    Meaningful and Attainable Reading Goals . . . . . . . . . . . . . 33
    Conclusion . . . . . . . . . . . . . . . . . . . . . . . . . . . . . . . . . 36

# 3 A System for Transitioning Schools to Evidence-Based Reading Practices . . . . . . . . . . . . . . . . . . . . . . .39

Form a Guiding Coalition . . . . . . . . . . . . . . . . . . . . . . . 40
Facilitate Job-Embedded Professional Development . . . . . . . . . 42
Use Schoolwide Norm-Referenced Assessment Data . . . . . . . . . 47
Find a Time for Intervention . . . . . . . . . . . . . . . . . . . . . . 51
Ensure Reciprocal Accountability . . . . . . . . . . . . . . . . . . . 53
Conclusion . . . . . . . . . . . . . . . . . . . . . . . . . . . . . . . 54

# 4 The Work of Teacher Teams . . . . . . . . . . . . . . . . . . . .57

Answer Question 1: What Is It We Want Our Students to Know
and Be Able to Do? . . . . . . . . . . . . . . . . . . . . . . . . . 58
Answer Question 2: How Will We Know If Each Student Has Learned It?. . 70
Answer Question 3: How Will We Respond When Some Students
Do Not Learn It? . . . . . . . . . . . . . . . . . . . . . . . . . . 75
Answer Question 4: How Will We Extend the Learning for Students
Who Have Demonstrated Proficiency? . . . . . . . . . . . . . . . 80
Plan Units of Instruction . . . . . . . . . . . . . . . . . . . . . . . . 80
Use the Science of Reading in Lesson Design . . . . . . . . . . . . . 81
Conclusion . . . . . . . . . . . . . . . . . . . . . . . . . . . . . . . 84

# Part 2: Classroom Implementation Using The Science of Reading . . . . . . . . . . . . . . . . . . . . . . 89

For Teachers: Applying Research-Based Instructional Practices
For Student Reading Success . . . . . . . . . . . . . . . . . . . . 89
For Leaders: Ensuring Schoolwide Implementation of Effective Reading
Practices . . . . . . . . . . . . . . . . . . . . . . . . . . . . . . 90

# 5 Phonological Awareness . . . . . . . . . . . . . . . . . . . . . .91

The Meaning of Phonological and Phonemic Awareness . . . . . . . . 92
Why We Should Teach Phonological Awareness . . . . . . . . . . . . 93
How to Assess Phonological Awareness . . . . . . . . . . . . . . . . 96
How to Teach Phonological Awareness . . . . . . . . . . . . . . . . 98
Conclusion . . . . . . . . . . . . . . . . . . . . . . . . . . . . . . .102

# 6 Phonics . . . . . . . . . . . . . . . . . . . . . . . . . . . . . . .105

The Meaning of Phonics . . . . . . . . . . . . . . . . . . . . . . . .106
Why We Should Teach Phonics . . . . . . . . . . . . . . . . . . . .106
How to Assess Phonics . . . . . . . . . . . . . . . . . . . . . . . .107
How to Teach Phonics . . . . . . . . . . . . . . . . . . . . . . . . .111
Conclusion . . . . . . . . . . . . . . . . . . . . . . . . . . . . . . .115

# 7 Fluency . . . . . . . . . . . . . . . . . . . . . . . . . . . . . . .117

The Meaning of Reading Fluency . . . . . . . . . . . . . . . . . . .118
Why We Should Teach Reading Fluency . . . . . . . . . . . . . . . .119
Prerequisite Skills for Fluency . . . . . . . . . . . . . . . . . . . . .120
How to Assess Reading Fluency . . . . . . . . . . . . . . . . . . . .121
How to Teach Reading Fluency . . . . . . . . . . . . . . . . . . . .127
Conclusion . . . . . . . . . . . . . . . . . . . . . . . . . . . . . . .131

Table of Contents | vii

## 8 Vocabulary . . . . . . . . . . . . . . . . 133
The Meaning of Vocabulary . . . . . . . . . . . 133
Why We Should Teach Vocabulary . . . . . . . . 134
How to Assess Vocabulary . . . . . . . . . . . 138
How to Teach Vocabulary . . . . . . . . . . . . 141
Conclusion . . . . . . . . . . . . . . . . . . 148

## 9 Reading Comprehension . . . . . . . . . . . 151
The Meaning of Reading Comprehension . . . . . . 152
Why We Should Teach Reading Comprehension . . . 152
How to Assess Reading Comprehension . . . . . . 152
How to Teach Reading Comprehension . . . . . . . 158
What to Teach Before, During, and After Reading . . . 162
Conclusion . . . . . . . . . . . . . . . . . . 165

## Epilogue . . . . . . . . . . . . . . . . . . . 169

## Appendix A: Phonological Awareness Lesson Plans . . . 171
*Syllable Clap* . . . . . . . . . . . . . . . . 172
*Onset and Rime Time* . . . . . . . . . . . . . 173
*Where's the Sound?* . . . . . . . . . . . . . . 177
*Say the Sound* . . . . . . . . . . . . . . . . 181
*Blend It!* . . . . . . . . . . . . . . . . . . 185
*Take Away* . . . . . . . . . . . . . . . . . 190
*Sound Count* . . . . . . . . . . . . . . . . 194
*Sound Switch* . . . . . . . . . . . . . . . . 200

## Appendix B: Phonics Lesson Plans . . . . . . . . 205
*Sorting Words* . . . . . . . . . . . . . . . . 206
*Tap, Map, Blend* . . . . . . . . . . . . . . . 214

## Appendix C: Fluency Lesson Plans . . . . . . . . 221
*Onset and Rime* . . . . . . . . . . . . . . . 222
*Sentence Fluency* . . . . . . . . . . . . . . 228
*Emphasize It!* . . . . . . . . . . . . . . . . 233
*Punctuation Practice* . . . . . . . . . . . . . 235

## Appendix D: Vocabulary Lesson Plans . . . . . . . 239
*Building Vocabulary* . . . . . . . . . . . . . . 240
*Name the Word Family* . . . . . . . . . . . . 242
*Understanding Morphemes* . . . . . . . . . . . 244

## Appendix E: Reading Comprehension Lesson Plans . . . 247
*Summarizing Text* . . . . . . . . . . . . . . 248
*Making the "Clunk" Click* . . . . . . . . . . . 250

## Glossary of Terms . . . . . . . . . . . . . . 253

## References and Resources . . . . . . . . . . . 261

## Index . . . . . . . . . . . . . . . . . . . . 283

# ABOUT THE AUTHORS

**George Georgiou** is a full professor in the Faculty of Education at the University of Alberta and the director of the J. P. Das Centre on Developmental and Learning Disabilities. In the past, George also worked as an elementary school teacher and as an advisor to Alberta Education. His research focuses on the prevention and remediation of reading difficulties across ages and languages. He has also been examining the developmental dynamics between environmental (that is, home literacy environment) and affective (that is, motivation) factors with literacy acquisition.

George has received several research awards in his career. In 2015, he received the prestigious Richard E. Snow Award from the American Psychological Association (Division 15); in 2018, the Alberta Teachers' Association Educational Research Award; in 2020, the Killam Professorship; and in 2024, the Confederation of Alberta Faculty Associations (CAFA) Distinguished Academic Award. Because of the impact of his work on the society, in 2018 he was inducted into the Royal Society of Canada, and in 2022 he received the Queen Elizabeth II Platinum Jubilee Medal.

George received a bachelor's degree in primary education from the University of Cyprus and master's and doctorate degrees in educational psychology from the University of Alberta.

**Greg Kushnir** is an educational leader and presenter with over three decades of dedicated service in public education. He earned both his bachelor's and master's degrees from the University of Alberta, specializing in oral language, reading, and writing disabilities. This foundational expertise has fueled his lifelong commitment to enhancing educational outcomes for all students. Throughout his career in Edmonton Public Schools in Alberta, Canada, Greg consistently demonstrated exemplary leadership and a deep commitment to educational excellence. He has led three schools: Terrace Heights

Elementary School, Ellerslie Campus, and Esther Starkman School. Under his guidance, each was transformed into a Model Professional Learning Community (PLC) at Work® and acclaimed for dramatic improvements in student achievement. This remarkable transformation is a testament to his visionary leadership and his ability to effectively implement educational strategies that foster significant and sustainable improvement.

Greg's contributions to education have been widely recognized. He has been nominated for educational excellence in Alberta four times. In 2010, his innovative approaches were honored with the Alberta ASCD Award for Innovative Practice. Furthermore, in 2014, he was a nominee for the Learning Partnerships Award of Excellence, distinguishing him as one of Canada's outstanding principals.

Since 2005, Greg has also excelled as an educational consultant. His expertise is particularly focused on helping schools develop the culture of a PLC, enhancing response to intervention (RTI) systems, and supporting the improvement of priority schools. His work in these areas has not only bolstered the operational success of numerous schools but also significantly enriched the educational experiences of countless students.

To book George Georgiou or Greg Kushnir for professional development, contact pd@solutiontree.com.

# FOREWORD
By *Mike Mattos*

Have you ever traveled to a country where you have no understanding of the native language? Every sign you read or menu you peruse is unintelligible. Directions from helpful strangers are incomprehensible. Simple daily tasks can become monumental challenges. If you have faced this experience, how did it make you feel—incompetent, overwhelmed, apprehensive, helpless? This is the same experience that students have at school when they can't read.

Reading is the language of learning. When students can competently turn symbols into words and meanings, the entire curriculum opens up to them. They are not dependent on others to translate critical information and instead are empowered to lead their own learning. Helplessness is replaced with confidence, apprehension with efficacy. Building strong literacy skills has a profound impact on overall brain development, future success in school, and lifelong learning (Hanover Research, 2016; Voyager Sopris Learning & Hasbrouck, 2023). The best way to ensure all students succeed in school is to get every student reading early, often, and well.

Literacy skills are also essential for our students in their adult lives. There is a strong correlation between literacy skills and higher wages (Hughson, 2022). Margaret L. Kern and Howard S. Friedman (2008) find that early literacy skills are accurate predictors of lifelong academic achievement and longevity, while illiteracy is a strong indicator of future incarceration (Thompson, 2022). The difference between being literate and being illiterate is quite literally the difference between thriving and surviving, imprisonment and freedom, life and death.

And collectively, an argument can be made that the abilities to read and write are the most important cognitive skills that humans have developed. We are the only species that communicates through a written language. Historians delineate our ancestors' development of a written form of communication as the difference between history and prehistory. Sharing information through symbols—instead of solely through an oral tradition—caused human knowledge to expand exponentially, as ideas could spread across communities, countries, and generations much more quickly and dynamically. This power has only magnified with the internet and the World Wide Web—a nearly endless amount of information at our fingertips for those who can accurately read and comprehend it.

With such life-altering consequences in the balance, how can we ensure every student becomes a confident reader? The ability to read involves discrete skills that cannot be self-taught, unlike learning how to play the piano by ear. You can't surround students with lots of quality books and expect them to break the code on their own. Literacy skills must be purposely and effectively taught and practiced. And while students certainly benefit from early exposure to reading at home, professional educators are best trained and positioned to ensure every student learns how to read effectively.

As professionals who have been tasked with this lifesaving work, we have an obligation to commit to the practices proven most effective. To this end, viewing the research from two perspectives is critical. The first is at the micro level: Which specific instructional practices are proven to work best? Luckily, over the past three decades, more research has been conducted in the teaching of reading than in any other subject. This has created a base of research—the science of reading—that provides educators with proven pedagogy to teach specific literacy skills. If every student receives highly effective reading instruction every school day, more students will become literate.

The second perspective is the macro level: How would we organize a school—or district—to ensure that the entire faculty develops collective efficacy of best teaching practice? Buying a research-based instructional program and expecting teachers to follow it with fidelity is counterproductive to this outcome. Instead, it requires an ongoing, collaborative process that ensures adult learning—it requires educators to function as a true professional learning community (PLC). Being a PLC is a never-ending process in which educators commit to working together to ensure higher levels of learning for every student. They achieve this outcome by learning together about the best practices proven to increase student learning, applying what they have learned, and using actual evidence of student learning to make decisions and revisions in practice to help even more students learn at higher levels (Mattos, DuFour, DuFour, Eaker, & Many, 2016). To this end, educators work collaboratively to determine the following (adapted from DuFour et al., 2024).

1.  What are the essential literacy standards that all students must learn?

2.  How will we know that every student is learning these essential literacy skills?

3.  What will we do if some students are not learning these literacy skills?

4.  What will we do when students have learned the literacy skills to stretch them further?

Continuously answering and reconsidering these four critical questions guides adult learning and unites a school's collective efforts to ensure all students become literate.

The purpose of this outstanding book is to help educators leverage the micro and the macro—the science of reading and the PLC process—to ensure all students become literate. These processes are complementary. A true PLC seeks out best practice—the science of reading. And even if a teacher is well versed in the science of reading, there is no way an individual teacher has all the time, skills, and knowledge to ensure every student becomes literate. It will require a schoolwide, collaborative process in which students benefit from the collective knowledge and skills of the entire staff: the PLC process. The authors represent the collective power of these two processes. George Georgiou is an expert in the science of reading, and Greg Kushnir is a leading authority in PLCs. Equally important, they are practitioners who understand how to transform powerful research into specific, doable actions.

I thank you for investing your precious professional time to read this exceptional book. A student who cannot read is like an eagle with a broken wing—endless blue skies above but unable to fly. We can change that!

# INTRODUCTION

How can I teach my students to read? What are some evidence-based instructional practices I could use to teach reading? What reading assessments shall I use? How do I know my students are progressing well? What should I do if my students are not progressing as expected in reading? If you are having the same questions, you are not alone. These are questions we have heard over and over again in our own practice, and we aim to provide you with answers in this book.

*Better Together* comes at a crucial point in time as schools face three significant obstacles in their endeavors to develop proficient readers. First, the number of students reading at proficiency level has decreased significantly from the years 2000 to 2024. For example, the number of students in Alberta achieving Level 1 (functionally illiterate) has doubled from 7.9 percent in 2000 to 14.7 percent in 2022 according to data from the Programme for International Student Assessment (PISA; OECD, 2023). Second, teachers graduating from most universities or colleges feel ill prepared to teach reading and address the needs of their diverse learners. In fact, several studies show that most teachers (pre-service and in-service) have limited knowledge of the language and literacy constructs their students need to become competent readers (Fielding-Barnsley, 2010; Parrila, Inoue, Dunn, Savage, & Georgiou, 2024; Washburn, Binks-Cantrell, Joshi, Martin-Chang, & Arrow, 2016). Finally, Human Rights Commission reports for the right to read made their appearance, and specific states in the United States (like Ohio) have banned certain reading programs, as they have been found to be ineffective in improving struggling readers' performance (Chapman & Tunmer, 2015; Hansford, Dueker, Garforth, Grande, King, & McGlynn, 2024).

In the midst of all this, there is a body of research, often collectively referred to as *the science of reading*, that tells us what practices are effective in improving students' reading performance. *Better Together* aims to bring this knowledge to every teacher by providing multiple examples of how teachers can assess and teach the necessary foundational literacy skills to their students. In addition, this book provides a framework for schools to follow that allows them to address and overcome the significant challenges faced when managing a change like shifting to structured literacy. Combining the knowledge contained within the science of reading with a framework that guides school leadership teams toward successful implementation is what makes this book unique.

## How We Came Together

Good things can happen when you mow your lawn. That could be the headline of the story that led to this book. On a beautiful summer day, George, who had just moved to his new house in Edmonton, went out to mow his lawn. Greg, living in the house next door, also went out to mow his lawn, and we introduced ourselves as new neighbors. After George mentioned he is a professor in the Faculty of Education at the University of Alberta specializing in the teaching of reading assessment and intervention, Greg, a principal at that time in one of Edmonton's largest K–9 schools, reacted by asking a blunt question: "How come you guys do not produce anything useful that teachers can use in their class to improve students' reading performance?" That very direct question caught George by surprise, as he certainly did not expect such a "welcoming" first interaction with his new neighbor.

Greg's provocative question marked the beginning of a beautiful journey in teacher training, resource development, program implementation, and policy advocacy that changed many things about how we teach reading and how we assess and intervene with students who struggle in learning to read. Fourteen years after that first question, we wrote this book together.

## The Purpose of This Book

When people ask us if our book is tailored toward teachers or principals, our answer is always the same: Yes! What we have learned through our experience working with schools is that teacher practice and improved reading outcomes don't occur when we compartmentalize knowledge. Changing ineffective reading instruction and shifting long-held beliefs regarding how students learn to read is a collaborative effort. Both principals and teachers must learn about the science of reading alongside each other if successful implementation is to be realized.

Chapters 1 through 4 of this book deal with two fundamental questions. First, Why should we change? And second, How should we implement the change at the leadership level? Traditionally, teachers would see the first four chapters as an administrative responsibility, especially if they view their administrators as the sole instructional leaders of the school. However, instead of waiting to be told what to do, we advocate for teachers to be active participants in leading the implementation efforts of the school. For this distributed leadership to occur, teachers need to understand not only why change is necessary but also what steps the school must take to facilitate the successful transition of reading instruction. Teacher participation in the decision-making process is essential if we want teachers to commit to changing their reading instruction and take ownership of improving student reading outcomes.

Chapters 5 through 9 address the question of *how* we should change by offering direct instruction for educators. These chapters provide a comprehensive look at the evidence-based instruction, assessment, and intervention outlined in the science of reading. Traditionally, administrators would view this information as solely belonging to the domain of teachers, and as a result, they may shy away from learning about the science because they are not responsible for providing classroom instruction. However, we argue that this information is vital for administrators as well. How can they effectively lead a change in reading instruction based on the science of reading if they have no knowledge of what the science tells us? Administrators have an obligation to learn about effective reading instruction so they can monitor implementation, determine instructional effectiveness, and identify areas where teachers need support. Learning alongside teachers about the science of reading sends a powerful message to staff regarding the priorities of the school. This act communicates to teachers that not only is it important for them to learn and implement evidence-based reading instruction, but the administration will walk with them as they do.

We consider our book to be a bridge between the science of reading and educational practice. If the science outlines a clear pathway to reading success, then teachers and administrators need to possess the knowledge it contains. We were intentional in bringing together the knowledge we have gained by working together to move the needle on literacy instruction in K–12 education. This book provides a pathway for teachers, principals, schools, and districts that hope to improve reading outcomes for the students they serve.

## About This Book

*Better Together* is split into two parts: The first four chapters present information on why we need to change our reading instruction and how the PLC process can ensure it happens. Chapters 5 through 9 present each of the five pillars of literacy instruction as identified by the National Reading Panel (phonological awareness, phonics, reading fluency, vocabulary, and reading comprehension). Each of these chapters discusses why the construct is important for reading, how to assess it (presenting both informal and formal assessments as well as individualized and group assessments), and how to teach it to the whole classroom by providing multiple examples of lesson plans. Importantly, wherever applicable, we also offer a scope and sequence that teachers can follow in teaching these skills. A description of each chapter is provided here.

**Chapter 1, "The Case for Change,"** outlines the critical importance of literacy as a basic human right and points out that reading performance in K–12 schools leaves much to be desired in ensuring this right. We challenge traditional and ineffective instructional approaches to reading and provide a case for the adoption of reading practices supported by research in the science of reading. We present an overview of what the science tells us about effective reading instruction.

**Chapter 2, "Successful Schoolwide Implementation of the Science of Reading,"** addresses the importance of having an implementation strategy to ensure the successful adoption of the science of reading. The implementation strategy must break down teacher isolation, address ongoing teacher learning, provide an opportunity to develop teacher motivation, and build a culture of continuous improvement. We recommend adopting the Professional Learning Communities at Work® (PLC) process developed by Richard DuFour and colleagues (2024) as a model for successful implementation.

**Chapter 3, "A System for Transitioning Schools to Evidence-Based Reading Practices,"** identifies the need for collaborative leadership. By establishing a guiding coalition comprised of both administrators and teachers, a school can take advantage of the collective talents of the team through distributed leadership. A framework is presented to help guide the work of the guiding coalition to ensure teacher teams are provided with the necessary supports to effectively change reading instruction.

**Chapter 4, "The Work of Teacher Teams,"** introduces the PLC process and how it can be used by teacher teams to learn about and implement the science of reading. To implement a structured approach to reading instruction, teams must build shared knowledge in curriculum, assessment, intervention, and extension. This process is used to reduce the variance of teacher effectiveness that exists when teachers work in isolation or are members of ineffective collaborative practices focused on the wrong work. Finally, we identify the need for good lesson design, outlining a framework supported by research that teachers can use to increase instructional effectiveness.

**Chapter 5, "Phonological Awareness,"** describes the first pillar of literacy instruction (that is, phonological awareness) and why it is important for literacy acquisition. We also provide a scope and sequence and recommendations on the frequency and length of each phonological awareness lesson. Finally, we describe formal and informal assessments of phonological awareness and provide sample lesson plans for the different phonological awareness subskills.

**Chapter 6, "Phonics,"** addresses phonics instruction. We start with a definition of phonics, and then we explain why it is important for literacy acquisition. Next, we provide a scope and sequence and recommendations on the frequency and length of each phonics lesson. Finally, we describe formal and informal assessments of phonics, and we provide examples of a phonics lesson.

**Chapter 7, "Fluency,"** focuses on reading fluency, which is often described as the most neglected component of literacy instruction. After defining fluency and describing why it is important for literacy acquisition, we review assessments of the different fluency components, and we provide examples of lesson plans for teaching fluency at the word and sentence level.

**Chapter 8, "Vocabulary,"** is devoted to vocabulary and elaborates on how teachers can select Tier 2 words to teach in an explicit manner. Similar to previous chapters, we provide recommendations on formal and informal assessments of vocabulary and a vocabulary lesson plan. Because of the close connection between vocabulary and morphological awareness, in this chapter we also review morphological awareness, and we specifically refer to Structured Word Inquiry (Bowers, 2009) as a way to teach bases and affixes.

**Chapter 9, "Reading Comprehension,"** focuses on the ultimate goal of reading, which is reading comprehension. Readers of this chapter will obtain information on the different ways of assessing comprehension and the complexities associated with each task. They will also learn about different comprehension strategies that they can practice with their students and two instructional approaches (collaborative strategic reading [CSR; Klingner, Vaughn, Argüelles, Hughes, & Ahwee Leftwich, 2004] and self-regulated strategy development [SRSD; Graham & Harris, 1993]) that involve different comprehension strategies.

Each chapter also features a "key readings and resources" section to provide access to some of the key works in the science of reading body of research, as well as links to active resources you may implement in your lessons.

Throughout this book, forward slashes // are used to indicate the sound of a particular letter. For example, when you see /p/, say the letter's sound, not the letter's name. Long vowel sounds are marked with a macron (that is, /ā/, /ē/, /ī/, /ō/, /ū/). In turn, short vowel sounds are marked with a breve over the letters (that is, /ă/, /ĕ/, /ĭ/, /ŏ/, /ŭ/).

At the end of this book, you'll find a full glossary of important terms featured throughout all nine chapters for your own use. Full lesson plans organized by pillar of literacy and grade level application are featured in appendices A–E. Each activity addresses a key component or skill meant to be learned sequentially as part of a science-of-reading-based learning curriculum.

We acknowledge that reading is a complex skill and the product of interactions between multiple subskills, including, but not limited to, interactions between genetics and environment. This book is not intended to address every possible skill that is associated with reading. Instead, we focus on the five pillars of literacy instruction, as their teaching has been found to exert the highest impact on students' reading performance. This book aims to effectively communicate the need to make data-informed decisions about teaching reading. Science clearly shows that if we learn and implement high-quality evidence-based reading instruction, we can effectively teach 95 percent of our students how to read at grade-appropriate levels (Fletcher & Vaughn, 2009; Torgesen, 2004). It is our intention, through the writing of *Better Together*, to make this a reality for every school.

# PART 1

# LITERACY INSTRUCTION AT THE LEADERSHIP AND TEAMS LEVEL

Part 1 of *Better Together* outlines why we need to change reading instruction and how we can ensure it happens. In chapter 1 (page 9), we highlight the historical pattern of poor reading performance in North America and explain how the "Reading Wars" shaped our current thinking regarding reading instruction. The chapter dispels common misconceptions about reading skills development and lays a foundation for good reading instruction. We discuss the need for schools to tackle poor reading performance at the school level and present a school that successfully improved reading by accepting ownership for improving reading outcomes.

Chapter 2 (page 21) acknowledges the difficulty of change and explores why this is a challenge. This chapter outlines common mistakes schools and districts make that impede improvement and points to alternatives that will facilitate a positive change in teacher practice. The case for schools to develop the culture of a PLC is presented as a pathway that any school can follow to facilitate a successful change to evidence-based reading instruction.

Chapter 3 (page 39) examines the need for schools to move away from top-down leadership models and instead embrace a distributed leadership model to guide the implementation process. PLCs do this through the formation of a guiding coalition that includes teacher participation and voice in leading the change in reading instruction. In this chapter, we outline how the guiding coalition can lead and monitor progress toward improved reading instruction by examining a process we have successfully used with numerous schools.

Finally, chapter 4 (page 57) outlines the work of teacher teams to ensure all teachers learn about the science of reading and develop the confidence and skills to successfully shift their reading instruction.

## For Teachers: Understanding How Leadership Decisions Shape Literacy Instruction

When reading the title of Part 1, teachers might mistakenly believe that the information contained in this section is not for them. However, we contend that if we are to improve reading instruction and change reading outcomes, we need to think differently about the role teachers play in the school improvement process. We have to move away from an improvement model where teachers are told what and how to improve and instead move toward a model where teachers see themselves as active participants. If we are to successfully improve reading instruction, teachers must view themselves as the instructional leaders in the school. Considering teachers are the group of people responsible for providing all of the instruction, it makes intuitive sense that they should share responsibility for leading instructional improvement in reading. The information contained in part 1 of *Better Together* will help teachers understand how we developed our current approach to reading, why we need to change, and how they can help lead their school's transformation to evidence-based reading instruction.

## For Leaders: Creating Systems That Support Effective Literacy Instruction

According to John Hattie (2023), creating the conditions for collective teacher efficacy to flourish is the number-one factor impacting student achievement in schools. However, fostering this belief in school staff can only happen if the work they are collaboratively engaged in moves the needle on student achievement. When it comes to making a difference, there is no skill we can teach our students that has a greater impact on learning than the ability to read at grade level. Therefore, it is vital that principals hoping to have more students become proficient readers facilitate the shift to evidence-based reading instruction outlined in the science of reading. Not only does part 1 of *Better Together* provide a clear rationale for change, but it outlines the necessary steps school leaders must take to make it happen. It identifies common mistakes schools make when trying to implement change and encourages principals to chart a different path forward by embracing the culture of a PLC. It is our hope that reading this section of the book creates both a sense of urgency for action and a sense of optimism that following the steps outlined will lead to sustained reading improvement for all students.

CHAPTER 1

# The Case for Change

In January 2022, the Ontario Human Rights Commission in Canada published the results of a public inquiry looking into the rights of students with reading disabilities in the Ontario school system. In the "Right to Read" inquiry report, they made a bold statement that literacy was so connected to positive societal outcomes that learning to read was not a privilege but instead a basic human right (Ontario Human Rights Commission, 2022). A year after Ontario, the Saskatchewan Human Rights Commission (2023) released their report, "Equitable Education for Students With Reading Disabilities," which drew basically the same conclusion. Both reports determined that grade-level reading proficiency is a cornerstone of academic success, serving as the gateway to a multitude of educational and professional opportunities.

Mastering reading skills at the appropriate grade level ensures students can comprehend and engage with age-appropriate texts across all subjects. As students progress through their academic years, their reading competence becomes a linchpin for unlocking the doors to a rich and diverse world of literature, scientific texts, historical documents, and mathematical problems. Students who are poor readers struggle to keep up and ultimately are disadvantaged compared to their peers with strong reading skills. Unfortunately, this disadvantage can set in motion a vicious cycle of academic failure, which leads many students to drop out of school (Hernandez, 2011; Lesnick, Goerge, Smithgall, & Gwynne, 2010). Moreover, in the world of work, strong reading skills are indispensable. They empower individuals to navigate complex documents, communicate effectively, and stay informed in a rapidly evolving global context. Therefore, students who leave high school without strong reading skills struggle to compete and support themselves in the literacy-rich modern world. Compared to high school graduates, high school dropouts make 30 percent less income, are six times more likely to be incarcerated, live up to thirteen years less, and cost the North American economy billions in social

> **As students progress through their academic years, their reading competence becomes a linchpin for unlocking the doors to a rich and diverse world of literature, scientific texts, historical documents, and mathematical problems.**

assistance programs each year. When considering the impact a skill such as reading can have on quality of life, it is easy to see why the Ontario Human Rights Commission has concluded not only that providing equitable access to learning to read is a basic human right, but that it provides an equal right to a future (Ontario Human Rights Commission, 2022).

Given the incredible importance of grade-level reading proficiency, it should not surprise us that federal, state, provincial, and local school boards spend large sums of money each year on literacy resources and teacher professional development in an attempt to improve their students' reading outcomes. In the 2018–2019 school year alone, the United States spent $800 billion on elementary and secondary public education. Included in that total was $56 billion for supplies, which includes reading resources, and $88 billion for services, which includes professional development for teachers (National Center for Education Statistics [NCES], n.d.b).

According to American Public Media, an independent investigative journalism organization, more money was spent on the purchase of English language arts resources than all other subjects in middle and high school combined (Peak, 2022). If dollars spent indicate the relative importance of the expenditure to the people spending the money, then one thing is abundantly clear: Educators understand the importance of ensuring students become strong readers. Unfortunately, despite the money being spent and the universal belief in the importance of reading, the outcomes for our students are underwhelming.

As part of their congressional mandate, the NCES in the United States periodically administers a nationwide reading assessment in order to gauge the current level of reading proficiency of grade 4 students. On the 2022 national report card, only 33 percent of students performed at or above the expected level of reading proficiency. While many may use this shockingly poor number to highlight the impact of the COVID-19 pandemic on students' academic achievement, this conclusion is inaccurate. In fact, reading rates have remained relatively unchanged; in the 30 years between 1992 and 2022, the number of proficient grade 4 readers ranged between a low of 29 percent and a high of 37 percent.

Is this a uniquely American problem, or are reading outcomes poor in Canada as well? National reading data are much harder to find in Canada, as there is no federal department of education; however, each province collects data on reading proficiency yearly on their Provincial Achievement Tests. As a case study, let's examine grade 6 reading proficiency in the province of Alberta. According to the Alberta Ministry of Education, 89.8 percent of grade 6 students achieved proficiency on the reading portion of the 2022 English Language Arts Achievement Test. On the surface this looks to be a very favorable result that aligns with research done by Joseph K. Torgesen in 2004. According to Torgesen (2004), approximately 95 percent of students should be able to learn to read if they are provided the right instruction. However, if we dig a little deeper into the data, there is cause for concern. The cutoff score used to determine the acceptable standard of proficiency is a score of 23 out of 50, which means that a student could fail this reading comprehension test and still be deemed a proficient reader. Understanding less than half of what was read should not be the benchmark for reading proficiency.

In the face of substantial investments of both time and financial resources aimed at enhancing reading scores, a perplexing question lingers: Why do reading outcomes often fall short of expectations? Despite the commendable efforts of teachers proficient in delivering reading instruction and the acknowledgment that 95 percent of students possess the capability to learn to read, the disconnect between investment and outcomes raises concerns. Perhaps we have been looking in the wrong place in our efforts to solve the reading achievement gap. Instead of blaming teachers or students, we contend that it's time to focus our attention on the ineffectiveness of current reading instruction. The predominant methodology for teaching reading in North America in 2025 is based on insufficient and ineffective practices rather than instruction based on research evidence. Teachers have been trained to deliver instruction that is having a disastrous impact on students' reading proficiency. Perhaps it is time to acknowledge that our profession has got it wrong and to truly embrace the extensive body of research outlining effective methods for teaching reading. This chapter offers a brief overview of the fraught history of literacy instruction, introduces the body of research known collectively as the science of reading, and argues for a change in the way we think about and approach literacy instruction internationally.

## The Reading Wars

Educators have long been engaged in a vigorous debate about how students learn to read and the best methods of teaching reading (Castles, Rastle, & Nation, 2018; Seidenberg, Borkenhagen, & Kearns, 2020). While this debate can trace its origins back to the beginnings of public schools, it picked up steam in the middle of the 1990s. The Reading Wars, as this debate became known, had two main characters who held opposing views on how to teach reading. On one side was Jeanne S. Chall, who published a synthesis of experimental reading studies titled *Learning to Read: The Great Debate* (1967). In this book, she concluded that better reading comprehension could be achieved when reading instruction emphasized *word decoding* (Chall, 1996). Decoding refers to a student's ability to recognize printed words by connecting the letters or groups of letters with the sounds they produce. Countering Chall's conclusion was Kenneth S. Goodman, who argued that reading did not require the explicit teaching and learning of letter-sound correspondences. Instead, learning to read was a psycholinguistic guessing game, where readers developed skill in "selecting the fewest, most productive cues necessary to produce guesses which are right the first time" (Goodman, 1967, p. 127). Goodman postulated that good readers did not have to decode words using letter-sound correspondences; instead, students should be taught to use "context clues and background knowledge to predict, confirm, and guess at the identification of new words" (J. Kim,

2008, p. 373). This whole language view of reading was influenced by the belief that reading development was a natural process akin to how people develop oral language. Whole language proponents labeled phonics instruction as tedious and unnecessary, while promoting their belief that a love of reading could be developed by simply immersing students in a literacy-rich environment. This was a compelling argument to teachers, and it gave them the freedom to move away from direct instruction of phonics and instead adopt a whole language approach in their classrooms. Throughout the 1980s and 1990s, momentum quickly gathered as a growing number of teachers adopted this approach (Ryan & Goodman, 2016). As more school districts and teachers moved to adopt whole language–based reading instruction, it seemed that in the minds of these educators the Reading Wars had a clear winner.

However, a group of reading researchers remained unswayed by the wave of enthusiasm behind the whole language movement. They continued to look at the growing body of evidence being accumulated through ongoing research that was painting a clearer picture of how to effectively teach reading and once again pushed back. By the middle of the 1980s, there was a growing concern regarding reading performance, as well as a growing acknowledgment that teaching reading should not be a "one side or the other" proposition. The publication of *Becoming a Nation of Readers* by the National Institute of Education (NIE) helped shift thinking by encouraging a more balanced approach to reading instruction (Anderson, Hiebert, Scott, & Wilkinson, 1985). Balancing out whole language instruction meant that teachers needed to provide direct instruction in both phonics and reading comprehension (Anderson, Hiebert, Scott, & Wilkinson, 1985). This idea of combining phonics intervention and whole language instruction became known as the "balanced literacy" approach to teaching reading and has influenced reading instruction and curriculum design from the 1990s through the 2020s.

Despite adopting balanced literacy as a "best of both worlds" approach, reading achievement in the classrooms in the United States and Canada never improved. Unfortunately, despite its name, it turns out that balanced literacy instruction was never really balanced but rather a rebranding of the whole language approach aiming to reduce criticism from the proponents of phonics instruction (Moats, 2000). While the guessing strategies from whole language instruction made their way into the balanced literacy approach, instruction in phonemic awareness and phonics was implicit rather than explicit. Balanced literacy and spin-off approaches like Leveled Literacy Intervention, Reading Recovery, and Readers Workshop have been heavily criticized for including too many elements of whole language instruction and too little of phonics instruction. It seems that the failed reading instruction of the 1970s and 1980s is still being used and is not any more effective than it was then. The real issue with reading instruction is not that we don't know how to effectively teach reading; it's that we have settled for popular practices instead of evidence-based practices.

## The Science of Reading

The science of reading is not a new program or one-size-fits-all philosophy, or even the latest educational fad. Instead, this term refers to the large body of scientific research conducted relating to the skill of reading. It outlines how humans learn to read, the breadth of skills required to become a proficient reader, and the most effective instructional strategies for teaching reading. Its scope extends past the field of education to include research from cognitive psychology, communication sciences, developmental psychology, education, special education, implementation science, linguistics, neuroscience, and school psychology (Reading League, 2022). The science of reading not only outlines how the brain connects oral and written language as it learns to read, but also provides clarity regarding how students should be taught. Understanding and incorporating the findings of this scientific research is the key to changing the reading fortunes of our students. To do this, we must understand how difficult it truly is for human beings to learn how to read and review the history of literacy policy based on the collective science of reading.

### Reading Is Not Natural

The production of human speech is a genetically endowed biological subsystem that has been part of the human condition for approximately 100,000 years (Berwick et al., 2013; Miyagawa, Berwick, & Okanoya, 2013). As a result, learning to communicate with oral language develops naturally, requiring nothing more than exposure to other humans who can speak. Conversely, written text has existed for only about 5,000 years, making reading and writing a relatively recent human development (Coulmas, 2003). Unlike oral language, evolution has not been as kind when it comes to communication via written text, as no innate genetic advantage is available when learning to read. This difference in evolutionary development makes reading a much more difficult task to learn than speaking and disproves the foundational premise of whole language reading instruction. It turns out that learning to read is not a natural process as Kenneth S. Goodman (1967), "Founding Father" of whole language, and his followers theorized. Learning to read is in fact a difficult task for most students.

### Instruction Is Key

Despite reading not being an innate ability, research suggests that 30 percent of students will learn to read regardless of how they are taught (Lyon, 1998). Considering proficiency levels have only hovered slightly higher than that since the 1990s, incorporating the learning found in the science of reading is long overdue. For the other 70 percent of students, exposure to quality reading instruction based on evidence of effectiveness will determine their reading proficiency. For these students to be successful, reading instruction must be structured, as this type of instruction "works best for students who must be taught how to read, write and use language: this is any student who cannot learn just from exposure to text or from incidental feedback" (Moats, 2020a, p. 254). A structured literacy approach would include the following five principles.

1. **Explicit:** Explicit instruction involves the teacher directly conveying the desired knowledge to the students. The teacher clearly and succinctly explains a concept, then demonstrates its application ("I do"), guides the students as they initially apply it ("we do"), and finally offers practice exercises ("you do") to ensure proficiency.

2. **Systematic and cumulative:** Systematic teaching is planned and follows a carefully designed sequence. This sequence introduces reading concepts and skills in an order that moves from simpler to more complex. Cumulative instruction builds on previously learned concepts and skills over time.

3. **Multimodal:** Instruction includes multiple modes of communication and expression including visual, audio, digital, kinesthetic, and textual.

4. **Diagnostic and responsive:** The teacher uses a variety of assessment methods to monitor student progress toward instructional goals and adjusts practice, pacing, and methodology accordingly. Assessment methods are varied and include observations of student work, conversations with students about learning, and students' products.

5. **Multilinguistic content:** Multiple layers of literacy are woven together in each lesson. For example, lessons are repeated and might include instruction on grapheme-phoneme correspondences, morphology, and comprehension of texts.

### Learning to Read Is Multifaceted

In 1997, Congress asked the National Institute of Child Health and Human Development (NICHD) and the U.S. Department of Education to study the current body of reading research to determine the best ways to teach reading. In 2000, the National Reading Panel released their findings in a report called *Teaching Students to Read: An Evidence-Based Assessment of Scientific Literature on Reading and Its Implications for Reading Instruction*. This definitive review of the science of reading clearly outlines that excellent reading instruction requires students to receive direct instruction in the following five key areas.

1. **Phonological awareness:** The ability to identify and manipulate the units of sound in a spoken language.

2. **Phonics:** The ability to understand the letter (graphemes) and sound (phonemes) correspondences in a language.

3. **Fluency:** The ability to read text accurately, at an appropriate speed, and with expression.

4. **Vocabulary:** The ability to increase the volume of words a person recognizes and comprehends when reading written text.

5. **Comprehension:** The ability to understand and make meaning of a variety of texts.

Moving the needle on reading proficiency will require teachers to provide effective and direct instruction in all five pillars while incorporating the principles of structured literacy. They must understand the relationship between the pillars at each grade level, as well as how the emphasis on each pillar changes throughout the grades. However, as pointed out by Jeffrey S. Bowers and Peter N. Bowers (2017), they also need to have a deep understanding of how their language and writing system works.

### Teaching Reading Requires Training

Unfortunately, this level of instructional knowledge is rather uncommon in North American classrooms. According to David A. Kilpatrick (2015), the problem begins with the inadequate training of pre-service teachers. In a study conducted by R. Malatesha Joshi and colleagues (2009), university professors tasked with preparing pre-service teachers were asked questions on their general philosophy for teaching reading, what causes students to suffer from poor reading ability, and their understanding of the effective reading instruction outlined by the National Reading Panel.

Regarding the most effective instructional approach to reading, 100 percent of respondents indicated that balanced literacy and whole language were the best approaches for classroom instruction. In addition, they failed to recognize that poor reading instruction was the cause of poor reading performance. Instead, they focused on low socioeconomic status, poor family background, and English as a second language as the leading causes. However, the most surprising result was their poor level of understanding of the science of reading. Only 20 percent of respondents were able to correctly answer basic questions like the definition of phonemic awareness (Joshi et al., 2009). Considering that this study was conducted sixteen years ago, it raises an important question: Is this still true? Are pre-service teachers still inadequately prepared to provide effective reading instruction grounded in science of reading?

Unfortunately, the North American reading data outlined earlier and more recent studies looking at teacher preparation programs point to a continuation of this issue (Ellis et al., 2023; Meeks, Madelaine, & Stephenson, 2020; Toste & Lindström, 2022; Xavier, 2022). For example, in a review of teacher preparation programs in the United States, Christie Ellis and colleagues (2023) found that only 25 percent of them were adequately addressing all five pillars of literacy instruction and that nearly one third of them did not provide any practice opportunities connected to the core components of reading. These studies confirm that the "Peter Effect" (Binks-Cantrell, Washburn, Joshi, & Hougen, 2012) continues to be a significant roadblock when preparing new teachers to provide evidence-based reading instruction. Based on a biblical verse, the Peter Effect states that you can't give what you don't have. In other words, pre-service teachers cannot provide effective reading instruction because they did not learn it at the university.

> Moving the needle on reading proficiency will require teachers to provide effective and direct instruction in all five pillars while incorporating the principles of structured literacy.

## School-Based Solutions

Even if all teacher preparation programs immediately began to teach pre-service teachers how to provide evidence-based reading instruction, it would still take decades for that shift to make its way into classrooms. In addition, relying on universities to change practice does nothing to solve our current reading instruction issues. In 2006, the Rose report was published in the United Kingdom. Written by Sir Jim Rose, the official title was the "Independent Review of the Teaching of Early Reading," and its purpose was to outline how the United Kingdom could improve reading through a systemic and structured approach that applied the science of reading. While the report confirmed that implementing effective reading instruction would require initial instruction for teachers on the five pillars, it also highlighted the need to provide ongoing professional development. The report acknowledged the pivotal role quality professional development would play in changing long-standing ineffective reading instruction.

However, the idea of improving classroom instruction through professional development is hardly a new concept for educators, as every year millions of dollars are spent on teacher professional development designed to improve instruction (Gore et al., 2017). Unfortunately, the long-term impact of this investment on instruction and student learning is questionable. As Robert J. Marzano, Timothy Waters, and Brian A. McNulty (2005) state, "Many, maybe even most, educational innovations are short-lived" (p. 65). Schools hoping to change their reading instruction must ask themselves a critical question: "How do we develop an effective approach to professional development so we can ensure our efforts aren't short lived?" According to Gemma E. Scarparolo and Lorraine S. Hammond (2018), achieving this goal will require a multifaceted professional development approach that takes into consideration several factors. First, teachers' current knowledge level must be considered, and professional development must be tailored to meet them where they are. Second, teacher attitudes toward the proposed change will impact their commitment to implementation. Therefore, time must be allocated to providing a clear rationale for why the change is necessary. Third, the administration must be all-in. Administrators communicate their commitment to the change through their actions. When principals are visible and attend professional development alongside their staff, they demonstrate their belief in its importance. Fourth, teachers must be provided with opportunities to practice, receive feedback, and learn with their colleagues. Finally, evidence of effectiveness must be gathered in the form of student performance data. These data must inform instructional practices. These observations build on earlier work by Kwang Suk Yoon, Teresa Duncan, Silvia Wen-Yu Lee, Beth Scarloss, and Kathy L. Shapley (2007) who examined studies that significantly impacted students' learning. Yoon and colleagues note that these studies share the following four characteristics.

1. Programs of professional development must extend for fourteen hours or more.

2. Experts or thoroughly prepared researchers should lead instruction.

3. There should be a modest number of participants, typically not more than forty-four, across one or a few school locations.

4. Schools should implement systems of ongoing support and feedback for the educators involved.

While these four characteristics provide an outline for effective professional development, specificity will help educators effectively apply them. Let us take a closer look at some more specific practices. In 2020, George K. Georgiou, Greg Kushnir, and Rauno Parrila (2020) sought clarity on the most impactful practices undertaken by language arts teachers at Esther Starkman School in Alberta, Canada. This school was unique in that the staff not only successfully shifted reading instruction to instruction based on the science of reading but also consistently improved students' reading outcomes over time. Language arts teachers were surveyed for the purpose of gathering their perspective on actions undertaken by the school to facilitate their successful shift in reading instruction. The questionnaire included sixteen items measuring support for factors that occurred both externally and within the school. The top ten are listed as follows.

1. Weekly collaborative team meetings focus on job-embedded professional development.

2. Grade-level teams give common formative assessments.

3. The school focuses on improving reading schoolwide.

4. Common team planning time is available outside the weekly requirement.

5. Schools use data to inform areas for growth, not evaluate teachers' performance.

6. School-based colleagues are available to support changes in reading practice.

7. The school believes in continuous improvement.

8. There is access to quality reading resources.

9. There is professional development focusing on the five pillars of reading.

10. The school has a reciprocal accountability process.

The results of this survey point to the multifaceted nature and complexity of developing a sustained improvement effort. However, the most interesting aspect of these results is the degree to which teachers valued school-based decisions and practices. Except for professional development on the five pillars provided by a literacy expert, the teachers attributed their success to factors under school control. Although it was important to participate in the information sessions on the five pillars, how the teachers interacted with the new knowledge back at the school was significantly more important.

*Teacher and Team Accountability*

For this job-embedded learning to occur, structures must be created to support the continuous learning required. First, there is a required belief in the power of ongoing weekly collaboration. By taking a team approach, teachers are able to learn together, support each other during implementation, and provide each other with continuous feedback on how to improve. Second, assessment must become predominantly formative in nature and be viewed as part of the instructional process instead of just a method of gathering grades. A substantial body of research (Frey & Fisher, 2009; Stiggins & DuFour, 2009; Yan & Chiu, 2023) demonstrates significant gains in student learning when formative assessment strategies are employed effectively. The frequent real-time data gathered from team-created common assessments allow them to evaluate the effectiveness of instruction and respond quickly to student learning needs. Third, the educators must embrace the need to not only improve reading instruction but see continuous improvement as a professional obligation. This common mission helps to keep major goals a priority, allowing for the discontinuation of competing initiatives. Finally, they must embrace the concept of reciprocal accountability. Teachers understand that for all students to achieve grade-level reading outcomes, they need to be accountable in three distinct ways.

1. Team accountability ensures that decisions made in collaboration with their colleagues are to be implemented in their classroom.

2. Grade-level accountability not only ensures that prerequisite skills are learned by every student before they move to the next grade, but also ensures a continuity of effective instructional practices based on the science of reading continued between grades.

3. School-level accountability ensures that teacher teams share their practices with the leadership team, allowing a team of educators to monitor progress, provide feedback, and offer necessary support.

*Professional Learning Communities*

Emulating the type of teacher efficacy demonstrated by Esther Starkman's language arts teachers should be the goal of any school effort. However, based on the many failed improvement efforts that litter the educational landscape, it is obviously easier said than done. Just like with reading instruction, we advocate following the research when attempting a school improvement initiative. Is there an approach that schools can embrace that has consistently provided successful outcomes across all demographics and socioeconomic conditions? Research consistently points to the operation of schools as PLCs, when they are developed properly, as the best pathway for schools to embrace teacher learning, implement effective instruction, and improve students' outcomes (Affandi, Ermiana, & Makki, 2019; Lutfia, Sa'ud, Nurdin, & Meirawan, 2022; Sigurðardóttir, 2010; Voelkel & Chrispeels, 2017). It is important to understand that developing the type of school culture that embraces the principles of adult learning, continuous improvement, and collective responsibility does not happen by chance. Instead, these cultures develop as a result of the deliberate actions of the adults in the school. This is why we advocate for schools that desire to become PLCs to follow a proven framework to guide their journey. PLCs are schools that prioritize using collective inquiry and action research to improve student achievement. To that end, it is our opinion that there is no more proven approach schools can follow for the successful development of a PLC than the PLC at Work process developed by DuFour and colleagues (2024). This is the process we use in our work with schools to implement the science of reading, and in subsequent chapters we will explore in greater detail how a school can implement the science of reading successfully using this process.

## Conclusion

There is no skill taught in school more important than reading. The consequences of poor reading are devastating for academic success and successful outcomes in life. Yet despite the acknowledgment of this fact and the amount of money and resources focused on closing the reading gap, our results have fallen far below expectations. If we are truly to change this result, educators must stop repeating harmful or ineffective practices. Whole language instruction and the reading approaches that have sprung up based on its theories need to be abandoned in favor of evidence-based practice. The science of reading clearly outlines the type of instruction, assessment, and intervention that needs to be embraced to ensure grade-level reading is a reality for all students. Changing practice won't be easy, and it won't happen by chance or in a heartbeat. Schools wanting to make this change will need to design an implementation strategy that not only provides teachers with the required knowledge on the five pillars but also supports the classroom implementation of learned skills. This book was written to help with both areas by providing the knowledge teachers need to learn and a process of implementation that will support a change in classroom instruction.

# Key Readings and Resources

- Ellis, C., Holston, S., Drake, G., Putman, H., Swisher, A., & Peske, H. (2023). *Teacher prep review: Strengthening elementary reading instruction*. Washington, DC: National Council on Teacher Quality.

- Georgiou, G., Kushnir, G., & Parrila, R. (2020). Moving the needle on literacy: Lessons learned from a school where literacy rates have improved over time. *Alberta Journal of Educational Research, 66*(3), 347-359. https://doi.org/10.55016/ojs/ajer.v66i3.56988

- Moats, L. C. (1999). *Teaching reading is rocket science: What expert teachers of reading should know and be able to do*. Washington, DC: American Federation of Teachers.

- Moats, L. C. (2000, October). *Whole language lives on: The illusion of "balanced" reading instruction*. Washington, DC: Thomas B. Fordham Foundation.

- National Reading Panel. (2000). *Teaching students to read: An evidence-based assessment of the scientific research literature on reading and its implications for reading instruction: Reports of the subgroups* (NIH Publication No. 00-4754). Washington, DC: National Institute of Student Health and Human Development. Accessed at https://www.nichd.nih.gov/sites/default/files/publications/pubs/nrp/Documents/report.pdf on October 27, 2024.

- Seidenberg, M. S., Borkenhagen, M., & Kearns, D. M. (2020). Lost in translation? Challenges in connecting reading science and educational practice. *Reading Research Quarterly, 55*(S1), S119-S130. https://doi.org/10.1002/rrq.341.

- Torgesen, J. K. (2004). Avoiding the devastating downward spiral: The evidence that early intervention prevents reading failure. *American Educator, 28*(3), 6-47.

CHAPTER 2

# Successful Schoolwide Implementation of the Science of Reading

The effectiveness of implementing new reading practices in a school hinges on the methods and strategies employed during the implementation process. How a school chooses to introduce and support the integration of new teacher learning can dramatically influence the success or failure of the initiative. School leaders must develop a plan for schoolwide implementation, and that plan may need to challenge the existing school culture to be successful (Kierstead, Georgiou, Mack, & Poth, 2023). For instance, if a school adopts a collaborative and inclusive strategy, where teachers are actively involved in the learning and adaptation of new methods, there is a higher likelihood of positive outcomes. This involves continuous professional development, shared decision making, and regular feedback loops that keep all stakeholders engaged and accountable. Conversely, a top-down approach, where new practices are mandated without sufficient teacher input and where teachers are expected to "go it alone," often leads to varied responses, minimal adoption, and poor sustainability. Thus, the chosen implementation strategy affects not only the initial uptake of evidence-based practices but also their long-term viability and effectiveness in enhancing reading outcomes. Before digging into a successful implementation framework, we feel that it is important to highlight why some of the most common improvement strategies often fail to have the desired impact. If improving reading instruction is the goal of your school's professional development efforts, avoiding these common mistakes will dramatically improve your chances of success.

## Teacher Isolation and Learning Loss

In his book *Schoolteacher*, Dan Lortie (2002) explains that the field of education suffers from a unique phenomenon he calls "the apprenticeship of observation." According to Lortie, teachers begin their first 12,000 hours of job training when they meet their kindergarten teacher on their first day of school. Each school day, our future teachers observe how their current teachers apply their craft. While they most likely observe teachers engaging in polite and cordial hallway conversations with other teachers, when classroom instruction starts, their teachers almost always work alone. Students watch their teachers be the sole decision makers regarding what to teach, how to teach, how long to teach, how to assess, and what constitutes grade-level proficiency. What our early apprenticeship does is help to reinforce isolated teacher practice as the operational and cultural norm for our profession.

> **When teachers work in isolation, there is a noticeable variation in educational quality across different classrooms within the same school.**

Research has consistently shown the detrimental effects that teacher isolation has on the quality of education. When teachers work in isolation, there is a noticeable variation in educational quality across different classrooms within the same school. Educational scholar Jorge A'vila de Lima (2003) of the Universidade dos A'cores, Portugal, points out that such isolation can lead to stagnant, less innovative, and less effective educational practices that fail to meet the diverse needs of students. Additionally, Judith Warren Little, Maryl Gearhart, Marnie Curry, and Judith Kafka (2003) emphasize that isolation limits teachers' access to varied teaching strategies and collaborative problem solving, reducing both student engagement and the vitality of classroom environments. Teacher isolation not only hinders teachers' professional efficacy and development but also leads to a decreased interest in their work (Rigelman & Ruben, 2012). Finally, Christa Spicer and Daniel B. Robinson (2021) observe that isolation contributes to increased burnout and a sense of disconnection from the educational community, which further diminishes teaching enthusiasm and quality. This makes teacher isolation a significant barrier that needs to be addressed for successful implementation of the science of reading to occur. Unfortunately, the organizational structure of the typical school promotes isolation as teachers spend much of their day working by themselves in their classroom. As a result, isolation in the field of education is viewed as a normal and often desirable practice, which is why professional development for teachers is often organized around this concept.

The downfall of many school implementation efforts is that they are designed to support the culture of teacher isolation. Take, for example, the traditional professional development day. All districts schedule days throughout the school year that are dedicated to the professional development of teachers. This is a universal strategy based on the idea that if we expose teachers to new ideas or instructional methods, we will change and improve practice. What seems like a good idea in theory turns out to be less effective in practice. Even a well-thought-out professional development session that incorporates hands-on practice activities designed to increase initial learning will impact each participant differently. How much a teacher learns will vary depending on their level of interest, level of engagement, level of self-efficacy, and amount of background knowledge and experience they have. This means that each participant leaves the session with a different level of content knowledge, which often results in a different level of willingness to incorporate the new learning. Some teachers will feel confident enough to give it a try, while others will not be willing to risk the uncertainty of how students will respond given their limited exposure and understanding of the new approach. Once again, relying on individual teachers to apply new knowledge creates a variable response, which is why one-day professional development sessions are ineffective as a strategy for universal change in practice.

Compounding the variance in learning and confidence level is the fact that after people participate in professional development, they almost immediately begin to forget what they learned. The "forgetting curve" is a graphical model created by German psychologist Hermann Ebbinghaus based on memory retention research (Murre & Dros, 2015). The forgetting curve demonstrates the rate teachers can be expected to forget anything they learned after their professional development session. Regardless of how much information was learned during the professional development, the forgetting curve begins the moment the session is over. Learning loss is largest in the first few days with participants forgetting up to 60 percent of their learning, and 90 percent after a month (Woolliscroft, 2020). However, the good news is that there is an antidote for the forgetting curve. The solution to learning loss is to immediately revisit the material and to continue to do so at regular intervals. Expecting all teachers to continually revisit the new knowledge presented and slow the forgetting curve on their own is unrealistic. The isolated work environment and the busyness of the teaching day don't afford teachers the opportunity or time to review what they learned. Instead of being left up to individual teachers, the discussion and instructional planning opportunity must be deliberately incorporated into the professional development plan by the school's educational leadership team. Teachers need to participate in continuous job-embedded learning at their school almost immediately after the initial learning takes place. Engaging in job-embedded collaboration allows teachers to share their perspectives as well as increase their understanding of the presented content and pedagogical strategies (Weedle et al., 2020). If school leaders fail to plan for this step, uncertainty on how to implement the new learning grows as the forgetting curve kicks in, causing teachers to fall back to their familiar practice.

Consider how this knowledge applies to your school's efforts as you implement the evidence-based reading instruction contained within the science of reading. Providing opportunities for teachers to learn about instruction, assessment, and intervention on each of the five pillars of reading is an important but insufficient first step. Increasing the amount of information teachers retain and, in turn, implement will require an organizational shift from isolation to collaboration. Providing weekly opportunities for meaningful collaboration is a powerful tool to combat the negative and often demoralizing impact of teacher isolation.

## Scripted Versus Adaptive Instruction

When implementing evidence-based reading instruction, it is important to understand what the science of reading is, but it is equally as important to understand what it is *not*. It is not a program! We mentioned this in chapter 1 (page 9), but understanding this concept is key, so we are mentioning it again: The science of reading is not a program! However, this does not mean that programs cannot be created based on the science. One of our goals in writing this book is to equip teachers with the knowledge they need to understand why they are being asked to change their instructional approach. Understanding the "why" behind a change helps to increase commitment and strengthen implementation (Razali, 2020). Therefore, we encourage schools and districts looking to implement the science of reading to abandon the "quick fix" in favor of building teacher knowledge and capacity by having them learn about the science rather than simply telling teachers to implement a program. As Louisa Moats (2000) nicely puts it, informed teachers are our best insurance against reading failure. Although programs are very helpful tools, programs don't teach; teachers do. Learning the science behind evidence-based reading instruction and applying this science effectively in a classroom will take some time. Teachers must be skillfully guided through this process using an implementation strategy that promotes teacher learning. When this is done well, teachers develop a sustained capacity to improve the reading performance of their students. To highlight the stark difference between these two different approaches in terms of the outcomes for teachers and students, we can consider the research on scripted versus adaptive instruction.

### Scripted Instruction

Scripted instruction is a method of teaching that uses predetermined scripts and lessons that teachers follow explicitly. We have worked in countless districts that believe they can reduce the complexity of teaching and learning down to one-size-fits-all instruction. This practice usually follows a predictable pattern. A district is dissatisfied with their reading results and has decided that something needs to be done. Rather than investing the time it takes to build teacher capacity through job-embedded collaborative practices, they contact several publishers of "high-quality instructional materials" so they can conduct a review of the resources and select a new resource to be implemented districtwide. Limited professional development is provided to the teachers regarding how to use the resource, but the teachers are told that they must teach the resource with "fidelity." Teachers are told that the resource is their curriculum (it's not) and that the resource aligns perfectly with their standards (it doesn't). Teachers begin to follow the script and quickly discover that this top-down, one-size-fits-all approach to instruction fails to take into consideration the diversity of learning needs of the students in their classroom or the differences from school to school (Ankrum et al., 2020). This can be especially detrimental for schools serving students in low socioeconomic neighborhoods, as the method of instruction can create a bigger problem, since the pace of instruction is often far too quick (Athanases, Bennett, & Wahleithner, 2015). Instead of ensuring learning, teachers become content coverers, leaving students behind and increasing gaps in foundational knowledge. This results in the exact opposite of what was intended; namely, it results in increased teacher frustration and poor student performance (Dresser, 2012). When scripted instruction fails to produce a desired result, rather than abandoning this approach, we have worked in districts that choose to double down. They assign a district instructional coach to meet weekly with a grade level of teachers so they can go over the script together, assuming the poor reading scores are a product of not teaching the script with enough fidelity rather than admitting to flawed methodology. Inevitably, this approach leads to the replacement of the resource with a different scripted resource, and the process begins again. To be fair, scripted instruction can serve a purpose if the script is better than the instruction it replaces. In these situations, following the script usually leads to a slight uptick in achievement that tapers off quickly (Dresser, 2012). If this is the approach schools take when implementing the science of reading, they are unlikely to see the gains in reading instruction they desire. Improving classroom practice will not happen if teachers are removed from the learning process, which is part of the reason why adaptive instruction is preferable.

### Adaptive Instruction

According to Margaret Vaughn (2019), "Adaptive teaching is considered a cornerstone of effective literacy teaching" (p. 1). Unlike scripted instruction, *adaptive instruction* aims to tailor classroom educational experiences to meet the diverse needs of learners from classroom to classroom. Teachers who provide this type of instruction possess the following characteristics (Vaughn, Parsons, Gallagher, & Branen, 2016).

- **Flexible:** They are flexible in their approach to learning. They understand that students in their classroom are unique and that ensuring grade-level reading for all will require a variety of instructional approaches tailored to the learners.

- **Data driven:** They are driven by data and use informal assessment of learning to determine the effectiveness of instruction. Educators who provide adaptive instruction can use data to make necessary instructional corrections.

- **Reflective:** They reflect on their practice and take proactive steps to continuously learn and improve.

In other words, they don't follow a script. They are teachers who have developed into highly skilled educators by learning how to provide instruction that places an emphasis on student learning instead of delivering canned instruction. Their decisions about the effectiveness of their instructional approach are based on formative assessment data collected during the instructional process. Based on the collection of real-time classroom data, they make course corrections in their instruction to ensure they are not continuing to consume valuable class time with ineffective reading instruction. This is the type of instructional skill that teachers need to develop if they want to effectively implement the science of reading. In chapters 5 through 9, we outline what research tells us about how to teach and assess reading. Applying this knowledge effectively requires a schoolwide commitment to building the organizational structures to support adult learning. Teachers need to dig into the research evidence by participating in weekly collaborative opportunities. As members of a collaborative team, teachers learn together so they can develop the knowledge and skills necessary to provide adaptive reading instruction for their students.

## Motivation for Change

Promoting effective change in practice requires an understanding that teacher motivation is paramount. Unfortunately, far too often, teachers are subject to implementation strategies that produce the opposite effect. Therefore, the improvement process teachers participate in must encourage the development of *intrinsic motivation* (when one is driven to complete an action because of the inherent satisfaction they will feel when doing so, and not driven by an external incentive), as motivated teachers are more likely to engage in the learning that is necessary to change their instructional practice. Motivation serves as a driving force for change, and according to psychologists Richard M. Ryan and Edward Deci (2017), building motivation is intricately tied to three fundamental psychological needs: autonomy, competence, and relatedness. Autonomy is the sense of volition and control over one's decisions and plays a pivotal role in fostering motivation by increasing a person's ownership and commitment to their actions. In educational terms, this means that teachers must have some say in the decisions that affect their classroom instruction. Ensuring teachers participate in the decisions that impact their work leads not only to increased motivation but also to increased ownership of results. Competence is a byproduct of tackling challenges and mastering the skills necessary to overcome them.

According to Arif Sarıçoban and Güven Mengü (2008), motivation occurs when teacher practice results in improved student achievement. Therefore, teachers not only need to feel competent in delivering evidenced-based reading instruction but need this competence to be validated through improved student reading outcomes. Sustained motivation won't be realized if the time, energy, and effort put forth by teachers to change their reading instruction doesn't ensure grade-level reading performance for more of their students. Finally, relatedness refers to the human need for meaningful connections with others. Collaborating with others toward a shared goal not only enhances the sense of relatedness but also amplifies the motivational impact. Satisfying the need for relatedness means abandoning isolated teacher practice in favor of a collaborative approach. However, relatedness also applies to the relationship between collaborative teams in a school. We must acknowledge that improved reading results are not the product of one team's efforts. Implementation of evidence-based practices must occur in every grade and requires clarity on behalf of every team with relation to their role in supporting grade-level reading for every student. Successful implementation of the science of reading will require teachers' participation in an improvement framework that satisfies all three of these psychological needs.

## A Professional Learning Community

Changing reading practice in schools is a difficult undertaking. It requires a coordinated universal approach to shift from a culture based on teacher isolation to a culture based on collaborative learning. When it comes to improving reading outcomes, adult learning precedes student learning. Only if adults learn more can they be expected to see a significant shift in instruction. However, simply putting teachers into collaborative teams doesn't guarantee a change in practice. Collaborative teams must be developed, monitored, and supported as they work to apply new learning. Educators and leaders must communicate clear expectations regarding our professional obligation not only to learn the research evidence but to incorporate that learning into our classroom instruction. For example, consider the role the following two factors, identified in chapter 1 (page 9), played in moving the needle on reading instruction at Esther Starkman School.

> **When it comes to improving reading outcomes, adult learning precedes student learning.**

1. A schoolwide focus on improving reading

2. The school's belief in continuous improvement

The school put reading improvement at the top of their priority list, and the teachers recognized how important it was to change practice. They also understood that change was not going to be instantaneous and that the only way change would occur was if they committed to continuous improvement of their practice. If we put it all together, schools hoping to successfully shift to the science of reading need to break down teacher isolation, promote collaboration and continuous learning, make reading their top priority, and create the conditions for teachers to develop collective efficacy (motivation). This is a tall task and the reason we recommend using a process like the PLC at Work process to guide your school. In our opinion, adopting and working within the PLC at Work process—originally developed by Richard DuFour, Rebecca DuFour, Robert Eaker, and Thomas Many (2006)—represents a school's best option for successfully navigating a change in reading instruction (DuFour et al., 2024).

Becoming a PLC creates the conditions for continuous improvement to become a reality. PLCs afford teachers the opportunity to engage in pedagogical discussion, exchange knowledge and experience, collaboratively address educational challenges related to student achievement, and offer each other emotional support (Ohayon & Abulescu, 2023). PLCs address isolated teacher practice by forming teams of teachers and providing them with frequent (weekly) opportunities to collaborate within the working day. This weekly collaboration provides a continuous job-embedded professional development model capable of overcoming the impact of the forgetting curve. With this model, teachers can support each other as they work to incorporate evidence-based reading instruction in their classrooms. When done well, teacher collaboration is a powerful force that not only enhances teachers' professional knowledge and experience but also significantly boosts student learning and achievement (Ostovar-Nameghi & Sheikhahmadi, 2016). This is why we embrace the development of a PLC as the pathway to sustained reading improvement.

### A Strong Foundation

It is important to understand that attempting to improve reading outcomes without addressing the school culture responsible for the current poor results is likely to fail. Cultures represent the model of the status quo, or "how we do things around here." They encompass everything from daily instructional practices to teachers' attitudes and beliefs regarding a student's ability to learn. Moving the needle on reading achievement will require all members of each collaborative team to not only share a common goal but commit to the necessary learning to make attaining the goal possible. If and only if all teachers have clarity of the purpose and commitment are they likely to engage in effective collaboration capable of changing long-standing ingrained practices.

All strong school cultures are built on a foundation of shared beliefs. The foundation of a PLC is that all educators work to accomplish a shared mission and vision, and they make commitments to each other for how they will work together to accomplish a shared goal. This is a crucial step for schools looking to make significant changes to their reading instruction. Building a shared foundation promotes clarity of purpose and provides clarity around what you are collectively trying to accomplish. This clarity occurs when a school establishes a shared foundation in the following four domains.

1. **A shared mission:** A shared mission defines why you come to work every day. It provides clarity around what the staff are working to accomplish collectively and is used to help determine whether existing practices should be continued. For a PLC to continue with an existing practice there must be evidence that the practice is helping the school get closer to accomplishing their mission. If no evidence is available, the practice must be replaced with something more effective. Simplicity is the key to success when developing a mission. If you have to look it up or you can't define the criteria for success, you don't have a mission. Consider the following mission statement.

   *It is the mission of our school to ensure*
   *all students achieve at grade level or better.*

   This mission is clear: The staff will work toward having all students achieve at grade level, which includes reading. If the school is not achieving grade-level reading proficiency with their students, this mission necessitates a conversation regarding instructional effectiveness. This clarity of purpose helps to open a conversation about the science of reading.

2. **A shared vision:** A vision statement is fundamentally different from the mission statement. While the mission statement addresses "why" we exist, the vision statement asks "what" we hope to become. A vision statement is an opportunity to engage staff in a conversation to gain clarity around the compelling future you want to create. Think five years down the road and imagine a school that has changed for the better. Here are some questions you may ask yourself.

   - What type of school do you want to work in?

   - What changes must be made for our school to improve students' achievement?

   - What is our place in our community?

   - How is it different from our current reality?

   - What does reading instruction look like?

   - What does reading achievement look like?

   - What state or national awards do we covet?

   Creating a vision allows the school to dream and think outside of their current reality. It encourages the staff to embrace the idea that a better reality for all stakeholders can be accomplished through their collective work.

3. **Shared collective commitments:** The collective commitments help to define how we must work together and what work we must do to become a learning organization focused on continuous improvement. Collective commitments require the participation of all staff and are written as "will" statements, without qualifiers like "hope to" or "try to," to indicate that the following action will in fact occur. When we commit to doing something, we are making a promise to follow through. Some examples of "we will" collective commitments are as follows.

   - We will ensure all teachers are members of a collaborative team.

   - We will commit to weekly job-embedded professional development on research-based best practices to improve student learning.

   - We will create and teach a guaranteed and viable curriculum.

   - We will ensure equitable assessment of student progress by creating and administering common formative assessments.

   - We will make decisions based on the collection of evidence of student learning by analyzing data from common assessments.

- We will commit to becoming problem solvers instead of problem identifiers.
- We will collaboratively plan regular cycles of inquiry focused on the four critical questions (see page 58).
- We will create, monitor, and refine SMART goals and growth targets.
- We will take collective responsibility for every student.
- We will speak respectfully about our students.
- We will celebrate student success on a regular basis.
- We will actively involve all students in personal goal setting and planning how they can achieve grade level or above.
- We will model, teach, and apply schoolwide behavioral expectations.

When considering what commitments your staff will make, a good place to start is to write commitments that reflect how a school can live the three big ideas and four critical questions of a PLC. However, a school focused on implementing the science of reading will want to write commitments specifically targeting this goal. Successful implementation will require the following "we will" commitments.

- We will create and implement a guaranteed and viable reading curriculum in our school.
- We will vertically align essential reading standards to ensure we reduce gaps in foundational knowledge.
- We will collectively monitor students' reading progress through the creation and delivery of common formative assessments.
- We will learn about and implement the evidence-based instruction contained within the science of reading.
- We will collectively provide additional time and support for students who read below grade-level proficiency.
- We will evaluate instructional effectiveness based on students' reading data.

These commitments form the basis of a plan for changing practice and outline the shared knowledge a team must build in order to improve reading results.

4. **Write SMART goals:** In John Hattie's (2023) meta-analysis of educational research, collective teacher efficacy is proven to be the single biggest factor in moving the needle on student learning. This means that if a school staff believes they are making a difference, it has a positive impact on the achievement of their students. In their mixed methods study, Georgiou and colleagues (2020) also report that collective teacher

efficacy is one of the highest-ranked factors among teachers of Esther Starkman School. Given its importance and positive impact on teacher practice, creating the conditions for collective efficacy to flourish should be a priority for any school looking to improve reading results. However, it is essential to understand that for collective efficacy to be developed, actual improvement must be realized. It is unlikely that a school whose mission is to help more students read at grade level will believe they are making a difference if more students don't read at grade level. Therefore, schools need to gather evidence that demonstrates that their collective efforts are having a positive impact on student learning. One way to demonstrate effectiveness is to write achievement targets that get achieved, as the achievement of our common goals provides clear evidence that our work is making a difference.

### The Three Big Ideas

Building on the foundational domains, PLCs use three big ideas to facilitate the shifts in thinking that will be required to successfully implement change that leads to continuous improvement. Communicated in conjunction with one another, these big ideas ask educators to rethink the role of the classroom teacher, how teachers will be expected to work, and the outcome of our collective efforts. They are as follows.

1. **A focus on learning, not teaching:** Teachers working within a PLC understand that the fundamental purpose of their school is not the act of teaching. Their school exists for one purpose and only one purpose, to improve student learning. Although learning the best ways to teach reading as outlined in the reading research is obviously important, focusing on learning extends beyond the individual teacher's classroom. A PLC seeks to create equity for students in curriculum, assessment, intervention, and enrichment. The PLC member teachers do this by working collaboratively as a team to answer four critical questions.

   1. What is it we want our students to know and be able to do?

   2. How will we know if each student has learned it?

   3. How will we respond when some students do not learn it?

   4. How will we extend the learning for students who have demonstrated proficiency?

   Answering these questions helps the team design the instructional supports required to increase the effectiveness of each teacher's classroom instruction. How a teacher team answers these questions will be explained in detail in chapter 4 (page 57).

2. **A focus on collaboration:** PLCs embrace collaboration as the pathway to improvement. They understand that collaborative teams are the engine that drives adult learning and that the continuous job-embedded learning

of the adults is the key to improved student learning. They take collective responsibility for all students, which ensures each student benefits from the collective wisdom of the team. As a result, highly effective collaborative teams are able to move the needle on student learning in ways an individual teacher cannot.

3. **A focus on results:** PLCs base their decisions on results, not intentions or feelings. They embrace the collection and analysis of student data to help determine the effectiveness of their instruction and use the data to collectively determine the next steps. Focusing on results prevents the continuous repetition of ineffective practice and promotes the adoption of practices that increase student learning.

Using the Common Core State Standards as an example, let's examine how these three big ideas focus the work of a teacher team looking to improve reading instruction. Contained in the Reading: Foundational Skills domain, you will find the exact same standard for kindergarten through grade 3, "Know and apply grade-level phonics and word analysis skills in decoding words" (National Governors Association Center for Best Practices & Council of Chief State School Officers [NGA & CCSSO], 2010). Underneath this umbrella standard each grade contains several targeted supporting standards that attempt to define the specific skills students need to know in each grade. However, upon closer examination, the supporting standards are not as clear as one would hope, and they make assumptions regarding teacher knowledge and competence. In kindergarten, the first two are here (NGA & CCSSO, 2010).

- **RF.K.3.A:** Demonstrate basic knowledge of one-to-one letter-sound correspondences by producing the primary sound or many of the most frequent sounds for each consonant.

- **RF.K.3.B:** Associate the long and short sounds with the common spellings (graphemes) for the five major vowels.

To ensure equitable learning (big idea 1), a team of kindergarten teachers tasked with teaching these standards must consider the following items.

- **Teacher content knowledge:** Do all teachers know which of the twenty-six letters (graphemes) produce each of the forty-four sounds (phonemes) associated with the English language? Both consonants and vowels can produce multiple sounds. For example:

  - The consonant *C* can make a /k/ sound (as in *cat*) and a /s/ sound (as in *cent*).

  - The vowel *A* can make an /ă/ sound (as in *cat*), an /ɑː/ sound (as in *father*), an /ā/ sound (as in *cake*), and an /ə/ sound (as in *sofa*).

- **Scope and sequence:** Are all teachers clear on the scope of work that has to be learned and the sequence in which it needs to be taught? Without a common scope and sequence, it is impossible for a team to create and analyze data from common formative assessments.

- **Assessment strategies:** Do all teachers agree on how best to assess students' knowledge of the agreed-upon content?

- **Proficiency:** Do all teachers agree on how many times a student needs to demonstrate their learning to be considered proficient?

- **Time and support:** How will the team guarantee additional time and support for students who need it, regardless of which teacher the student has?

When teacher teams focus on learning and implementing effective reading instruction (big idea 1), they create equity for students in what they learn, how they are assessed, and intervention support. For equity to be achieved, they have to embrace collaboration (big idea 2) as the medium. Collaborative inquiry by teacher teams into the science of reading is the only way to ensure all students in the school experience the most effective reading instruction possible. Finally, teacher teams need to collectively examine the results (big idea 3) from common reading assessments so they can determine instructional effectiveness. This is how teachers develop the instructional tool kit required to move away from scripted instruction. When the data say their instruction is not achieving the desired outcome, they are compelled to change the course of their instruction. All reading teachers understand that time is a commodity that is often in short supply; therefore, frequently measuring progress and listening to what the data tell you prevents wasted instructional time on non-impactful reading strategies. These three philosophical guiding principles don't stand alone; rather, they are interconnected ideas used to guide teacher practice and ensure effective instruction.

## Meaningful and Attainable Reading Goals

Writing goals is not an unfamiliar educational practice, as most districts require schools to write improvement goals as part of their yearly improvement plans. Usually, the goals are written by the principal or a leadership team using data from some form of standardized assessment. More often than not, the process follows a predictable pattern. First, the principal or leadership team looks at last year's reading results; second, based on the data, they select an improvement target and write a goal; and finally, the goal is communicated to the staff. Usually, there are some action steps shared with teachers that are included in the school plan indicating the work the school will do to achieve the goal. Unfortunately, this annual practice has done little to improve reading results and is often little more than a compliance exercise. Goals written using a top-down process like the one we just described suffer from the following three main issues.

1. **The wrong people are writing the goal:** If the school is going to achieve their reading goal, it will be the work of teachers that has the most direct

impact on its success or failure. When teachers are involved in the goal-setting process, they are more likely to be committed and motivated to achieve the goals. Deciding the goal for them does not create ownership for the goal and does little to inspire teachers to make the instructional changes necessary to achieve it.

2. **The goal is not attainable:** We have worked with countless schools that have ignored the fact that goals need to be attainable. Often, the improvement target is set artificially high and is plucked out of thin air in an attempt to portray that the school has high expectations for themselves and the students they serve. However, this practice is self-defeating. If teachers don't believe a goal is attainable, they are likely to dismiss it.

3. **The goal was not determined based on student learning needs:** Goals are only relevant when they are based on an analysis of the learning needs of the students in the school. Before we can determine if we can improve reading, we need to understand what reading skills need to be improved. This requires a determination of the skills each student will need to learn compared to the capacity of the people in the school to fill in the gaps within the time frame of a single academic year.

Writing meaningful reading goals begins from the bottom up instead of the top down. This means that teacher teams, not administrators, need to write the goals for the school. Here are the four steps to the process that we have used with schools to write meaningful goals that avoid the common mistakes listed previously.

1. Have grade-level teams use a formative assessment to measure the reading performance of their incoming students. Before an improvement target can be established, we need to know the number of students who are currently reading at grade level. Teams can use a variety of assessments, but we suggest using the three norm-referenced reading screeners listed in chapter 3 (page 39).

2. For students not at grade level, the team needs to examine the learning profile of each student to determine the specific skill deficits that are preventing them from achieving grade-level reading. For example, do they have a decoding deficit or a comprehension deficit? Understanding the area of need allows the team to develop a specific plan of action.

3. Based on the analysis of each student's learning needs, the team determines if they believe they can fill in the missing reading skill gaps and return the student to grade-level reading performance during the school year. These students are grouped together to determine the level of improvement the team will commit to when writing the goal.

4. The goal is determined by adding the group of students in the improvement group to the baseline number of students currently reading at grade level.

See figure 2.1 for an example of a reading goal. In this example, there are fifty-six students in the grade that are currently reading at grade level. Another forty-four (totaling 100 students) are not reading at grade level; the team has determined they can move fifteen students up to grade level by the end of the year. When done this way, the team is writing a goal that they believe is possible. They are making a commitment to work together but, most importantly, to change their practices so their instruction and intervention will successfully accelerate the learning for these fifteen students. This bottom-up goal-writing process allows for the creation of targeted schoolwide reading goals by adding together the individual goals of each grade-level team.

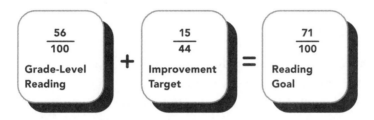

**Figure 2.1: Reading goal formula.**

Once the target has been established, write a good SMART goal to ensure you have a plan. The SMART acronym first appeared in an article written by George T. Doran (1981) titled "There's a SMART Way to Write Management's Goals and Objectives" that was published in the *Management Review*. Doran uses the SMART acronym to outline the characteristics of a well-written goal.

- **Specific:** The goal must clearly outline what the team hopes to improve and must be narrow enough so the team can identify the necessary steps to accomplish it. Being specific means that the goals should be written by using numbers of students rather than percentages. When writing a goal that states the number of students we are intending to reach, it necessitates a conversation about each individual student. No such conversation is required when we use percentages.

- **Measurable:** The goal must clearly state the measurement instrument that will be used to determine success. This may include state assessments, team-generated common assessments, and more.

- **Attainable:** The goal must be realistic. Attainability is essential for collective efficacy to be developed, as efficacy requires a successful outcome.

- **Relevant:** Relevance means that the goal must not only address a current need but also reflect the most important skills necessary for student success. If you want to improve reading achievement, you should write reading goals.

- **Time bound:** The goal must define the time frame for achievement as a goal without a time frame breeds no urgency. Assigning a time for improvement to occur also prevents the endless application of failed strategies. If a goal is to be accomplished in three weeks and the time comes with no improvement, the reason why must be explored.

Although the architect of the SMART goal process defined clear criteria for the writing of an effective goal, the architects of the PLC process made one revision. The *Handbook for SMART School Teams* (Conzemius & O'Neill, 2014) changed the *R* from *relevant* to *results oriented*. When thinking of a goal as results driven, we have to think about the specific actions required to successfully achieve the goal. To attain positive results, the goal will be driven by the following action—a subtle yet important distinction.

## Conclusion

While the science of reading holds the promise of dramatically improving reading outcomes for students, its implementation will be a significant challenge. Asking teachers to abandon their existing practice requires a well-thought-out implementation approach that incorporates the development of intrinsic motivation and collective teacher efficacy. This is the fundamental flaw in traditional school improvement approaches. They rely on a top-down hierarchy for decision making that expects teachers to implement decisions in isolation that they seldom believe in or understand. At best, these improvement plans elicit compliant teacher behavior that falls short in building a commitment to change practice or an ownership of results. This is the power of becoming a PLC. PLCs are built through a symbiotic relationship between the leadership team (guiding coalition) and the teacher teams. They develop a simultaneously loose and tight decision-making structure that defines who should take responsibility for making the decision. The guiding coalition can be tight about ensuring the PLC process is implemented but loose about allowing teachers to make decisions that impact the effectiveness of their practice. As a result, they create a collaborative culture that makes previously impossible achievement possible. This is the pathway to the successful implementation of the science of reading. Traditional implementation approaches are bound to fail.

# Key Readings and Resources

- Athanases, S. Z., Bennett, L. H., & Wahleithner, J. M. (2015). Adaptive teaching for English language arts: Following the pathway of classroom data in preservice teacher inquiry. *Journal of Literacy Research, 47*(1), 83-114. https://doi.org/10.1177/1086296X15590915

- DuFour, R., DuFour, R. B., Eaker, R. E., Mattos, M. W, & Muhammad, A. (2021). *Revisiting professional learning communities at work: Proven insights for sustained, substantive school improvement* (2nd ed.). Bloomington, IN: Solution Tree Press.

- Murre, J., & Dros, J. (2015). Replication and analysis of Ebbinghaus' forgetting curve. *PLoS ONE, 10*(7), Article e0120644. https://doi.org/10.1371/journal.pone.0120644

- Ohayon, A., & Albulescu, I. (2023). Influence of teachers' participation in professional learning communities on their teaching skills. In I. Albulescu & C. Stan (Eds.), *Education, Reflection, Development* (ERD 2022, vol. 6): *The European Proceedings of Educational Sciences* (pp. 445-451). London: European Publisher. https://doi.org/10.15405/epes.23056.40

- Ostovar-Nameghi, S. A., & Sheikhahmadi, M. (2016). From teacher isolation to teacher collaboration: Theoretical perspectives and empirical findings. *English Language Teaching, 9*(5), 197-205. http://dx.doi.org/10.5539/elt.v9n5p197

- Ryan, R. M., & Deci, E. L. (2022). *Self-determination theory: Basic psychological needs in motivation, development, and wellness.* New York: Guilford Press.

CHAPTER 3

# A System for Transitioning Schools to Evidence-Based Reading Practices

Successful implementation of reading instruction based on the science of reading can be a challenging task for any school. While some staff may be open to learning about the research evidence, many more may experience cognitive dissonance due to their long-held ingrained beliefs about reading instruction. According to Dilakshini and Kumar (2020), this dissonance produces tension, which can then lead to the development of coping strategies like this one: "rejecting the new information, explaining away or avoiding new information" (p. 54). Combating this phenomenon requires leaders to chart a clear path forward that leads staff toward the adoption and implementation of the new knowledge. Within the structure of the PLC process, this chapter presents a set of action steps we developed that has a proven track record of successfully transitioning schools to evidence-based reading instruction supported by the science of reading (Georgiou et al., 2020). The following leadership action steps are not intended to be a buffet where schools select items that they like, but rather all steps need to be implemented as part of a systemic approach to improving reading success.

1. Form a guiding coalition.
2. Facilitate job-embedded professional development.
3. Collect valid and reliable schoolwide reading data.
4. Create time for intervention.
5. Create a system of reciprocal accountability.

Although we recommend implementing these steps in the order they are presented, apart from step 1 it is not essential. For example, a school can collect benchmark data while planning for the delivery of professional development, but for each of the last four action steps to be successful, a guiding coalition must first be in place.

## Form a Guiding Coalition

There is a large body of research evidence that supports distributed leadership as an essential component of school improvement (Galdames-Calderón, 2023; Kierstead et al., 2023; Ling et al., 2023; Obadara, 2013; Zheng et al., 2019). Distributed "leadership implies a social distribution of leadership where the leadership function is stretched over the work of a number of individuals and the task is accomplished through the interaction of multiple leaders" (Day, Sammons, & Gorgen, 2020, p. 20). Stated in simpler terms, principals should not try to implement change alone; instead, they need to share the responsibility for reading improvement with teachers in the school. Since teachers are the ones being asked to implement an instructional change, it makes both logical and practical sense that including a teacher voice in the implementation process will increase the likelihood a change occurs. A study conducted by Mohd Izham Mohd Hamzah and Mohd Fadzil Jamil (2019) reveals distributed leadership to be not only an essential component of developing a PLC but also "a significant factor in driving the school towards excellence" (p. 2738).

> **Principals should not try to implement change alone; instead, they need to share the responsibility for reading improvement with teachers in the school.**

Central to the success of all PLCs is the distribution of leadership through the formation of a guiding coalition. This team, comprised of teachers and administrators, is charged with leading, monitoring, and supporting a school's transition to evidence-based reading instruction. It must include the right individuals, be well structured, and consistently support those impacted by the change (Maximini, 2015). According to Bill Hall (2022), a successful guiding coalition takes responsibility for the following actions.

- **Lead the process by example:** The team digs into the research. They embrace the opportunity to learn about evidence-based reading instruction, assessment, and intervention.

- **Provide support for teacher teams:** The guiding coalition supports teams as they transition from their existing practice to reading instruction supported by the science of reading. This includes monitoring the effectiveness of implementation so areas requiring support can be identified.

- **Design and deliver professional development:** The team commits to learning about the five pillars of reading and provides job-embedded professional development for the staff.

- **Commit to continuous improvement:** The team demonstrates a commitment to continuous learning as a pathway to improve their support for teams. As they learn more, they incorporate their new learning into their support structures for teacher teams.

When selecting members for the guiding coalition, it is important for the team to have considerable representation from the teaching staff. If you are going to ask teachers to make a significant change in practice, it is essential that they are represented at the table. As educational leadership expert and author Douglas Reeves (2006) notes, "leaders can make decisions with their authority, but they can implement those decisions only through collaboration" (p. 52). Although teacher representation is essential, it is not essential to have a member from each teacher team. Team size is an important consideration when forming a guiding coalition. If a team is too large, it becomes difficult to manage a meeting effectively enough to ensure meaningful participation from all members. Research into the nature of leadership suggests that the size of a school's guiding coalition should range between four and seven members in order to maximize team productivity (Karlgaard & Malone, 2015).

Selecting members for the guiding coalition is ultimately the responsibility of the school's principal. Since this team will be in charge of leading all aspects of the change management process, it is essential to ensure the right people are selected. As Jim Collins (2001) notes, the leaders who are successful in leading transformational change are adept at getting the "right people on the bus". When deciding who should be on the bus, consider selecting staff with the following characteristics.

1. **Commitment to the change:** Staff understand both the importance of grade-level reading for every student and the need to change reading instruction to achieve it.

2. **Diverse skill sets and perspectives:** Diversity of perspective can help ensure multiple points of view are considered prior to making decisions. Including a diverse set of skills helps ensure the right people are available to support and overcome any issues that arise during implementation.

3. **Leadership and influence:** A title isn't necessary to lead. Some people have influence over the staff for a variety of reasons—for example, instructional competence, willingness to support others, professional behavior, willingness to learn, and so on.

4. **Capacity for collaboration:** Staff have demonstrated a capacity to work with others not only to learn together but also to support adoption of best practice.

5. **Openness to learning:** Staff are constantly learning and growing as professionals. They understand that continuous adult learning is the pathway to improved student reading success.

Once formed, the guiding coalition assumes lead responsibility for implementing the remaining four steps in the system.

## Facilitate Job-Embedded Professional Development

According to Amy A. Germuth (2018), studies on traditional teacher professional development indicate that while teachers often learn new strategies, only 10 percent implement them into practice without additional support. As noted earlier, designing and delivering professional development that will lead to a change in reading instruction is the responsibility of the guiding coalition. So what pitfalls will they need to avoid in order to embrace instruction based in the science of reading? There is good news in that research supports an effective framework for professional development design that can ensure increased teacher implementation resulting in increased student learning (Desimone & Garet, 2015). There are seven features of effective professional development that the guiding coalition must incorporate when planning reading professional development for their staff (Darling-Hammond, Hyler, & Gardner, 2017).

1. **Is content focused:** Professional development must target teaching strategies linked to specific subject matter. This approach emphasizes targeted curriculum development and teaching methods specific to the science of reading such as phonemic awareness, phonics, fluency, vocabulary, and comprehension. It is important for the guiding coalition to recognize that for change to happen, teachers cannot have their focus watered down. If reading improvement is the focus, then professional development in other areas such as writing should be delayed until competence in reading is achieved. Trying to implement too many things at once can cause teachers to feel overwhelmed and frustrated, and it is the role of the guiding coalition to ensure this doesn't occur.

2. **Uses models and modeling of effective practice:** The modeling that is provided during professional development provides clear examples of best practice. The models that the guiding coalition shares may be examples of unit or lesson plans, instructional strategies to address a pillar, samples of how to assess a particular reading skill, or models of research-supported intervention.

3. **Incorporates active learning utilizing adult learning theory:** Active learning in professional development involves teachers in learning and practicing teaching strategies, allowing them to experience the type of learning they design for their students. This includes the use of real-world artifacts and interactive activities to provide embedded context-specific professional learning. Active learning moves away from the traditional yet ineffective sit-and-get lecture style of professional development.

4. **Provides coaching and support:** Members of the guiding coalition can provide individualized support to teachers. Since all teachers will possess different levels of understanding of evidence-based reading instruction

> Studies on traditional teacher professional development indicate that while teachers often learn new strategies, only 10 percent implement them into practice without additional support.

when the school begins the transition, different teachers may require significantly more support than others.

5. **Is of sustained duration:** Professional development opportunities are ongoing and provide teacher teams ample time to learn and incorporate new practices. Monitoring the progress of teacher teams so proper learning supports can be put in place and sufficient time for learning can be provided is a key responsibility of the guiding coalition.

6. **Supports collaboration, typically in job-embedded contexts:** High-quality professional development extends learning past initial exposure to incorporate frequent opportunities for teachers to participate in job-embedded collaboration.

7. **Offers opportunities for feedback and reflection:** Collaborative teacher teams build in opportunities for peer feedback on each member's instructional implementation.

Here is an example of what reading professional development that incorporates the aforementioned seven elements might look like.

- The guiding coalition meets to plan a professional development session for staff and determines the title of this session will be "What Is Effective Phonics Instruction?"

- An introductory session on phonics includes a definition of phonics, a rationale for why phonics is important, some common misconceptions about phonics, and research to support phonics instruction.

- A possible scope and sequence for phonics instruction is outlined and connected to each grade's reading standards. This clarifies the phonics skills that are expected to be mastered in each grade level.

- A live demonstration of effective phonics instruction is provided to help participants see what direct and systematic phonics instruction looks like in a classroom. As an alternative to live modeling, they may choose to present videos of experts providing phonics instruction. This gives the members of the guiding coalition an opportunity to learn alongside the participants.

- Working in teams, participants are given an opportunity to discuss the key elements of the phonics lesson they just observed.

- In teams, teachers are engaged in a role-playing activity where they are given the opportunity to practice delivering phonics instruction to their colleagues.

- After each role-playing session, the "teacher" is given feedback from the other participants.

- To close the session, each teacher team discusses their key takeaways from the session and has an opportunity to ask and answer questions from the group.

- Ensuring the forgetting curve does not have an opportunity to slow progress, the guiding coalition plans an opportunity for each grade-level team to meet and review what they learned.

- During this meeting, teams clarify the scope and sequence of phonics skills they will commit to ensuring their students learn. They review different phonics resources to determine which lessons might effectively provide an effective structure for direct instruction.

- The team agrees to begin phonics instruction immediately so they will have an opportunity to deliver instruction to their students before their next team meeting.

- At a follow-up meeting, they discuss what went well and ask for clarity and assistance from their team on self-identified areas of struggle. This support may take the form of having an opportunity to watch a team member teach their class or hosting a team member in their classroom to give feedback on their phonics lesson delivery.

- The guiding coalition continues to check in on each teacher team, providing support when necessary.

When planning professional development for staff, members of the guiding coalition can use the template in figure 3.1 as a guide.

Developing a collective responsibility for reading improvement comes when schools embrace learning as their fundamental purpose. PLCs understand that improved reading outcomes for students are driven by adult learning. There is no school that universally improves student learning without first engaging the teachers in a process of continuous job-embedded professional development. Harvard researcher Roland Barth (2001) states, "I have yet to see a school where the learning curves . . . of the adults were steep upward and those of the students were not. Teachers and students learning go hand in hand . . . or they don't go at all" (p. 23). Therefore, effective ongoing professional development to facilitate teacher learning is essential for successful schoolwide implementation of the science of reading.

Key to the successful implementation of evidence-based reading instruction will be the guiding coalition's ability to support teachers as they learn new instructional methods. Moving away from familiar practice is often uncomfortable and uncertain for teachers. In addition to providing professional development on evidence-based practices in reading, the guiding coalition must explicitly state that there is an expectation that the knowledge and skills learned during the professional development must be implemented. In chapter 4 (page 57), we will discuss teacher team actions that will ensure the team has clarity around how to answer the four critical questions of a PLC; however, to assist teacher teams, the guiding coalition should consider creating a practice and feedback loop for each new skill.

This idea is modeled after the concept of Japanese lesson study (Cheung & Wong, 2014). There is tremendous power when a team accepts ownership of instructional

# A System for Transitioning Schools to Evidence-Based Reading Practices | 45

**Session Logistics**

| | |
|---|---|
| • When and where will the PD take place?<br>• Who do we need to contact to arrange to use the facility? | • Who will be required to attend?<br>• Which staff members will benefit from this PD?<br>• How will staff be released for this PD? |
| **What materials are needed for this PD?**<br>• Instructional materials<br>• Technology (microphone, projector, and so on) | **What amenities are needed?**<br>• Coffee, water, or juice<br>• Snacks<br>• Lunch |

**Session Design**

| | |
|---|---|
| **What is the focus of this PD?**<br>• Phonological awareness<br>• Phonics<br>• Fluency<br>• Vocabulary<br>• Comprehension<br>• Screening data | **Who will be conducting the PD?**<br>• An outside expert<br>• Members of the guiding coalition |
| **Define the topic:**<br>• What is meant by the term phonological awareness?<br>• What is its role in evidence-based reading instruction?<br>• How does this pillar connect to the other pillars of reading?<br>• What research will we highlight that provides a clear rationale for change? | **How will we model best instructional practice? (I Do)**<br>• What strategies are considered to be best practice for teaching this pillar?<br>• What does direct and systematic instruction look like? |
| **How will we model best assessment practice? (I Do)**<br>• How can a collaborative team formatively assess this pillar?<br>• What does grade-level performance look like? | **How will we incorporate opportunities for practice? (We Do)**<br>• What does active learning look like for the participants?<br>• How will we provide feedback during collaborative practice? |
| **Session Outcomes:**<br>• For this professional development to be successful, all participants will leave knowing how to do what? | **Session Feedback:**<br>• How will we collect feedback from participants regarding session outcomes? |

**After-Session Support**

| | |
|---|---|
| **Applied Learning:**<br>• When will teacher teams meet to discuss implementation of new learning?<br>• What elements of the PD session will teams be expected to implement?<br>• By when should this implementation occur?<br>• How will we monitor the implementation of new learning? | **Team Support:**<br>• How will we support teams as they implement new learning?<br>• How will we provide feedback to teams?<br>• How will we differentiate support for individual teachers? |
| **Team Data:**<br>• What are our team expectations for the collection and analysis of data?<br>• How will we support teams in the collection and analysis of data?<br>• How will teams track student progress? | **Session Feedback Reflection:**<br>• When will we review and reflect on session feedback? |

**Figure 3.1: Professional development planning template.**

*Visit **go.SolutionTree.com/literacy** for a free reproducible version of this figure.*

improvement through practice and feedback. Lesson study occurs when a team of teachers targets a particular area for improvement, in our case reading skills, and through a series of observations and reflections continuously improves instruction and student learning outcomes. In 2014, University of Hong Kong researchers Wai Ming Cheung and Wing Yee Wong reviewed nine separate studies related to the effectiveness of lesson study on improving instruction and student learning. They concluded that "the studies that we have reviewed systematically here provided compelling evidence to support the view that lesson study and learning study worked in classrooms and improved student learning outcomes" (Cheung & Wong, 2014, p. 9). According to Sarah Seleznyov (2018), the typical lesson study process involves seven steps. Here is an example of how a team might apply these steps.

1. **Identify a focus:** In this phase, the teacher team identifies an area of reading instruction that they wish to collectively improve. For example, the SRSD model, outlined in chapter 9 (page 151), may be used to support students in building a deeper understanding of a selected text.

2. **Plan collaboratively:** The team collaboratively plans a sequence of lessons using this strategy, which includes the intended lesson outcome, how the skill will be directly taught (I Do), how to provide guided practice (We Do), independent student practice (You Do), and formative assessment strategies.

3. **Teach the lesson:** One of the team members teaches the lesson while being observed by the other members of the team. The observers are looking for the strengths and weaknesses of the lesson in terms of how well students engage with the content.

4. **Hold post-lesson discussion:** The team meets to discuss their observations, as well as to reflect on how the lesson can be improved.

5. **Repeat cycles of instruction:** The team repeats this process with a different teacher using the same strategy to provide instruction on the next lesson.

6. **Engage outside expertise:** The team can invite an outside expert or the members of the guiding coalition who provided the initial professional development to observe. This provides the perspective of an educator with more background knowledge or expertise.

7. **Mobilize knowledge:** The team agrees to share their process and what they learned with the rest of the staff.

Organizing a classroom visitation schedule for teacher teams to engage in the lesson study process is one way the guiding coalition can support teams as they implement new skills. For example, if a team is focusing on enhancing students' phonemic awareness, they might observe one another teaching lessons on identifying, blending, or segmenting individual sounds, providing feedback on instructional clarity and student engagement. Having teams identify a skill to implement and then having team members observe and provide feedback reinforces the idea that the team will learn together. Individual self-reflection is a powerful improvement process for teachers; however, having the added bonus of reflecting on feedback from other professionals provides another important layer to teacher learning. One key consideration when implementing this process is that staff serving as observers should not include any staff member (such as the principal) who has the responsibility to supervise teacher performance. The goal is to promote self-reflection, adult learning, and, most importantly, support for teachers as they learn and implement new instructional practices.

Regrettably, due to budget constraints and difficulty in securing substitute teachers, some schools may face significant resource challenges as they try to engage their teachers in the collaborative study of reading strategies. Fortunately, technology has an answer to enable resource-strapped teams to benefit from this impactful professional practice. Teams still identify the area for improvement, but rather than visiting classes, the teacher records the lesson with a conferencing platform or can simply record it with their phone. The video can be shared with team members to watch in advance of their collaborative team meeting, enabling the same powerful feedback and reflection process to take place.

## Use Schoolwide Norm-Referenced Assessment Data

Although teacher teams will be responsible for the collection of ongoing student data in their classroom, it is essential that data be collected at the school level as well. Having a focus on results means that PLCs need to monitor the effectiveness and progress of all practices within the school against their core purpose of student learning. Undertaking a fundamental shift in reading instruction requires the guiding coalition to collect data so they can identify whether or not their implementation process is having the desired impact on student reading performance. They need a way to identify teams that are successfully adopting and implementing the science of reading strategies learned in their professional development sessions. Conversely, the guiding coalition also must identify individual teachers or grade-level teams that are struggling to provide effective reading instruction so they can provide additional support.

An effective way to determine the impact of reading instruction on student reading outcomes is to collect data by screening all students three times a year. Screening with this frequency provides valuable comparative data for teams and the guiding coalition without significantly impacting time teachers have for reading instruction. In addition, it allows enough time between measurement points so the implementation of evidence-based reading practices in the classroom can lead to measurable gains in reading. For this process to provide actionable data, it is essential to select reading screeners that contain the following characteristics.

1. **They are norm referenced:** Norm-referenced screeners compare a student's score against a representative norm of students who have approximately the same chronological age. The norms age range is dependent on the age and developmental stage of the students being assessed. Younger students have smaller age ranges, which represents the fact that they can experience a significant change quicker than older students. If the range was too large, this would have a significant negative effect on students at the bottom end of the age range. For example, the norms for students who are six years old are calculated every month. This means that there are norms for students who are six years and one month, six years and two months, six years and three months, and more. As students get older, the need for such tight norms is not required because developmental changes take place over a longer period of time.

2. **They produce a standard score:** A standard score is a score that has been statistically transformed from a raw score to allow comparison of an individual's performance to their normative group. Standard scores also allow comparisons across reading subskills (decoding versus fluency or fluency versus comprehension). This will tell us if a student does better in one reading skill than another, which then allows teachers to tailor their instruction to improve the reading skill that is weaker.

3. **They are quick and easy to administer:** Instructional time is a valuable commodity in all schools that shouldn't be significantly impacted by testing procedures. Procedures for screening should be easily understood so they can be administered by classroom teachers.

4. **Their data can be interpreted at the school:** The data from the assessment should be analyzed and interpreted by school staff without having to send them to a third party.

5. **They have no yearly fee:** While it is unlikely for a school to find effective screeners for free, many effective screeners exist with a one-time cost.

6. **Their research supports test validity and reliability:** Accurate screening data are essential for schools to make impactful data-driven decisions. Therefore, it is imperative that the accuracy of the selected screeners be supported by research. A screener is considered valid if it accurately measures what it purports to measure. In other words, a comprehension screener that effectively measured comprehension would have high validity. An assessment is considered reliable if the same test can be administered to the same group of students at different times or by different examiners and yield consistent results. This means that different teachers could give the assessment to a group of students, and the performance of the students would be the same.

## Recommended Reading Screeners

There are three age-based norm-referenced screeners that meet all the listed criteria and that we have successfully used to collect valid and reliable reading data across different schools in the United States and Canada. They are listed here.

- **The Test of Word Reading Efficiency (TOWRE)** is a reading screener that contains two subtests, a nonword test and a real-word test, that measure a student's reading efficiency. The nonword reading task also serves as a good indicator of students' phonics skills.

- **The Test of Silent Word Reading Fluency (TOSWRF)** is a fluency screener that assesses a student's ability to read words fluently and accurately.

- **The Test of Silent Reading Efficiency and Comprehension (TOSREC)** is used as a proxy for reading comprehension.

In addition to providing excellent reading data, these screeners are not time consuming and are easy to administer. Each subtest in the TOWRE is administered individually for forty-five seconds while both the TOSWRF and TOSREC are delivered to the whole class for three minutes each (plus one to two minutes for providing instructions). This means that whether a school has classroom teachers assess their own students or whether they designate specific staff members to screen all of the students, minimal instructional time is lost. Raw scores from each of these screeners are converted to standard scores, which are used to track individual students' reading performance three times each school year.

Without getting too deep into statistics, a standard score is a measure of performance that can be tracked over time using these three assessments. Standard scores ranging from 85 to 115 represent the middle 66 percent of the norm with a standard score of 100 representing the mean of the norm. The standard score of each student can be used to determine their relative reading strength for the pillar being assessed. Table 3.1 can be used to determine where a student fits relative to their age-appropriate norm. Note that we created these four categories combining both properties of the bell curve distribution (one standard deviation below the mean of 100 gives you 85) and pedagogical reasons (anyone scoring above 120 is considered to have superior reading performance).

**Table 3.1: Reading Performance Scores**

| Standard Score | Reading Performance |
|:---:|:---:|
| 0–85 | Severe |
| 86–100 | Below Average |
| 101–119 | Above Average |
| 120+ | Superior |

Scores below 85 indicate that this student struggles in the assessed reading skill and may require more specialized instruction (including perhaps a more comprehensive assessment in the targeted reading skill). Students scoring in the Severe category can read but must be on the teacher's radar as they will most likely require continued instruction and some intervention to improve. It is important to note that there can be a significant difference in student performance from the bottom of this range to the top.

### Student Growth Goals

The goal of all teacher teams should be to improve the reading performance for all of the students they serve. However, having a valid and reliable method of measuring student growth has been a challenge. Charting student reading growth using the reading screeners is a simple comparison of their beginning, midyear, and end-of-year scores. Students who demonstrate a year's reading growth in one academic year will have a standard score that remains the same during each assessment period. For example, a student who scores 100 during the September baseline assessment, 100 on the January midyear assessment, and 100 on the May end-of-year assessment has demonstrated one year of academic growth during the school year. A stable standard score means that the student is growing at the same rate as the rate of improvement of their comparison norm. Therefore, a student wishing to grow at the same rate as the norm must also demonstrate the same level of performance as the comparison group. This increased performance represents normal growth.

Since a standard score is a measure of growth, it can also be used to measure significant improvement or decline. If a student scores 7 standard points better or worse as compared to their last score, they are demonstrating statistically significant growth or decline. In other words, a student who scores 100 in September but scores 93 or lower in January is not growing at a rate to make a year's growth. A student scoring 100 in September who scores 107 in January is on pace to grow more than one academic year in this school year. A gain or loss of about 7 or more standard points is outside of the margin of chance, which means that the factor impacting changes this large is likely classroom instruction. The guiding coalition can use these data to paint a picture of the effectiveness of instruction for each student. The student who declined by 7 points is being negatively impacted by their classroom experience, while the student who gained 7 points is being positively impacted by classroom instruction. These data are key for teacher teams and the guiding coalition to look at the best ways to meet the learning needs of each student.

In addition to individual student data, reading screener standard scores can be used to track the performance of individual classes as well as the performance of the entire grade. For example, if the mean standard score of a class was 100 on the September assessment, but the class recorded a mean of 107 in May, the teacher and the guiding coalition would know that students in that class received instruction that positively impacted the reading performance of the students. If a class declined by 7 or more points, this would represent ineffective instruction and would be an indication that the guiding coalition may need to provide additional support to that classroom teacher. If a grade level had a teacher who significantly outperformed their colleagues, this would point to a teacher who had been providing effective instruction and would signal a need for the collaborative team to learn from that teacher.

We believe that all teachers want to improve their students' reading performance. However, doing this requires good data that can be tied to the effectiveness of instruction. Without good data (as in data derived from informal assessments), teachers will often be oblivious to whether their instruction is having a positive or negative impact on their students' performance. Making a change for the better begins with knowing what to change.

## Find a Time for Intervention

One of the things that all teachers agree on is that there is no "one size fits all" way to ensure all students learn to proficiency the first time. Typically, effective instruction ensures that 75 to 80 percent of students in a class learn a given skill to proficiency after initial instruction. However, despite their best efforts, all teachers have students who will require additional time and support in order to reach grade-level proficiency. The number of students requiring supplemental support is a byproduct of instructional effectiveness and pacing. In a traditional school the responsibility to provide this additional support rests solely with the individual classroom teacher. PLCs understand that this approach creates variance in teacher response and, as a result, variance in student outcome. Therefore, PLCs build a system that guarantees additional time and support is provided for all students regardless of which teacher they have. Learning to read at grade level is too important to be left to chance. That is why the three-tiered approach and intensive intervention are available as methods of stepping in.

### A Multitiered System of Supports

It is a realistic goal for any school providing effective instruction in the five pillars of reading and supplemental support as part of a multitiered system of supports (MTSS) to expect the majority of their students to score in the Above Average and Superior categories. An MTSS is a comprehensive framework used by schools to provide targeted support to all students based on their individual needs (Mattos et al., 2025). A typical MTSS framework is comprised of three distinct layers of support based on high-quality, scientifically based instructional strategies and interventions. The framework contains the following.

- **Tier 1:** All students receive reading instruction using the proven methods outlined in the science of reading.

- **Tier 2:** Students who need additional time and support to learn grade-level reading standards are provided with access to research-based interventions.

- **Tier 3:** Students who have gaps in foundational reading skills that should have been learned previously are provided with intervention on the missing skills.

PLCs provide support for students through a system that takes a three-tiered approach. Tier 1 refers to whole-classroom instruction, and the goal of Tier 1 instruction is to prevent learning issues from occurring by providing high-quality classroom instruction on grade-level core standards. Teachers working in a PLC understand that you can't expect a student to perform at grade level if you teach them below grade level all year. This is the primary work of teacher teams in a PLC as the teams work to prevent issues before they occur. In an effective system, approximately 80 percent of students should benefit from Tier 1 instruction and should not require Tier 2 instruction (Buffum et al., 2017). Tier 2 refers to supplemental support (often delivered in small groups) on grade-level core standards. When students need additional time and support to learn grade-level standards, the grade-level team responds by working together to collectively provide this support. In an effective system, educators can expect that approximately 15 percent of students require small-group Tier 2 instruction but not Tier 3 (one-to-one and more intensive) instruction. Teacher teams in a PLC take primary responsibility to plan and deliver instruction for both Tier 1 and Tier 2.

The guiding coalition plays a key role in developing this tiered system of support. As mentioned previously, they create the conditions for the successful transition to the science of reading during Tier 1 instruction. Second, they ensure the time for additional support at Tier 2 exists within the master schedule. Ideally, this will be thirty minutes set aside each day that can be used by teacher teams to work with small groups of students who need additional time and support. (How teacher teams plan for this thirty minutes of intervention will be covered in more detail in chapter 4 [page 57]). Third, the guiding coalition takes the lead on providing support for students who are not responding as expected after they have received initial instruction and supplemental support. Students who do not respond after Tiers 1 and 2 require much more targeted and intensive support. Often these students have much greater challenges when learning to read than is experienced by the typical student. Students requiring this level of support may have learning disabilities. The role of the guiding coalition in Tier 3 is to identify the students requiring intensive intervention and to provide them with the specialized support they need.

### Intensive Intervention

Data from reading screeners are an excellent way of quickly identifying students who have much more complex reading challenges. Students requiring Tier 3 support will be the students who consistently score below a standard score of 85 despite having experienced excellent classroom instruction and effective intervention. Helping students at this tier requires staff with specialized skills (such as special education teachers). When addressing reading issues, this is where a teacher with specialized training in reading will provide the necessary intervention. We wish to emphasize this point because in the past we have seen principals assigning staff to deliver Tier 3 intervention simply based on their time availability and not based on their skill set. This will reduce the effectiveness of the intervention.

The goal of any Tier 3 approach in reading is to remediate specific skills and return students to grade-level proficiency. Too often, students in Tier 3 intervention are provided with additional reading instruction that is ineffective at overcoming their deficit. As previously mentioned, students qualifying for Tier 3 score significantly below a standard score of 85 on the reading screeners (Johnson, Pool, & Carter, 2011). In fact, it is quite common for these students to have a standard score in the low 60s or 70s. An effective Tier 3 reading intervention would provide targeted instruction at sufficient intensity to see gains of 15 or more standard points. This rate of growth would represent a full standard deviation from the normal rate of growth and would equate to about two full years of academic growth in a calendar year (Buffum et al., 2017). Selecting an instructional approach that effectively backfills missing skills and accelerates learning is needed to return Tier 3 students to grade-level reading proficiency. The next step for our guiding coalition is to develop a system of reciprocal accountability that can be used to facilitate ongoing conversations regarding the effectiveness of our implementation efforts.

## Ensure Reciprocal Accountability

Facilitating the instructional improvement of teacher teams is a key responsibility of the guiding coalition. According to Phillip Hallinger and Ronald H. Heck (2010), instructional improvement can be realized if the collaborative leadership team establishes a strategic, schoolwide organizational process focused on improvement that incorporates the concept of reciprocal accountability. Reciprocal accountability promotes the idea that reading improvement is a shared responsibility between the guiding coalition and teacher teams. In such a system, each participant is accountable to the others, and they, in turn, are accountable back. A PLC embraces this concept as a pathway to developing a collective responsibility for the reading outcomes of every student.

One way a guiding coalition can promote this concept is through the establishment of regular accountability meetings between the guiding coalition and each teacher team tasked with incorporating evidence-based reading instruction. Occurring a minimum of four times a year, these meetings provide an opportunity for the guiding coalition to monitor the work of teams so they can determine the effectiveness of reading implementation. They also provide an opportunity to hear directly from teacher teams on how they are implementing the practices learned during their professional development sessions. These meetings clearly communicate the priorities and values of the school and convey a clear expectation that teams improve their practice. For teacher teams, these meetings are an opportunity to receive feedback as they implement new reading instruction. However, equally as important is the opportunity for teacher teams to articulate the support they need from the guiding coalition to successfully overcome any implementation challenges they are experiencing. In addition, this face-to-face two-way flow of information affords an excellent opportunity to share successes and best practices so they can be distributed schoolwide.

We can speak from personal experience of the power of this process to improve reading instruction and promote teacher confidence and efficacy. When beginning this process, it is important to establish with teachers that these meetings are an opportunity to learn together, not an evaluation process. The goal of these meetings is to determine successes and struggles experienced by each team so we can provide praise and support. How a guiding coalition responds to ineffective practice or poor data will either promote organizational trust or increase teacher pushback.

We recommend that an accountability meeting be about an hour in duration for each teacher team held once per quarter. From a team perspective, meeting each quarter provides ample opportunity to dig into the work so they can determine support they need from the guiding coalition. From the guiding coalition's perspective, the timeframe ensures you are allowing teams some autonomy while also not going too long without monitoring team progress. Prior to holding an accountability meeting, it is important for the guiding coalition to be open and transparent regarding the goal of the meeting. The guiding coalition can do this by sharing a list of topics and artifacts they wish to see a week or two prior to the meeting date. Topics and artifacts may include those listed here.

- A team-developed scope and sequence for reading instruction
- The essential reading standards and learning targets currently being taught
- The instructional strategies used to teach them
- Lesson design feedback
- Key learnings for the team based on lesson design feedback
- Copies of the team's common assessments to determine their validity to assess the current learning targets
- Data from the common assessments
- Data from the reading screeners
- The team's plan for intervention
- The team's process for tracking student progress
- Celebrations of team success
- Areas in which the team needs support from the guiding coalition

The strategic implementation of regular accountability meetings within a framework of reciprocal accountability significantly enhances the instructional capabilities of teacher teams. By fostering an environment where feedback, support, and mutual responsibility are central, the guiding coalition not only promotes continuous improvement in reading instruction but also builds a robust PLC.

## Conclusion

Changing long-held beliefs and practices within a school is not an easy task. Considerable pushback from people both outside and inside the school who wish to hang on to their existing practice can be significant. Developing a guiding coalition of teachers and administrators to share the burden and confront resistance dramatically increases the chance that positive change will occur. A guiding coalition that takes ownership of implementing a plan based on continuous learning, instructional support, data collection, timely intervention, and accountability will build the collective capacity necessary for successful implementation of evidence-based practices in reading. In the next chapter we will outline how teacher teams, led by the guiding coalition, collaboratively build shared knowledge of the science of reading and how they can apply this knowledge in their classrooms.

# Key Readings and Resources

- Cheung, W. M., & Wong, W. Y. (2014). Does Lesson Study work? A systematic review on the effects of Lesson Study and Learning Study on teachers and students. *International Journal for Lesson and Learning Studies, 3*(2), 137-149. https://doi.org/10.1108/ijlls-05-2013-0024

- Darling-Hammond, L., Hyler, M. E., & Gardner, M. (2017). *Effective teacher professional development.* Palo Alto, CA: Learning Policy Institute. https://doi.org/10.54300/122.311

- Hall, B. (2021). *Powerful guiding coalitions: How to build and sustain the leadership team in Your PLC at Work.* Bloomington, IN: Solution Tree Press.

- Hallinger, P., & Heck, R. H. (2010). Collaborative leadership and school improvement: Understanding the impact on school capacity and student learning. *School Leadership & Management, 30*(2), 95-110. https://doi.org/10.1080/13632431003663214

- Hamzah, M. I. M., & Jamil, M. F. (2019). The relationship of distributed leadership and professional learning community. *Creative Education, 10*(12), 2730-2741. https://doi.org/10.4236/ce.2019.1012199

CHAPTER 4

# The Work of Teacher Teams

Classroom instruction can be described as equal parts art and science. As it relates to reading, "science" refers to the body of research evidence contained in the science of reading. It encompasses the knowledge, skills, and strategies that define how best to provide reading instruction, assessment, and intervention. "Art" refers to how each individual teacher applies their craft, the everyday performance teachers deliver to their students that relies on finding the right mix of intuition, creativity, tolerance, compassion, high expectations, and understanding of human motivation. Whether a student learns to read at grade level is directly impacted by a teacher's ability to balance all of these factors as they implement the science. This is a considerable challenge; however, it is a challenge that can be met if teachers work as part of a grade-level, subject-specialty, or vertical team within the PLC process. In a PLC, teacher collaborative teams are the engine that drives a culture of continuous improvement. They engage in weekly job-embedded professional development to both learn the science and perfect the art of classroom instruction.

Research has consistently demonstrated the power of working in a team: "In comparison to working alone, team members show as much as a 50 percent increase in performance during teamwork" (Karlgaard & Malone, 2015, p. 98). However, simply grouping teachers together once a week is not a guarantee that students' learning will improve. According to Richard DuFour, Rebecca DuFour, Robert Eaker, Thomas W. Many, and Mike Mattos (2020), school improvement will not occur simply by assigning teachers to collaborative teams. The act of collaboration is insufficient unless the collaborative efforts of the teams are focused on the right work. For collaboration to be effective, teams must move past the simple sharing of ideas and focus on building shared knowledge and mutual accountability.

In a PLC, highly effective collaborative teams are developed over time by working through the PLC process. The PLC process can be defined as what the learning

> **In a PLC, teacher collaborative teams are the engine that drives a culture of continuous improvement.**

57

teams must do to answer each of the four critical questions, listed here (DuFour et al., 2020, p. 59).

1. What is it we want our students to know and be able to do?

2. How will we know if each student has learned it?

3. How will we respond when some students do not learn it?

4. How will we extend the learning for students who have demonstrated proficiency?

These questions provide the process for teacher collaboration in a PLC and help to focus teacher collaboration on the right work. PLC schools all have a tight expectation that collaborative team time is focused on answering these four critical questions; therefore, topics that do not move the needle on student learning and teacher effectiveness must be excluded. Without a process to follow, collaborative time can easily be derailed. It is not uncommon for teachers to come to a meeting wanting to discuss an issue that is bothering them. For example, I (Greg) once had a kindergarten team spend an entire collaborative team meeting discussing two topics of importance: "How can we get our students to line up and walk quietly in the hallway?" and "How can we get our students to stop digging holes in the playground sand at recess?" It was clear that these two topics were bothering one or more members of the team, but solving them didn't help one additional kindergarten student learn how to read. Administrative tasks or operational issues like recess supervision schedules, Halloween parades, who gets the laptop cart, or whether students should be allowed to eat in class must be excluded from the collaborative team meetings. Although there may be value in having these discussions, they need to occur at another time, as the collaborative teacher time in a PLC is sacred and is solely focused on improving students' learning. Having a framework for teams to work through helps to ensure this happens. We can begin developing this framework by asking ourselves the four critical questions when it comes to literacy instruction and answering them systematically throughout this chapter. Ensuring teams focus on answering the four critical questions will make each collaborative meeting a valuable experience that helps every team member excel in both the art and the science of classroom instruction.

## Answer Question 1: What Is It We Want Our Students to Know and Be Able to Do?

At first glance, the answer to this question seems self-explanatory. Obviously, we want our students to learn the reading standards or outcomes contained within the state or provincial curriculum documents. Unfortunately, these standard documents contain far too many standards for all students to learn to grade-level proficiency. As a result, when teachers try to teach them all, they are forced to sacrifice in-depth learning in the name of content coverage. While true of all schools, it is especially true of schools that serve students in low socioeconomic neighborhoods as these students often enter school with significant academic disadvantages compared to students from middle-class homes (Chung, 2015). This is a realization that classroom teachers know too well. So to deal with this reality, teachers are forced to make decisions about what standards they will teach, how long they will teach them, and what to leave out when time becomes an issue. Left alone to do this work, it is very possible that individual teachers will make very different decisions than the teacher across the hall even though they teach the same subject and grade. Unfortunately, this variance in teacher decision making can have a profoundly negative impact on student learning. Another reason to select essential standards is to focus the work of a collaborative team on fewer standards so deeper teacher learning can occur. Given the limited time most teacher teams have for collaboration (approximately one hour per week), focusing on fewer standards allows the team members to gain a deeper understanding and gain more clarity regarding the knowledge and skills each standard contains. Collective study of these standards increases teacher clarity and content knowledge, which directly impacts the effectiveness of classroom instruction (Didion, Toste, & Filderman, 2020). However, the distinction between "essential" and "nice to know" does not mean that a teacher has to completely omit the "nice to know" standards. Agreeing that a standard is essential means that ensuring learning on this standard will be the focus and responsibility of the collaborative team. If an individual teacher has the time and wishes to provide instruction on standards not deemed essential, they are welcome to do so. However, for all standards deemed essential, each member of the team agrees to take collective responsibility for grade-level learning for all students taught by their team.

Answering question 1 is all about teachers working together to create a guaranteed and viable curriculum: guaranteed to be taught to every student and viable in that each student can learn it to grade-level proficiency in the time you have (Marzano, 2003). Creating a guaranteed and viable curriculum is crucial to reducing the number of students moving between grade levels with gaps in foundational skills. To do this, a teacher team must build shared knowledge in four areas.

1. Selecting essential reading standards

2. Aligning the essential reading standards

3. Creating a reading year plan

4. Analyzing cognitive tasks

The combination of knowledge and application in these four areas will most often guarantee teachers and teams will successfully answer question 1 together. Selecting essential reading standards is the first step in building a solid understanding of what teams will want students to do, and the particulars are detailed in the following section.

*Selecting Essential Reading Standards*

It will be impossible for a school to create a guaranteed and viable curriculum unless this task is done by the teacher teams within the school. After all, it is the teachers who have to make the guarantee that it will be implemented. In this step of the PLC process, teacher teams are tasked with studying the standards documents to determine which standards are essential and which are just nice to know. When selecting essential standards, it is important to have a common set of criteria that teams can use to determine if a standard is essential. We like the R.E.A.L. criteria outlined by Larry Ainsworth (2015b).

1. **Readiness:** Has this standard been identified as an essential prerequisite skill in the next course or grade level?

2. **Endurance:** Are students expected to retain the knowledge and skill beyond the unit and the course?

3. **Assessment connected:** Is this a concept or skill that students are most likely to encounter on state exams, college entrance exams, or occupational competency exams?

4. **Leverage:** Will the student be able to apply the standard in more than one subject area?

Selecting essential standards for the school begins with the guiding coalition. This team takes lead responsibility for determining the process teams will use, teaching the process to teams, establishing a timeline for the work to be completed, and preparing any materials teams will need to complete the task. We recommend using a common template like the one featured in figure 4.1, which has been filled out with sample standards. The process we use to determine essentials is as follows.

1. Give each team member a copy of the standards template.

2. Select a domain to start with, such as Reading: Literature.

3. In silence, each team member will use the R.E.A.L. criteria to determine the standards they feel are essential. Up to, but no more than, ten minutes should be allotted for individual decisions.

4. At the completion of the allotted time, the team chair will use a new blank template to record the team decisions.

5. Starting with the first standard, work through all of the standards in the domain. If all team members are in agreement that a standard is essential, a brief discussion can be had to explain why. If there is not complete agreement on a standard, the team must come to consensus on a path forward. The teachers on both sides will be given an opportunity to defend their decision. Then, the team will work through this process until they reach consensus.

6. Repeat this process for the remaining domains.

It is important in any collaborative endeavor to ensure the participation of all teachers and ensure all opinions are heard. Buy-in and ownership for the decisions

The Work of Teacher Teams | 61

**Reading: Literature**

**Key Ideas and Details:**

| ☐ Readiness | ☐ Endurance | ☐ Assessment | Leverage |
|---|---|---|---|
| **RL.3.1**<br>Ask and answer questions to demonstrate understanding of a text, referring explicitly to the text as the basis for the answers. | | | Essential |

| ☐ Readiness | ☐ Endurance | ☐ Assessment | Leverage |
|---|---|---|---|
| **RL.3.2**<br>Recount stories, including fables, folktales, and myths from diverse cultures; determine the central message, lesson, or moral and explain how it is conveyed through key details in the text. | | | Essential |

| ☐ Readiness | ☐ Endurance | ☐ Assessment | Leverage |
|---|---|---|---|
| **RL.3.3**<br>Describe characters in a story (e.g., their traits, motivations, or feelings) and explain how their actions contribute to the sequence of events. | | | Essential |

**Craft and Structure:**

| ☐ Readiness | ☐ Endurance | ☐ Assessment | Leverage |
|---|---|---|---|
| **RL.3.4**<br>Determine the meaning of words and phrases as they are used in a text, distinguishing literal from nonliteral language. | | | Nice to Know |

| ☐ Readiness | ☐ Endurance | ☐ Assessment | Leverage |
|---|---|---|---|
| **RL.3.5**<br>Refer to parts of stories, dramas, and poems when writing or speaking about a text, using terms such as chapter, scene, and stanza; describe how each successive part builds on earlier sections. | | | Nice to Know |

| ☐ Readiness | ☐ Endurance | ☐ Assessment | Leverage |
|---|---|---|---|
| **RL.3.6**<br>Distinguish their own point of view from that of the narrator or those of the characters. | | | Nice to Know |

**Integration of Knowledge and Ideas:**

| ☐ Readiness | ☐ Endurance | ☐ Assessment | Leverage |
|---|---|---|---|
| **RL.3.7**<br>Explain how specific aspects of a text's illustrations contribute to what is conveyed by the words in a story (e.g., create mood, emphasize aspects of a character or setting). | | | Nice to Know |

| ☐ Readiness | ☐ Endurance | ☐ Assessment | Leverage |
|---|---|---|---|
| **RL.3.8**<br>(Not applicable to literature) | | | Not Applicable |

| ☐ Readiness | ☐ Endurance | ☐ Assessment | Leverage |
|---|---|---|---|
| **RL.3.9**<br>Compare and contrast the themes, settings, and plots of stories written by the same author about the same or similar characters (e.g., in books from a series). | | | Nice to Know |

**Range of Reading and Level of Text Complexity:**

| ☐ Readiness | ☐ Endurance | ☐ Assessment | Leverage |
|---|---|---|---|
| **RL.3.10**<br>By the end of the year, read and comprehend literature, including stories, dramas, and poetry, at the high end of the grades 2–3 text complexity band independently and proficiently. | | | Nice to Know |

**Figure 4.1: Sample essential standards selection.**

continued ▶

## 62 | BETTER TOGETHER

### Reading: Informational Text

**Key Ideas and Details:**

| ☐ Readiness | ☐ Endurance | ☐ Assessment | Leverage |
|---|---|---|---|
| **RI.3.1** Ask and answer questions to demonstrate understanding of a text, referring explicitly to the text as the basis for the answers. | | | Essential |
| ☐ Readiness | ☐ Endurance | ☐ Assessment | Leverage |
| **RI.3.2** Determine the main idea of a text; recount the key details and explain how they support the main idea. | | | Essential |
| ☐ Readiness | ☐ Endurance | ☐ Assessment | Leverage |
| **RI.3.3** Describe the relationship between a series of historical events, scientific ideas or concepts, or steps in technical procedures in a text, using language that pertains to time, sequence, and cause/effect. | | | Essential |

**Craft and Structure**

| ☐ Readiness | ☐ Endurance | ☐ Assessment | Leverage |
|---|---|---|---|
| **RI.3.4** Determine the meaning of general academic and domain-specific words and phrases in a text relevant to a grade 3 topic or subject area. | | | Nice to Know |
| ☐ Readiness | ☐ Endurance | ☐ Assessment | Leverage |
| **RI.3.5** Use text features and search tools (e.g., key words, sidebars, hyperlinks) to locate information relevant to a given topic efficiently. | | | Nice to Know |
| ☐ Readiness | ☐ Endurance | ☐ Assessment | Leverage |
| **RI.3.6** Distinguish their own point of view from that of the author of a text. | | | Nice to Know |

**Integration of Knowledge and Ideas**

| ☐ Readiness | ☐ Endurance | ☐ Assessment | Leverage |
|---|---|---|---|
| **RI.3.7** Use information gained from illustrations (e.g., maps, photographs) and the words in a text to demonstrate understanding of the text (e.g., where, when, why, and how key events occur). | | | Nice to Know |
| ☐ Readiness | ☐ Endurance | ☐ Assessment | Leverage |
| **RI.3.8** Describe the logical connection between particular sentences and paragraphs in a text (e.g., comparison, cause/effect, first/second/third in a sequence). | | | Nice to Know |
| ☐ Readiness | ☐ Endurance | ☐ Assessment | Leverage |
| **RI.3.9** Compare and contrast the most important points and key details presented in two texts on the same topic. | | | Nice to Know |

**Range of Reading and Level of Text Complexity**

| ☐ Readiness | ☐ Endurance | ☐ Assessment | Leverage |
|---|---|---|---|
| **RI.3.10** By the end of the year, read and comprehend informational texts, including history/social studies, science, and technical texts, at the high end of the grades 2–3 text complexity band independently and proficiently. | | | Nice to Know |

| Reading: Foundational Skills | | | |
|---|---|---|---|

**Phonics and Word Recognition:**

| ☐ Readiness | ☐ Endurance | ☐ Assessment | Leverage |
|---|---|---|---|
| **RF.3.3** Know and apply grade-level phonics and word analysis skills in decoding words. | | | Essential |
| ☐ Readiness | ☐ Endurance | ☐ Assessment | Leverage |
| **RF.3.3.a** Identify and know the meaning of the most common prefixes and derivational suffixes. | | | Essential |
| ☐ Readiness | ☐ Endurance | ☐ Assessment | Leverage |
| **RF.3.3.b** Decode words with common Latin suffixes. | | | Essential |
| ☐ Readiness | ☐ Endurance | ☐ Assessment | Leverage |
| **RF.3.3.c** Decode multisyllable words. | | | Essential |
| ☐ Readiness | ☐ Endurance | ☐ Assessment | Leverage |
| **RF.3.3.d** Read grade-appropriate irregularly spelled words. | | | Essential |

**Fluency**

| ☐ Readiness | ☐ Endurance | ☐ Assessment | Leverage |
|---|---|---|---|
| **RF.3.4** Read with sufficient accuracy and fluency to support comprehension. | | | Essential |
| ☐ Readiness | ☐ Endurance | ☐ Assessment | Leverage |
| **RF.3.4.a** Read grade-level text with purpose and understanding. | | | Essential |
| ☐ Readiness | ☐ Endurance | ☐ Assessment | Leverage |
| **RF.3.4.b** Read grade-level prose and poetry orally with accuracy, appropriate rate, and expression on successive readings. | | | Nice to Know |
| ☐ Readiness | ☐ Endurance | ☐ Assessment | Leverage |
| **RF.3.4.c** Use context to confirm or self-correct word recognition and understanding, rereading as necessary. | | | Essential |

*Source for standards: NGA & CCSSO (2010).*

*Visit **go.SolutionTree.com/literacy** for a free reproducible version of this figure.*

require an opportunity to participate in the process. This is why step 3 involves individual decision making and step 5 ensures both sides of the argument are given an opportunity to state their case. If the team starts by having an open discussion, they run the risk of having some teachers sit in silence while others make all the decisions.

Schools beginning this process often ask how many essential standards they should select. Although we have heard different opinions on the number, we are reluctant to tell a school how many they should choose. The reason we feel this way is that each school is unique, and the number of standards that can be learned to grade level is contextual. Consider the following three schools: School A serves a population of students who come from upper-middle-class homes with well-educated parents. School B serves a population of students from a low-socioeconomic, high-social-vulnerability neighborhood with parents who are working two jobs to survive. School C contains large numbers of English learners and students who are refugees, many who come to school carrying considerable trauma. Should all three of these schools select the same number? If we were to tell them that all schools must select fifteen essentials, school A would probably be fine with that number, but schools B and C might see that number as unrealistic. Therefore, our advice is to select a number that the teachers believe is viable. If they do not believe the number is attainable, it is unlikely they will commit to the work of ensuring students attain grade level for each essential. Schools with significant learning challenges may need to start small and build their way up. It is important to remember that the list is not written in stone and can always be modified as you work your way through the process. Figure 4.2 shows sample grade 3 essential standards.

### Aligning the Essential Reading Standards

When grade-level teams have reached consensus on what is essential, it is time to align the essentials vertically throughout the school. This is a step that cannot be ignored if a school wishes to reduce the number of students who move from grade to grade with gaps in foundational skills. Improving reading schoolwide requires the essential grade-level reading standards be connected so standards taught in one grade ensure students leave with the prerequisite knowledge to be successful in the next grade. For example, if the grade 3 team selects standards 3a, 3b, 3c, and 3d under the Foundational Skills domain, their chances of ensuring grade-level proficiency are greatly increased if the kindergarten, grade 1, and grade 2 teams also select those standards.

The process a school chooses when aligning standards has a lot to do with the structure and amount of collaborative time allotted. If the school has time to meet as a staff, then a whole-staff process can be selected. However, we have worked in districts that have collective agreements that don't allow time for the staff to meet at the same time. Clearly, in this case an alternative process needs to be conducted.

#### Option 1: Whole Staff

Having the opportunity to align standards with all English language arts teachers is a great way to create a common understanding of what will constitute the school's guaranteed and viable reading curriculum. It allows all teachers to see the big picture and clarifies how their grade-level work supports the work of other school teams. Having all staff see the macro view allows for a broader voice in standards selection and encourages the creation of a collective responsibility and ownership for the final decisions.

The Work of Teacher Teams | 65

**Grade 3 Team Essential Reading Standards**

| Domain | Subcategory | |
|---|---|---|
| **Reading: Literature** | **Key Ideas and Details** | |
| **Essential Standard** | **R.E.A.L. Criteria** | **Rationale** |
| **RL.3.1** Ask and answer questions to demonstrate understanding of a text, referring explicitly to the text as the basis for the answers. | Readiness Assessment Connected | Essential for developing comprehension skills. Prepares students for more advanced reading. Often assessed. |
| **RL.3.2** Recount stories, including fables, folktales, and myths from diverse cultures; determine the central message, lesson, or moral and explain how it is conveyed through key details in the text. | Endurance Leverage | Understanding the central message and summarizing are skills that remain necessary over time. Skills applicable across various subjects. |
| **RL.3.3** Describe characters in a story (e.g., their traits, motivations, or feelings) and explain how their actions contribute to the sequence of events. | Readiness Leverage | Enhances understanding of narrative structures. Supports readiness for more complex literature. Leverages skills in social-emotional learning across curricula. |
| **Domain** | **Subcategory** | |
| **Reading: Informational Text** | **Key Ideas and Details** | |
| **Essential Standard** | **R.E.A.L. Criteria** | **Rationale** |
| **RI.3.1** Ask and answer questions to demonstrate understanding of a text, referring explicitly to the text as the basis for the answers. | Readiness Assessment Connected | Fundamental for extracting explicit information. Prepares students for more complex comprehension tasks. Often directly tested in academic assessments. |
| **RI.3.2** Determine the main idea of a text; recount the key details and explain how they support the main idea. | Readiness Assessment Connected | Crucial for long-term academic success. Commonly featured in standardized testing. |
| **RI.3.3** Describe the relationship between a series of historical events, scientific ideas or concepts, or steps in technical procedures in a text, using language that pertains to time, sequence, and cause/effect. | Leverage Readiness | A vital skill for understanding complex texts in content areas. Prepares students for interdisciplinary learning and future academic challenges. |

**Figure 4.2: Example of grade 3 essential standards.**

continued ▶

| Domain | Subcategory | |
|---|---|---|
| **Reading: Foundational Skills** | **Phonics and Word Recognition** | |
| **Essential Standard** | **R.E.A.L. Criteria** | **Rationale** |
| **RF.3.3** Know and apply grade-level phonics and word analysis skills in decoding words. **RF.3.3.a** Identify and know the meaning of the most common prefixes and derivational suffixes. **RF.3.3.b** Decode words with common Latin suffixes. **RF.3.3.c** Decode multisyllable words. **RF.3.3.d** Read grade-appropriate irregularly spelled words. | Readiness Endurance Leverage | Phonics and word recognition are foundational for decoding. Crucial for the development of reading skills. Decoding skills ensure the ability to understand unfamiliar words in text throughout school and life. |

| Domain | Subcategory | |
|---|---|---|
| **Reading: Foundational Skills** | **Fluency** | |
| **Essential Standard** | **R.E.A.L. Criteria** | **Rationale** |
| **RF.3.4** Read with sufficient accuracy and fluency to support comprehension. **RF.3.4.a** Read grade-level text with purpose and understanding. **RF.3.4.c** Use context to confirm or self-correct word recognition and understanding, rereading as necessary. | Assessment Connected Endurance | Fluency is directly linked to comprehension. Crucial for future academic success. Necessary for assessments where understanding and speed are tested. |

*Source for standards: NGA & CCSSO (2010).*

*Visit **go.SolutionTree.com/literacy** for a free reproducible version of this figure.*

This process is best used during a schoolwide professional development day rather than done in parts over several staff meetings. Give the process time, and the result will be a deeper understanding of what students should learn by all who participate. The process is as follows.

1. Have each English language arts team transfer their essential standards from each domain to a separate piece of chart paper.

2. Line the chart paper up on the wall from lowest grade to highest grade in your school.

3. Conduct a gallery walk where each team is given an opportunity to look at the big picture to determine initial alignment and look for places where standards divergence exists between grade levels.

4. Provide an opportunity for each team to give a rationale for the decisions they made.

5. Facilitate a discussion regarding a path forward. As a general rule, you have standards alignment when each grade selects the prerequisite standard for the grade level above within the same domain subcategory. For example, to have alignment in the phonics and word recognition subcategory of the Foundational Skills domain, the skills selected in kindergarten would need to support grade 1, grade 1 would need to support grade 2, and so on.

### Option 2: Above Grade Level and Below Grade Level

If whole-staff professional development days are not available, a second, less inclusive process can be used that still will provide a rich learning opportunity for grade-level teams. Alignment can be achieved by having each English language arts grade-level team meet with the grade-level team above and below and use the following process.

1. Have the guiding coalition create a schedule for team meetings.

2. Have each grade-level team create a "wish list" of prerequisite skills for the three reading domains. This list answers the following question: In a perfect world, all students come into my grade knowing how to do what?

3. Hand this list to the grade level below, and give them an opportunity to check their essentials against the list.

4. During the meeting, the alignment process begins in much the same manner as the essential selection process. Pick a reading domain to start. Then, compare the essentials selected by each team in each of the domain subcategories, looking for similarities and differences. If there is disagreement on an essential standard, both teams provide the rationale for their decisions. Work to achieve consensus.

Though this is a lighter version of a full professional development day of aligning standards, the important takeaway is a consensus-built list of reading essentials across grade levels. This process will set up a team to generate a comprehensive reading year plan.

### Creating a Reading Year Plan

A year plan contains a comprehensive outline or overview of the standards to be taught for an entire academic year. It outlines the scope and sequence of essential and supporting standards to be covered over the course of the school year. It divides the work into manageable units of study and assigns a specific number of instructional days to each unit. When assigning instructional days, teams need to consider the following.

1. Total number of instructional days in the academic year.

2. The portion of days that will not be scheduled, from which the team can draw when unexpected circumstances occur (field trip, fire drill, reteach, and more). For example, the school has 190 days with students in school, so they hold back ten days and only map out 180.

3. The order of the essential standards.

4. Which supporting standards to group with essentials.

5. Some standards will repeat throughout the year.

6. Teams that are in state testing years must have all of the essentials plotted prior to the beginning of the state assessment window.

### Analyzing Cognitive Tasks

Cognitive task analysis (CTA) refers to the systemic process that teacher teams engage in to unpack the knowledge, skills, and mental processes contained within each grade-level standard. According to Winston Sieck (2021), CTA "helps you unpack the thought processes of experts, so you can teach them to others." The goal of the unpacking process is to deconstruct the standard into a scaffold of learning targets that you can share with your students. This is a very important step that often proves difficult the first time teacher teams attempt it. It is not uncommon for frustration to occur as teachers struggle to make sense of the ambiguity of certain standards. As a result, teams may be tempted to skip this step in favor of a less cognitively demanding task. However, it is imperative that teams do not succumb to this desire as this process provides invaluable clarity on what students need to learn and forms the basis of good assessment, instruction, and intervention. There are many ways for teams to work through the unpacking process. However, we have successfully used a process, with slight modifications, outlined by Sharon V. Kramer and Sarah Schuhl (2017).

1. **Identify and highlight the verbs in the standard:** The verbs in a standard provide valuable insights into the level of thinking and the type of skills students should demonstrate.

2. **Underline the nouns or noun phrases:** These represent the specific content knowledge or concepts students are expected to master.

3. **Put brackets around the context contained within the standard:** Context refers to any circumstances or conditions that must occur to learn the standard.

4. **Determine academic vocabulary:** Academic vocabulary refers to any specialized words or phrases that will need to be pretaught to assist students in their understanding of the standard.

The Work of Teacher Teams | 69

5. **Considering the context of the standard, combine the knowledge and skills together to form grade-level student-friendly learning targets:** Learning targets are specific and measurable statements that form a scaffold for what students are expected to know or be able to do as a result of instruction.

6. **Determine the cognitive rigor of each learning target:** *Cognitive rigor* refers to the level of mental complexity and intellectual challenge required to learn each target. Determining the level of rigor is important so the team can plan instruction and assessment that match the requirements of the standard. It can be determined by comparing each learning target to both Bloom's updated taxonomy (Anderson et al., 2001) and Webb's Depth of Knowledge (DOK) model (Webb, 1997). Originally created in 1956 by Benjamin Bloom, the taxonomy was revised in 2001 by Lorin Anderson and David Krathwohl to reflect our current understanding of cognitive processes and skill progression more closely. This tool is used to define and distinguish different levels of human cognition: In other words, it outlines the processes of thinking and learning. Webb's DOK model was developed by Norman Webb to categorize tasks according to the complexity of thinking required to successfully complete them. Bloom's taxonomy is broadly used for overall educational planning and assessment design, while Webb's DOK primarily aids in aligning standards with assessments to ensure cognitive demands are appropriately matched. Combining both tools allows teacher teams to determine the type of instruction they must provide and the type of assessments they must use to match the cognitive processes called for in the standard.

   We recommend using Karin Hess's (2014) cognitive rigor matrix (located online through this link: www.karin-hess.com/free-resources) as a tool to assist teams in determining cognitive rigor. Once learning targets have been determined, teams can compare their target to the criteria listed in Hess's matrix to determine the level of cognitive rigor required to be grade-level proficient on each target.

7. **Write one or two learning targets that extend learning:** Question 4 in a PLC refers to the extension of learning. This is often an overlooked question, as most teams are so busy trying to help students who don't learn that they forget about the needs of the students who learn quickly. Writing extension targets during the unpacking phase can help teachers be better prepared and plan in advance. Determining how to meaningfully extend learning on a standard can be a difficult task. Once again, Hess's matrix can be used to simplify this process for teacher teams. Using the target with the highest level of rigor as a starting point, teams will need to look to the criteria listed at the next highest level of Bloom's taxonomy or move over one DOK. The next-level criteria describe the high-level thinking required for extension to occur.

See figure 4.3 for a sample of how a team can unpack a reading standard into learning targets.

**Standard:**

**RL.4.1**
Refer to details and examples in a text when explaining what the text says (explicitly) and when drawing inferences from the text.

| Skills (Verbs) What students need to be able to do | Content (Nouns) What students need to know |
|---|---|
| Refer | To details<br>To examples |
| Explain | Explicitly what the text says |
| Draw | Inferences based on the text |

**Key Vocabulary:**

Explicit

Inference

| Student Learning Targets: | Bloom's | DOK |
|---|---|---|
| I can refer to details in a text when explaining what the text says explicitly. | Understand | 2 |
| I can refer to examples in a text when explaining what the text says explicitly. | Understand | 2 |
| I can draw inferences from the text to understand implied information. | Analyze | 3 |
| I can explain what the text says using explicit details and examples. | Analyze | 3 |
| **Extension** | | |
| I can analyze the author's choices in language and structure to evaluate the effectiveness of the text. | Evaluate | 4 |

*Source for standard: NGA & CCSSO (2010).*

**Figure 4.3: Unpacked essential reading standards sample.**

*Visit* **go.SolutionTree.com/literacy** *for a free reproducible version of this figure.*

## Answer Question 2: How Will We Know If Each Student Has Learned It?

Answering the second question requires teacher teams to gather evidence of student learning of the essential standards. For a PLC, evidence of learning is collectively gathered through the creation and administration of common assessments. Common assessments provide teacher teams with four key pieces of information necessary to improve student achievement. First, they help a team determine which students are on track for grade-level learning and which students are not. Second, common assessments provide a lens through which teacher teams can measure the effectiveness of their instructional practice. Comparing data from common assessments provides an invaluable opportunity for teacher teams to reflect on their instruction practice. Instructional approaches can be compared and analyzed to determine the most effective strategies for teaching the students they collectively serve. Third, common assessments can identify areas for team growth. Having consistently poor team data is a strong indicator that an instructional change is necessary. If the team is out of new ideas, they can engage in collective inquiry, dig into the research, and learn a different way. Finally, common assessments can be used to create a shared understanding of what grade-level achievement looks like for the assessed standards. If you know where you are going, it is much easier to design classroom experiences that take you there.

### Learn the Types of Assessment

Prior to the beginning of instruction, the teacher team creates an assessment plan that leans heavily on using assessment as a tool to improve learning. As Michael Fullan (2005) points out, "assessment for learning . . . when done well, . . . is one of the most powerful, high-leverage strategies for improving student learning that we know of. Educators collectively at the district and school levels become more skilled and focused at assessing, disaggregating, and using student achievement as a tool for ongoing improvement" (p. 71). A well-designed assessment plan consists of four different types of assessments.

1. **Preassessment:** It is not uncommon for literacy resources to contain preassessments that teachers are expected to give prior to teaching the unit. These assessments are based on the standards the students have yet to learn. The idea of giving this assessment is that after you teach the unit you can give the assessment again and the students will demonstrate growth. We would hope so! However, we fundamentally disagree with this form of preassessment. We have asked teachers all over Canada and the United States a simple question: "How do your students do on the unit preassessment?" The answer is predictable: They fail it. Why give an assessment that you know students are going to fail simply because they have never been taught the material? This practice is even more curious when you think of the negative impact on a student's belief in themselves as a learner when they are continuously set up to fail. A preassessment is an opportunity for teacher teams to find out if students are ready to learn new grade-level content. To do this, a preassessment needs to be based on prerequisite skills from the prior grade, not standards to be learned in the upcoming unit of instruction. This will allow teams to analyze data and make an immediate plan for intervention if students require a review or some lessons to activate prior knowledge.

2. **Daily checks for understanding:** PLCs do not require teachers to use lockstep instructional strategies. Students learn in different ways; therefore, the methods chosen by each teacher to gather evidence of learning and to provide feedback during daily classroom instruction

are up to each teacher. However, there is tremendous value in teachers discussing the methods they use with their teammates. This would be especially helpful to new teachers or teachers who are unfamiliar with daily formative assessment practices. Using learning targets to make lesson goals clear for students, monitoring progress toward target completion, providing feedback on next steps, and providing opportunities for peer and self-assessment are all powerful strategies that need to be learned and refined by each teacher (Pellegrino & Hilton, 2012). In addition, a team may decide to gather and quickly compare evidence of learning through daily formative assessments by creating and giving common exit tickets. Data from common exit tickets can provide teams with opportunities to have data conversations in between larger common assessments.

3. **Common formative assessments:** Common formative assessments are team-generated assessments given at least every three weeks. These assessments measure student performance on each individual learning target taught in a unit up to the assessment date. Data from these assessments will be formally analyzed by the team using a data protocol, and this analysis will inform next steps for classroom instruction. Most importantly, data from these assessments will be used to determine which students require additional time and support on which specific learning targets. These data will be used by the team to create a collaborative intervention plan that demonstrates the team's collective responsibility to ensure grade-level learning for all students.

4. **End-of-unit assessments:** These assessments are designed to assess all of the learning targets associated with the essential standards taught in the unit. They occur after instruction has been completed and should provide confirmation of the student learning evidence gathered throughout the unit. They are called end-of-unit assessments rather than summative assessments as an acknowledgment that learning can continue for students who continue to require additional time and support. There are no state standards that contain a caveat stating they must be learned in a particular amount of time. The only time teachers must make a summative judgment is at the end of the school year. Before that deadline, learning is fluid, and it is the responsibility of the team to make the best use of each instructional day. Once data from these assessments are analyzed by the team, they make a plan for how to proceed. This plan may include more intervention for some students who need it even though they are beginning a new unit of instruction. It's up to the team to determine the best course of action.

### Write a Common Assessment

When writing a common assessment, teams need to ensure that the assessment is both valid and reliable. A common formative assessment is valid when the assessment actually measures the intended learning targets, and it is reliable when the assessment can be given by any teacher and produce the same result. However, when creating a common assessment, the team must also consider the amount of evidence they will collect. The number of student responses must provide sufficient information for the team to make an informed judgment regarding a student's level of proficiency. As a first step in the assessment process, teams will need to establish congruence regarding what constitutes grade-level proficiency for each standard. We have found that asking teams to write a proficiency scale for each standard is a good framework for this discussion. When writing scales, we like to keep it simple by using the learning targets from the unwrapped standard as the benchmark for grade-level proficiency. Therefore, grade-level performance is the result when a student can successfully demonstrate knowledge of each learning target contained with the standard, while above-grade-level performance is defined by the extension targets written during the unpacking process. Close-to-grade-level performance is achieved if a student can successfully demonstrate they understand the targets on the lower level of cognitive rigor but not the higher-level skills. Finally, far-from-proficient performance occurs when the student is unable to demonstrate grade-level learning. See figure 4.4 for a sample of how the team determines grade-level proficiency for the unpacked standard from figure 4.3 (page 70).

---

**Essential Standard:**

**RL.4.1**
Refer to details and examples in a text when explaining what the text says (explicitly) and when drawing inferences from the text.

| | | Highest Level | |
|---|---|---|---|
| **Proficiency Scale** | | **Bloom's** | **DOK** |
| **Above Proficient** | **Understands above-grade-level content**<br>• I can analyze the author's choices in language and structure to evaluate the effectiveness of the text. | **Evaluate** | **Level 4** |
| **Proficient** | **Understands grade-level content**<br>• I can refer to details in a text when explaining what the text says explicitly.<br>• I can refer to examples in a text when explaining what the text says explicitly.<br>• I can draw inferences from the text to understand implied information.<br>• I can explain what the text says using explicit details and examples. | **Analyze** | **Level 3** |
| **Close to Proficient** | **Understands lower-level grade-level content**<br>• I can refer to details in a text when explaining what the text says explicitly.<br>• I can refer to examples in a text when explaining what the text says explicitly. | **Understand** | **Level 2** |
| **Far From Proficient** | **Does not understand grade-level content** | | |

*Source for standard: NGA & CCSSO (2010).*

**Figure 4.4: Essential standard proficiency scale.**

*Visit **go.SolutionTree.com/literacy** for a free reproducible version of this figure.*

Once the team has clarity on the scope of work required to perform at grade level on each essential standard, the team can write their common assessments using the learning targets. If we measure individual student performance on each target, we are better able to determine the specific areas students can do well and those where they require assistance. When writing a common assessment, the team must consider which targets to include on the assessment, what proficiency on each target looks like, and the type of assessment method to use for each target, and they must make sure the assessment method aligns with the cognitive demand of the target. Similar to the unpacking and the proficiency scale processes, teams can use a template to guide their team's thinking. Figure 4.5 provides an example of how a team can plan to assess target 1 of the unpacked essential standard. This template facilitates a conversation regarding how the team will assess each target so a team can write common assessments that align with each target in the standard.

| Grade 4 Common Formative Assessment | |
|---|---|
| **Assessment Date:** TBD | **Unit 1 Narrative Literature** |
| **Essential Standard**<br><br>**RL.4.1**<br>Refer to details and examples in a text when explaining what the text says (explicitly) and when drawing inferences from the text. | |

| **Target 1** | I can refer to details in a text when explaining what the text says explicitly. |
|---|---|
| **Bloom's** | **How will you assess learning?** |
| **Understand**<br>**DOK 2 Method:**<br>**Short Answer** | Students will read the short story called [insert story name] and answer the following questions:<br><br>What specific detail from the first paragraph supports the main idea of the text?<br><br>Teacher team will list possible answers.<br><br>According to the text, how does the main character feel in the second paragraph?<br><br>Teacher team will list possible answers.<br><br>The third paragraph describes a key event. What is that event? Use text evidence to explain how it impacts the main character.<br><br>Teacher team will list possible answers.<br><br>Locate a sentence in the text that directly states the problem the main character is facing. Explain this problem using the details provided in the sentence.<br><br>Teacher team will list possible answers.<br><br>Identify two facts mentioned in the fourth paragraph that explain how the main character resolved the conflict.<br><br>Teacher team will list possible answers. |
| **Proficiency** | Proficiency on this target requires a student to correctly answer 4 out of 5 questions. |

*Source for standard: NGA & C CSSO (2010).*

**Figure 4.5: Grade 4 target 1 common formative assessment.**

*Visit go.SolutionTree.com/literacy for a free reproducible version of this figure.*

## Answer Question 3: How Will We Respond When Some Students Do Not Learn It?

In a traditional school, answering this question is left up to each individual teacher as they are given sole responsibility for ensuring their students can read at grade level. Given the national reading data provided in chapter 1 (page 9), it is fair to assume that when it comes to teaching students to read, this approach has been disastrous. Every year, students are passed from grade level to grade level with foundation gaps because of the variance in individual teacher response.

The key to effective Tier 2 support is for the teachers to respond to student learning needs collectively rather than individually. Intervention should allow for flexible grouping of students so every student can benefit from the expertise of the team rather than just having access to their classroom teacher. The students and their specific learning needs are determined by the team analyzing the results of their common assessments. They use a data protocol to determine which students require support on which specific learning targets. This is why the common assessment is written to address each learning target rather than simply addressing the standard as a whole. We use a three-part data protocol. Part 1 we borrowed from Kramer and Schuhl (2017) as it provides an excellent way to determine which students require additional support on which targets. Part 2 was modified from Buffum and colleagues (2017) as it provides questions for the team to work through that help it dig deeper into the data. Finally, part 3 provides a process for intervention planning.

### Part 1: Identify Student Learning Needs by Target

Using the agreed-on target proficiency, teachers identify and plot the students in each class who were proficient, close to proficient, or far from proficient. Breaking the data down in this way provides a clear picture of the performance of each class, as well as which students require help on which targets. Figure 4.6 (page 76) is an example of how a team would group students by targeted learning need. For the sake of brevity, the number of students listed in each category has been limited.

### Discuss the Data

Use the following questions to dig deeper into the data and reflect on the effectiveness of the assessment.

1. **Did any teacher have significantly better results than the other teachers? If so, how can we learn from this teacher?** This question facilitates a conversation about effective instruction. If the performance of a class is considerably better than the others, we need to ask the teacher of the higher-performing class to share their instructional process.

2. **Are there any areas that the team collectively struggled with?** If a team consistently struggles to produce an acceptable result on a particular standard or target, this is an indicator that the team needs help.

## BETTER TOGETHER

**Learning Target 1**
I can recognize and use common consonant digraphs when reading words.

| | Proficient | Close to Proficient | Far From Proficient |
|---|---|---|---|
| **Ms. Johnson** | Ayaan P.<br>Lina N.<br>Carlos R. | Dante R.<br>Eleni P.<br>Lukas B. | Nora F.<br>Mateo J. |
| **Mr. Smith** | Mia K.<br>Tariq A.<br>Naomi W.<br>Raj S. | Finn M.<br>Amina Z. | None |
| **Ms. Malhotra** | Elena S.<br>Keon B.<br>Isabella R. | Sofia V.<br>Leo F.<br>Anaya G. | Omar N. |
| **Total Team** | | | |

**Learning Target 2**
I can recognize and use long vowel sounds in words with final -e and vowel teams.

| | Proficient | Close to Proficient | Far From Proficient |
|---|---|---|---|
| **Ms. Johnson** | Lina N.<br>Carlos R<br>Oliver S.<br>Yuto N. | Ayaan P.<br>Chloe T.<br>Ivan C.<br>Henri D. | Mateo J. |
| **Mr. Smith** | Mia K.<br>Tariq A.<br>Naomi W.<br>Raj S.<br>Priya N. | Layla F.<br>Nia D.<br>Stefan B. | None |
| **Ms. Malhotra** | Elena S.<br>Keon B.<br>Isabella R.<br>Youssef M. | Sofia V.<br>Leo F.<br>Anaya G.<br>Omar N. | None |
| **Total Team** | | | |

**Learning Target 3**
I can count how many syllables are in a word by recognizing that every syllable must have a vowel sound.

| | Proficient | Close to Proficient | Far From Proficient |
|---|---|---|---|
| **Ms. Johnson** | Lina N.<br>Carlos R.<br>Oliver S.<br>Yuto N. | Ayaan P.<br>Chloe T.<br>Ivan C | Mateo J. |
| **Mr. Smith** | Mia K.<br>Tariq A.<br>Naomi W.<br>Raj S. | Layla F.<br>Nia D.<br>Zoe C. | None |
| **Ms. Malhotra** | Elena S.<br>Keon B.<br>Isabella R.<br>Youssef M. | Zoe A.<br>Finnegan W.<br>Lila C. | None |
| **Total Team** | | | |

**Figure 4.6: Learning target proficiency charts.**

*Visit **go.SolutionTree.com/literacy** for a free reproducible version of this figure.*

When whole classes of students struggle, there is clearly a mismatch between instructional method and student need. To improve their practice, the team might seek support through consultation with a subject-area specialist or instructional coach, or the team can agree to review the research on effective instruction for the targeted area they wish to improve. This is a key question that takes the focus off the students and puts it back onto the actions of the team. Too often we have worked with teams that have blamed poor student performance on demographics or class composition. If a team blames the students, it is unlikely that anything will improve.

3. **If so, what is the team's plan to address this need?** If the team has made the decision to seek outside support, they need to make a plan for when, where, and in what form the support will come. This is an area where the guiding coalition can provide support by reaching out to experts on behalf of the team, scheduling professional development sessions, or compiling initial research for the team to review.

4. **Which instructional practices proved to be most effective?** It is essential for teachers to provide effective Tier 1 instruction for students. If a team is consistently having to provide support to large groups of students, the effectiveness of targeted Tier 2 support will suffer. Since instructional approaches are contextual, the team needs to determine which instructional approaches are most effective with their current groups of students. When a team answers this question, they begin the process of developing an effective tool kit of instructional approaches for the community of learners in their classes.

5. **What patterns can we identify from the student mistakes?** Examining student errors is a valuable exercise for teachers to undertake. Mistakes can reveal misconceptions in student understanding or gaps in student knowledge. In addition, they may uncover a misalignment between classroom instruction and the targets being assessed. Finally, error analysis can be used to help teachers determine an instructional approach to be used with a specific group during Tier 2 intervention.

6. **How can we improve this assessment?** Answering this question requires the team to examine each question for clarity of language using Lexile levels. If students struggled to answer a question correctly, this may indicate that the wording of the question isn't clear and, as a result, students are confused about how to answer the question. In addition, this question facilitates a conversation regarding the validity and reliability of the results.

Though collaborative time may be limited, it benefits the team to discuss and answer these questions together. Have someone record the answers in a manner everyone can access even after the meeting. You will need the final answers to create an intervention plan.

## Make an Intervention Plan

Each time a collaborative team gives a common assessment and analyzes data, they must make a plan for how they will respond to the data. The plan must outline how each student who needs additional time and support will receive it regardless of which teacher they have. This is best done using a flexible grouping model where the team designs and executes the intervention plan together. Working as a team reduces the burden of each teacher to individually provide intervention for all learning targets tested. Using the preceding example, if they were working in isolation, each teacher would need to provide an intervention on each of the three targets. However, working together allows students to be grouped by target with each teacher responsible for only one target.

The first step in planning the intervention is to determine a schedule that ensures all students who need help on more than one target receive it. This can be accomplished by planning for more than one round of intervention and grouping the students accordingly. Using the distribution of data from figure 4.6 (page 76), figure 4.7 provides a sample schedule.

Once we understand how many rounds of intervention to deploy, the team must plan how to address each specific target. This plan will include assigning a teacher to each targeted intervention group, determining which instructional method will be used, the frequency and the duration of the intervention, how the teacher will monitor student progress, and the criteria for proficiency. Figure 4.8 (page 79) is an example of a team plan.

As mentioned in chapter 3 (page 39), the ideal situation occurs when Tier 2 intervention time is part of the master schedule. This ensures that there is time available and conveys an expectation that teacher teams work together to use this time to effectively improve student learning.

In addition to providing support for struggling students, intervention time provides an excellent opportunity for student enrichment. One of the groups could be designated as an enrichment group with students

**Intervention Round 1**

| Target 1 | Target 2 | Target 3 |
| --- | --- | --- |
| Dante R. | Layla F. | Ayaan P. |
| Eleni P. | Nia D. | Chloe T. |
| Lukas B. | Stefan B. | Ivan C. |
| Henri D. | Sofia V. | Zoe C. |
| Sana K. | Leo F. | Zoe A. |
| Nora F. | Anaya G. | Finnegan W. |
| Finn M. | Omar N. | Lila C. |
| Amina Z. | Mateo J. | |

**Intervention Round 2**

| Target 1 | Target 2 | Target 3 |
| --- | --- | --- |
| Sofia V. | Ayaan P. | Layla F. |
| Leo F. | Chloe T. | Nia D. |
| Anaya G. | Ivan C. | Mateo J. |
| Omar N. | Henri D. | |
| | Sana K. | |
| | Nora F. | |

**Intervention Round 3**

| Target 1 | Target 2 | Target 3 |
| --- | --- | --- |
| Chloe T. | None | None |
| Ivan C. | | |
| Mateo J. | | |

**Figure 4.7: Sample of a multiple-round intervention schedule.**

*Visit **go.SolutionTree.com/literacy** for a free reproducible version of this figure*

The Work of Teacher Teams | 79

| Phonics Intervention Round 1 | | | |
|---|---|---|---|
| **Target 1** **Teacher:** Mr. Smith | **Target 2** **Teacher:** Ms. Malhotra | **Target 3** **Teacher:** Ms. Johnson | **Extension** **Teacher:** Support Staff |
| **Area of Focus** | | | |
| I can recognize and use common consonant digraphs when reading words. | I can recognize and use long vowel sounds in words with final -e and vowel teams. | I can count how many syllables are in a word by recognizing that every syllable must have a vowel sound. | Extension activity planned by teacher team. |
| **Instructional Method** | | | |
| **Digraph Sorting** • Review digraphs • Pronounce words and sort by digraph • Independent practice | **Silent -e and Vowel Teams** • Introduce the concept of the silent final -e • Flash card practice recognizing words (cap vs. cape) • Introduce vowel teams (ai, ea, oa, ie, ue) and long sound rule • Flash card practice reading vowel team words • Magic -e wand activity • Vowel team bingo | **Syllable Division** • Review what a syllable is and why they are important • Review three syllable division rules (vowel consonant/consonant vowel, vowel/consonant vowel, and consonant vowel/vowel). • Guided practice with syllable clapping • Independent dividing | The team can use the extension target they created during the unpacking process to design an extension activity for students. |
| **Frequency** | | | |
| 30 mins per day | 30 mins per day | 30 mins per day | 30 mins per day |
| **Duration** | | | |
| Two days | Two days | Two days | Two days |
| **Progress Monitoring** | | | |
| Observation and conversation | Observation and conversation | Observation and conversation | Assessment not required |
| **Expected Level of Proficiency** | | | |
| Students will be able to correctly identify digraphs sh, ch, th, and wh individually and within words. Students will be able to pronounce each diagraph correctly. Students will be able to decode words with diagraphs sh, ch, th, and wh. | Students must orally read and spell words with silent -e and vowel teams. Cloze test • "He likes to r_de his bike." • "I love to p__nt pictures in my art class." | Students will be able to orally identify the three syllable division rules. Students will correctly divide syllables using the rules on the provided worksheet. | Extension activities are not required to be grade-level proficient. They are provided to challenge thinking and foster a love of reading. |
| **Students** | | | |
| Dante R. Eleni P. Lukas B. Henri D. Sana K. Nora F. Finn M. Amina Z. | Layla F. Nia D. Stefan B. Sofia V. Leo F. Anaya G. Omar N. Mateo J. | Ayaan P. Chloe T. Ivan C. Zoe C. Zoe A. Finnegan W. Lila C. | All students not in intervention. |

**Figure 4.8: Intervention group planning chart.**

*Visit **go.SolutionTree.com/literacy** for a free reproducible version of this figure.*

moving into and out of the group when they are not part of a specific intervention group. One of the advantages of identifying enrichment targets during the unwrapping of standards is that the team will already have thought about how to provide effective enrichment.

## Answer Question 4: How Will We Extend the Learning for Students Who Have Demonstrated Proficiency?

If they were honest with themselves, most teachers would admit that they spend very little time planning for and delivering enrichment activities. They are far more worried about the students who do not learn, and planning for their needs consumes all of their time. This means that students who need enrichment often go without. This is why answering question 4 should be undertaken by the team in advance of the start of instruction. Writing extension targets is one way for the team to gain clarity on what meaningful enrichment would entail. Planning activities around these targets in advance would ensure teachers could respond to students in real time rather than having to come up with activities on the spot.

One of the tenets of a PLC is collective responsibility. This means every adult in the building should be considered a resource to be utilized when planning for Tier 2 support, including noncertified staff and building administrators. This is why our sample planning document has support staff taking lead responsibility for monitoring progress of the extension group. Since extension activities are in addition to grade-level outcomes, no formal evaluation of student progress needs to occur. The activities can be designed as low stakes with high engagement rather than achievement as the primary goal—learning for the love of learning instead of learning for the sake of earning a grade. If activities are well thought out, flexible in design, and based on student interest, it is possible to have staff other than the grade-level teachers supervise these activities. However, we understand that not every school has access to additional human resources. Therefore, in situations like this, the teacher team would run one fewer intervention group and adjust the intervention schedule accordingly.

## Plan Units of Instruction

The last thing the team must do prior to beginning instruction is combine what they have learned into units of instruction or instructional cycles. When planning a unit, the team pulls from their previous work. The year plan mapped out the standards to be taught and the length of every unit of instruction. But what it doesn't contain is what will be taught on each day of the unit and when the team will give common assessments. While there are some more detailed unit planning templates available, we have found that using a digital copy of your district's school calendar works quite well. On that calendar the team will plot the following.

- Link your proficiency map.

- Plot the learning targets for each of the instructional days.

- Plot the common formative assessments the team will give during the unit.

- Select and plot reading instructional materials.

- Identify and plot the days when you will analyze data and create an intervention plan.

- Add links to assessments and instructional materials.

- Write SMART goals on the first day of instruction based on preassessment data.

Figure 4.9 (page 82) features a unit plan template you can use as an example alongside your district's school calendar or any other pertinent document.

Creating a common unit plan helps ensure consistency and quality across classrooms while at the same time building a sense of collective responsibility and accountability for the educational outcomes of students. It supports data-driven instruction and shared Tier 2 intervention through the collective use of common formative assessments. However, most importantly, it reduces teacher isolation and promotes reflective discussion on instruction as a pathway to effectively implement evidence-based instruction. In the next section we discuss a framework classroom teachers can use that is supported by research to effectively deliver the instructional strategies outlined in chapters 5 through 9.

## Use the Science of Reading in Lesson Design

At their core, PLCs are based on the development of highly effective collaborative teams. Collaborative teams serve as the mechanism for continuous teacher learning regarding evidence-based practices including the science of reading. However, even though a team can learn together, instruction is still primarily the responsibility of each classroom teacher. Therefore, the focus of teacher collaboration must include practices that ensure all teachers are effective at lesson delivery. Research has consistently affirmed that teacher competence is a critical determinant of student achievement, emphasizing the necessity of proficient classroom instruction for achieving grade-level reading (Didion et al., 2020; Fadlun & Fatmawati, 2023; Johansson, Strietholt, Rosén, & Myrberg, 2014). Teacher competence when teaching reading is enhanced when teachers both possess pedagogical knowledge of effective instructional strategies and experience delivering the strategies. It is this knowledge that allows for real-time, effective, student-driven, adaptive instruction to occur. Effective teachers don't follow the script; they modify the script as needed to meet the learning needs of their students.

Collaborative teams looking to increase the effectiveness of their lesson delivery should plan together using an instructional literacy framework supported by research. An instructional framework is a detailed road map that outlines the concepts, strategies, and practices used to deliver effective instruction. It serves as a

> **Teacher competence when teaching reading is enhanced when teachers both possess pedagogical knowledge of effective instructional strategies and experience delivering the strategies.**

## Unit Plan

| SMART goal: [Insert SMART goal for this unit.] | | | Proficiency map: [Link to map.] | |
|---|---|---|---|---|
| **Day 1 Targets:** | **Day 2 Targets:** | **Day 3 Targets:** | **Day 4 Targets:** | **Day 5 Targets:** |
| [Insert learning targets] | [Insert learning targets] | [Insert learning targets] | [Insert learning targets] | [Insert learning targets] |
| **Instruction:** | **Instruction:** | **Instruction:** | **Instruction:** | **Instruction:** |
| What materials will be used for instruction? | What materials will be used for instruction? | What materials will be used for instruction? | What materials will be used for instruction? | What materials will be used for instruction? |
| **Daily Assessment:** | **Daily Assessment:** | **Daily Assessment:** | **Daily Assessment:** | **Daily Assessment:** |
| Daily formative check for understanding | Daily formative check for understanding | Daily formative check for understanding | Daily formative check for understanding | Daily formative check for understanding |
| **Tier 3 Intervention:** | **Tier 3 Intervention:** | **Tier 3 Intervention:** | **Informal Data Talk:** | **Tier 2 Intervention:** |
| Team helps students with gaps in necessary prior skills. | Team helps students with gaps in necessary prior skills. | Team helps students with gaps in necessary prior skills. | Team discusses student progress based on daily formative assessments. | Execute intervention plan during intervention block. |
| **Day 6 Targets** | **Day 7 Targets** | **Day 8 Targets** | **Day 9 Targets** | **Day 10 Targets** |
| [Insert learning targets] | [Insert learning targets] | [Insert learning targets] | [Insert learning targets] | [Insert learning targets] |
| **Instruction:** | **Instruction:** | **Instruction:** | **Instruction:** | **Instruction:** |
| What materials will be used for instruction? | What materials will be used for instruction? | What materials will be used for instruction? | What materials will be used for instruction? | What materials will be used for instruction? |
| **Daily Assessment:** | **Common Formative Assessment:** | **Daily Assessment:** | **Daily Assessment:** | **Daily Assessment:** |
| Daily formative check for understanding | Team-created assessment | Daily formative check for understanding | Daily formative check for understanding | Daily formative check for understanding |
| **Tier 2 Intervention:** | **Tier 2 Intervention:** | **Data Analysis and Intervention Planning:** | **Tier 2 Intervention:** | **Tier 2 Intervention:** |
| Execute intervention plan during intervention block. | Execute intervention plan during intervention block. | Team looks at data for common formative assessment and plans intervention. | Execute Intervention plan during intervention block. | Continue intervention. |
| **Day 11 Targets** | **Day 12 Targets** | **Day 13 Targets** | **Day 14 Targets** | **Day 15** |
| [Insert learning targets] | [Insert learning targets] | [Insert learning targets] | [Insert learning targets] | **End-of-Unit Assessment:** |
| **Instruction:** | **Instruction:** | **Instruction:** | **Instruction:** | Cumulative assessment |
| What materials will be used for instruction? | What materials will be used for instruction? | What materials will be used for instruction? | What materials will be used for instruction? | |
| **Daily Assessment:** | **Daily Assessment:** | **Daily Assessment:** | **Daily Assessment:** | |
| Daily formative check for understanding | Daily formative check for understanding | Daily formative check for understanding | Daily formative check for understanding | |
| **Tier 2 Intervention:** | **Tier 2 Intervention:** | **Tier 2 Intervention:** | **Tier 2 Intervention:** | |
| Continue intervention. | Continue intervention. | Continue intervention. | Continue intervention. | |

**Figure 4.9: Unit plan template.**

*Visit **go.SolutionTree.com/literacy** for a free reproducible version of this figure.*

blueprint for educators, helping them plan, implement, and assess teaching and learning processes. Douglas Fisher and Nancy Frey (2021) outline the advantages of teachers using a common instructional framework for lesson design and delivery.

- **Structural consistency:** Provides a clear, consistent structure for lessons, ensuring that all essential components of reading instruction are systematically addressed.

- **Optimal strategy selection:** Helps teachers make informed decisions about which strategies are most effective for different reading skills and student needs.

- **Common vocabulary:** Facilitates communication and collaboration among teachers by providing a common language to discuss instructional practices and student progress.

- **Scaffolded learning:** Supports the gradual release of responsibility from teacher to student, promoting independent reading skills.

- **Adaptability:** Allows for flexibility and adaptation to different instructional settings, including face-to-face, distance learning, blended, or hybrid models.

- **Targeted professional development:** Identifies specific areas for professional growth, enabling teams to seek out training and resources to improve their reading instruction.

- **Student engagement:** Organizes lessons in a way that keeps students engaged and motivated, making reading instruction more effective and enjoyable.

- **Holistic approach:** Ensures a comprehensive approach to teaching reading that integrates various components of the five pillars of literacy instruction (see chapter 1, page 9).

One of the most common and effective literacy instructional frameworks a team can use when planning for effective reading instruction is the gradual release of responsibility (GRR) model. Developed originally by P. David Pearson and Margaret C. Gallagher in 1983 (cited in Pearson, McVee, & Shanahan, 2019), the GRR model has stood the test of time with research consistently reinforcing its effectiveness for improving reading achievement in students with and without disabilities (Hall, Dahl-Leonard, Denton, Stevens, & Capin, 2021). During the implementation of this framework, reading instruction begins with teachers taking responsibility for learning through direct instruction. However, as the lesson progresses, the emphasis for learning is transferred from the teacher to the class, finally culminating with individual students. The end goal is a student who is able to independently demonstrate learning because they were effectively supported throughout the lesson. The original three stages of the GRR model contained an explanation and modeling stage, a guided practice stage, and an independent practice stage. These three stages were coined as "I Do, " "We Do," and "You Do" by Anita L. Archer and Charles A. Hughes (2011), which is how many educators have come to describe this framework. However, Douglas Fisher and Nancy Frey (2013) added a fourth stage to this framework to include a stage between the guided practice stage and the independent practice stage. This new stage, dubbed the "You All Do" phase, incorporates collaborative learning between pairs or small groups of students. Bridging the gap between guided practice and independent practice allows for more responsibility to be transferred to the students while still allowing for teacher feedback. A lesson using the GRR model contains the following (Hall et al., 2021).

1. **Focused instruction:** This stage is often referred to as the "I Do" stage where the teacher provides direct and focused instruction on a specific reading skill.

2. **Guided instruction:** This is the "We Do" stage where the class begins to practice the skill with the teacher.

3. **Collaborative practice:** This "You All Do" stage provides opportunities for students to practice the skill in pairs or small groups. The teacher is still able to monitor and support groups as needed.

4. **Independent practice:** The "I Do" stage shifts responsibility for learning to each individual student. They should be able to respond and practice independent of teacher support.

Working together as a team is a great way to learn about how to effectively design and implement lessons using this model. One of the advantages to designing lessons together is that the team is more likely to ensure all aspects of the instructional design are planned and implemented. One of the biggest challenges teachers encounter when using this model is the inadequate allocation of time on the practice stages of the model (Hall et al., 2021; Lin & Cheng, 2010; Okkinga, Steensel, Gelderen, & Sleegers, 2018). They either move too quickly to independent practice or spend too much time on teacher instruction. Working as a team would help mitigate this issue, especially if the team periodically made time to engage in collaborative reflection to examine the effectiveness of their lesson design and delivery. Figure 4.10 provides an example of how a lesson could be constructed using the GRR model.

## Conclusion

Teaching is an intricate blend of art and science. When educators grasp the scientific principles underlying their craft, they empower themselves to deliver more impactful instruction. When it comes to reading instruction, the science of reading stands out as a crucial guide, delineating the most effective methods for teaching the five pillars of reading to students. However, expecting teachers to learn and apply these strategies by themselves can be a significant challenge. Working as a member of a collaborative team affords teachers the opportunity to learn and develop their expertise in the science of reading within an environment of support and encouragement. Collaborative teacher teams can move the needle on student reading

The Work of Teacher Teams | 85

**Lesson Title:** Morphology

**Grade Level:** 3

**Subject:** English Language Arts

**Lesson:** 1

**Outcome Addressed:** The study of words and how they are formed (morphology) can support development of vocabulary and enhance comprehension.

**Learning Targets:**
I can understand that English words are made up of base words, prefixes, and suffixes.
I can understand that base words are complete words that stand on their own.
I can understand that suffixes are not words on their own and must be added to the end of base words.
I can understand that adding suffixes changes the meaning of a base word.
I can use the morpheme -er to change the meaning of a base to mean "more."
I can use the morpheme -er to change the meaning of a base to "one who does."

**Materials Needed:**
- Whiteboards and markers
- Word cards with base words (play, run, teach, drive, paint, and so on)
- Suffix cards with -er
- Paper and pencils

| Instructional Framework | Activities | Time |
|---|---|---|
| **Teacher Model ("I Do")** | **Teacher Script:**<br><br>• "Today, we are going to learn about how English words are made. Many words are made up of smaller parts called bases, prefixes, and suffixes."<br>• "A base is a complete word that can stand on its own." "What is a base? [Choral response.] For example, 'play' is a base word."<br>• "Prefixes and suffixes are added to bases to change their meaning. A prefix is added to the beginning of a base, and a suffix is added to the end."<br><br>**Teacher Example:**<br><br>• Write examples on the board (replay where re- is a prefix and playful where -ful is a suffix) and have students identify the base word, prefix, and suffix.<br><br>**Teacher Script:**<br><br>• "Now, let's learn about suffixes. A suffix is a group of letters added to the end of a base to change its meaning. A suffix cannot stand alone."<br>• "Adding a suffix to a base changes its meaning. Let's see how this works."<br>• "The suffix -er can be used to compare things. It can mean 'more.' For example, slow becomes slower to mean more slow."<br><br>**Teacher Example:**<br><br>• Provide pairs of adjectives and have students add -er to make comparisons (warm to warmer, quick to quicker, small to smaller).<br>• Write examples on the board (big to bigger, fast to faster) and explain the comparative meaning.<br><br>**Teacher Script:**<br><br>• "The suffix -er can also change a verb to mean 'one who does.' For example, teach becomes teacher to mean one who teaches."<br><br>**Teacher Example:**<br><br>• Write examples on the board (hunt to hunter, paint to painter) and explain the new meaning. | Ten minutes |

**Figure 4.10: Morphology lesson using an instructional framework.**

continued ▶

| | | |
|---|---|---|
| **Guided Practice ("We Do")** | **Student Activity:**<br><br>Have the students pull out their whiteboards.<br><br>Write a word on your whiteboard from the following list.<br><br><table><tr><td>faster</td><td>worker</td><td>baker</td></tr><tr><td>traveler</td><td>higher</td><td>player</td></tr><tr><td>starter</td><td>walker</td><td>lighter</td></tr></table><br><br>**For each given word, have the students do the following:**<br>• Write the word on their whiteboard.<br>• Put a plus sign between the base word and the suffix (-er).<br>• Write how the -er suffix changes the word.<br><br>**Example:**<br>Thinker<br>Think + er<br>Person | Fifteen minutes |
| **Collaborative Practice ("You All Do")** | **Have students work in pairs:**<br>• Using their whiteboards students each create a list of five to ten base + -er words.<br>• Students will exchange lists and see if they can separate the base from the suffix the same way they did during the guided practice portion of the lesson.<br><br>**Extension Activity:**<br>• Students work together to identify -er suffix words in a continuous piece of text.<br>• This activity includes words with prefixes and words that use spelling rules not explicitly covered in this lesson.<br>• This activity can serve as an introduction to working with these types of morphemes.<br><br>**Sample text:**<br>During recess, the third graders excitedly gathered on the field for a game of baseball. The pitcher stood ready, waiting for the batter to take a swing. The catcher crouched behind the plate, his eyes focused on the ball. As the batter hit the ball, the runner sprinted toward first base. The fielders quickly moved to catch the ball and throw it to the base. The outfielder ran fast to catch the fly ball, while the infielder scooped up grounders. Everyone cheered when a player made a good play. The teacher watched with a smile, proud of the effort and teamwork the students showed. | Ten minutes |
| **Independent Practice ("You Do")** | • Students complete a worksheet where they have to fill in the blanks to complete the line.<br>• Combine the base and suffix to make a new word.<br>• Break apart the word into base and suffix.<br>• Determine if the suffix changes the meaning of the word to more or a person.<br>• See the following worksheet. | Ten minutes |

| Base | | Suffix | | Word | Change [more] [person] |
|---|---|---|---|---|---|
| light | + | er | = | lighter | more |
| bake | + | er | = | | |
| | + | | = | worker | |
| own | + | er | = | | |
| call | + | er | = | | |
| | + | | = | longer | |
| | + | | = | talker | |
| fast | + | er | = | | |
| | + | | = | watcher | |

| quick | + | er | = | | |
|---|---|---|---|---|---|
| | + | | = | smarter | |
| few | + | er | = | | |
| | + | | = | younger | |
| Assessment | | | • Observation during guided practice<br>• Observation of group discussions<br>• Morphology worksheets | | |
| Differentiation and Accommodations | | | • Provide additional visual aids and manipulatives for students who need extra support (for example, precut cards with bases and suffix -er to be used instead of whiteboards).<br>• Have advanced students create their own words.<br>• Provide one-to-one support as needed. | | |
| Reflection | | | • What worked well?<br>• Areas for improvement. | | |

*Visit **go.SolutionTree.com/literacy** for a free reproducible version of this figure.*

achievement by using the PLC process to learn a consistent approach to reading instruction that encompasses the principles of structured literacy. Although this chapter has described how the PLC process can be used to build shared knowledge regarding what to teach, how to assess, how to intervene when students struggle, and how to extend learning when they do not, we have not directly addressed instruction. The subsequent chapters in this book will introduce instructional strategies to support each pillar that collaborative teams can learn and incorporate into daily instruction. By marrying the artistry of teaching with the insights of educational science within the supportive context of PLCs, educators can actually attain their goal of grade-level reading for all.

# Key Readings and Resources

- Ainsworth, L. (2015b, February 24). *Priority standards: The power of focus.* Accessed at https://www.edweek.org/teaching-learning/opinion-priority-standards-the-power-of-focus/2015/02 on June 19, 2024.

- Didion, L., Toste, J., & Filderman, M. (2020). Teacher professional development and student reading achievement: A meta-analytic review of the effects. *Journal of Research on Educational Effectiveness*, 13, 29–66. https://doi.org/10.1080/19345747.2019.1670884

- Hall, C., Dahl-Leonard, K., Denton, C., Stevens, E., & Capin, P. (2021). Fostering independence while teaching students with or at risk for reading disabilities. *Teaching Exceptional Children*, 54, 124–133. https://doi.org/10.1177/0040059921994596

- Kramer, S. V., & Schuhl, S. (2017). *School improvement for all: A how-to guide for doing the right work.* Bloomington, IN: Solution Tree Press.

- Mattos, M., Buffum, A., Malone, J., Cruz, L. F., Dimich, N., & Schuhl, S. (2025). *Taking action: A handbook for RTI at Work* (2nd ed.). Bloomington, IN: Solution Tree Press.

# PART 2

# CLASSROOM IMPLEMENTATION USING THE SCIENCE OF READING

Part 2 of *Better Together* addresses what the science of reading says about effective reading instruction and assessment. More specifically, we focus on the five pillars of literacy instruction (phonological awareness, phonics, fluency, vocabulary, and reading comprehension), and we present why each component is relevant and requires explicit teaching. Chapter 5 (page 91) focuses on phonological awareness, chapter 6 (page 105) on phonics, chapter 7 (page 117) on fluency, chapter 8 (page 133) on vocabulary, and chapter 9 (page 151) on reading comprehension. Although there may be additional skills involved in learning to read, these five pillars represent the most critical skills in learning to read English (August & Shanahan, 2006; National Reading Panel, 2000).

## For Teachers: Applying Research-Based Instructional Practices For Student Reading Success

For teachers, this section provides the knowledge to effectively provide direct and systematic reading instruction for their students. Each chapter begins with a comprehensive explanation of "why" the pillar is important and the role it plays in reading development. Providing a clear rationale is essential if we expect teachers to buy in and commit to learning how to implement evidence-based reading instruction. Next, each chapter focuses on "how" to teach one of the five pillars of reading so teachers can provide effective instruction in their classroom. Included in each chapter are assessment tools to help teachers assess and monitor the progress of their students as they develop into strong readers. Our goal in writing this section was to provide teachers with everything they need to increase their understanding and build their confidence so they can successfully transition their practice to evidence-based reading instruction.

## For Leaders: Ensuring Schoolwide Implementation of Effective Reading Practices

At first glance, school administrators may look at the content of part 2 and dismiss it as information only for teachers. Although it is unlikely that principals will be directly involved in delivering classroom reading instruction, the information contained in this section is essential for them to know. This book takes a whole-school approach to improving reading that requires principals to understand what they are asking their teachers to do. Without a clear understanding of what the science tells us is effective reading instruction and assessment, it is difficult to monitor the progress of implementation. School improvement is a collaborative effort that is enhanced when principals engage in learning alongside their teachers.

CHAPTER 5

# Phonological Awareness

Phonological awareness, the ability to hear and manipulate the units of sound in a spoken language, is one of the strongest predictors of reading ability and a core deficit in reading disabilities. Evidence in support of the crucial role of phonological awareness in reading and spelling acquisition comes from both correlational and intervention studies, including systematic reviews (Blachman, Tangel, Ball, Black, & McGraw, 1999; Galuschka, Ise, Krick, & Schulte-Körne, 2014; Landerl, Castles, & Parrila, 2022; Muter, Hulme, Snowling, & Stevenson, 2004; Webber et al., 2024). For example, the National Reading Panel (2000) concludes after reviewing fifty-two experimental studies published in peer-reviewed journals that phonological awareness instruction has statistically significant effects on reading and spelling and that explicit instruction is beneficial for typically developing students, for young students at risk for reading difficulties, and for poor readers. In his popular book *Visible Learning: The Sequel*, John Hattie (2023) also includes phonological awareness in a list of the top five most effective educational practices along with phonics. Thus, teaching phonological awareness to students is critical for their later reading and spelling development.

We wish to emphasize from the very beginning of this chapter that phonological awareness activities are to be performed orally (in the absence of written letters). In other words, they can be done with your eyes closed. At the same time, instruction in phonological awareness should never be considered an end in itself. According to the National Reading Panel (2000), phonological awareness instruction is most effective when students are taught to use letters as they manipulate phonemes (Erbeli, Rice, Xu, Bishop, & Goodrich, 2024; Stalega, Kearns, Bourget, Bayer, & Hebert, 2024).

In this chapter, we aim to describe phonological awareness, how to teach it, and how to assess it. Similar to any other skill described in this book, teaching phonological awareness should be explicit and systematic.

## The Meaning of Phonological and Phonemic Awareness

An important distinction we should make at this point is between phonological awareness and phonemic awareness. These terms are not the same and should not be used interchangeably. In essence, phonemic awareness is the most complex phonological awareness skill, the end tail of the phonological awareness continuum.

- **Phonological awareness:** It is a general concept used to describe an individual's ability to process large chunks of speech. It includes awareness of number of words in a sentence, rhyming and alliteration, syllables within words, and onset and rime (onset in a one-syllable word is the beginning consonant, and rime is the vowel and whatever comes after it within the syllabic boundaries). For example, when a teacher says, "Do *cat* and *mat* rhyme?," the teacher is asking the student to pay attention to the rhyming unit (*-at*), which means that the activity taps into phonological awareness.

- **Phonemic awareness:** It is the ability to identify and manipulate individual sounds (otherwise known as phonemes) in spoken language. It includes skills such as blending, segmentation, deletion, addition, and substitution. For example, when a teacher says, "What is left in the word *cat* after deleting the /k/ sound?," the teacher is asking the student to delete an individual sound (not a group of sounds), and this means the activity taps into phonemic awareness.

Phonological awareness is one of the components of *phonological processing* (an umbrella term referring to the use of the sounds in one's language to process spoken and written language), along with phonological retrieval (otherwise known as rapid automatized naming) and phonological short-term memory (Torgesen, Wagner, Rashotte, Burgess, & Hecht, 1997). We prefer to keep the term "phonological awareness" as the skill that is subsumed under phonological processing. Phonemic awareness is included in phonological awareness. That explains why assessment batteries of phonological processing like the Comprehensive Test of Phonological Processing, Second Edition (described on page 97), include measures of phonological awareness, rapid automatized naming, and phonological short-term memory (Wagner, Torgesen, Rashotte, & Pearson, 2013). Phonological awareness correlates significantly with rapid automatized naming and phonological short-term memory (Swanson, Trainin, Necoechea, & Hammill, 2003) but contributes to reading and spelling independently (Caravolas, Lervåg, Defior, Seidlová Málková, & Hulme, 2013; Ergül et al., 2022; Parrila et al., 2004; Powell & Atkinson, 2021).

As shown in Figure 5.1, phonological awareness is better conceptualized as a continuum of skills that develop over time (Al Otaiba, Allor, Werfel, & Clemens,

> Phonological awareness is better conceptualized as a continuum of skills that develop over time.

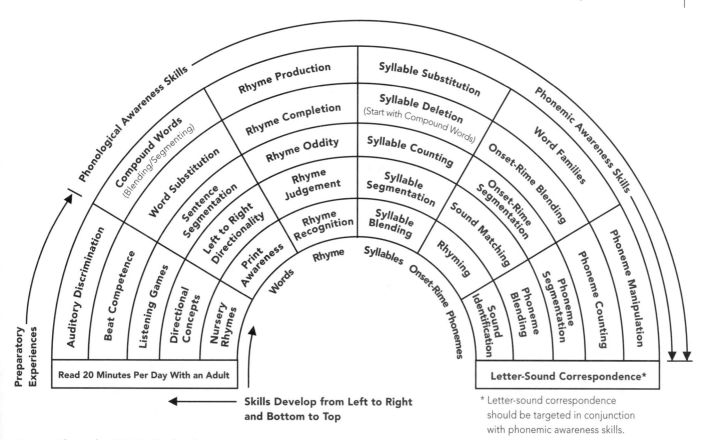

*Source: Schumacher (2013). Used with permission.*

**Figure 5.1: Continuum of phonological awareness.**

2016; Anthony & Francis, 2005). Initially, students are able to segment sentences into words (mastered by most students by age 5), and then they can identify syllables within words and blend or segment onset and rime within a syllable (mastered by most students by age 6). Finally, they can identify, blend, segment, and manipulate phonemes within syllables (mastered by most students by the age of eight). It is important to note that these skills do not develop in a lockstep fashion, meaning that one skill does not have to be fully developed before another may emerge.

It should be noted that this follows more or less the natural breakdown of a word into its sound units. For example, if we think of the word *black*, it has one syllable that can be broken down into an onset (*bl-*) and rime (*-ack*), representing four phonemes (/b/, /l/, /a/, and /k/). See figure 5.2 (page 94) for a visual sample of the breakdown. By being able to break down a word into its constituent phonemes, students can better understand the alphabetic principle, which is the basis of decoding (Foorman et al., 2016).

## Why We Should Teach Phonological Awareness

There are seven reasons why we should teach phonological awareness. They are as follows.

1. It is one of the best predictors of word reading and spelling in alphabetic orthographies like English, particularly at the beginning of learning

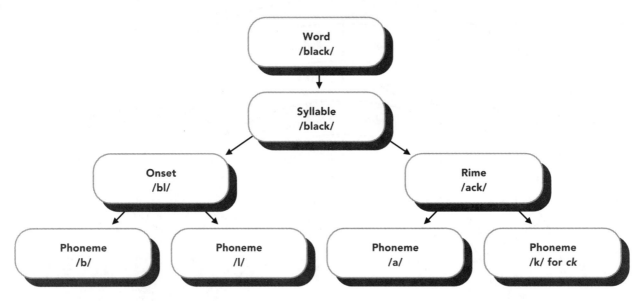

Figure 5.2: Word-to-phoneme breakdown.

> Phonological awareness is one of the best predictors of word reading and spelling in alphabetic orthographies like English.

to read and spell. In other words, if we know a student's score in phonological awareness in kindergarten, we can use their score to predict their reading and spelling ability in later grades and estimate the risk of that student developing reading difficulties. Importantly, the effect of phonological awareness on reading is independent of other key predictors of reading such as letter knowledge, vocabulary, automatized naming, and morphological awareness (Georgiou, Parrila, & Papadopoulos, 2008; Furnes & Samuelsson, 2011; Kirby, Parrila, & Pfeiffer, 2003; Parrila et al., 2004; Torgesen et al., 1997).

2. It is a core deficit in reading disabilities (Hulme & Snowling, 2014). This means that most students with word reading difficulties (dyslexia) experience deficits in phonological awareness. In a study we ran a few years ago with grade 2 and 6 struggling readers in Edmonton (Alberta, Canada), 82 percent of them scored more than a standard deviation below average in phonological awareness.

3. It is a prerequisite to phonics instruction. As you will learn in chapter 6 (page 105), in phonics, students must blend together the sounds of the letters in order to decode a word (/d/, /o/, /g/ → *dog*). For this to happen, students should be well versed in blending sounds. In addition, when asked to spell a word, students must first segment the sounds in the word and then convert the sounds they hear to their corresponding letters. For this to happen, students should be well versed in phoneme segmentation. Good blending and segmentation skills make it easier for beginning readers to understand that written words are composed of graphemes (letters or letter combinations) that correspond to phonemes, a concept called the "alphabetic principle." Researchers consider the alphabetic principle to be the bridge between phonological awareness and phonics.

4. It plays an important role in orthographic mapping. According to Ehri (1997), once a word has been identified through phonological decoding (sounding out), readers connect that new information (the newly identified written word) to an existing representation in long-term memory, namely the word's pronunciation. Access to the word's pronunciation must be made at the phoneme level in order to accurately distinguish between words that share many of their sounds (such as *winner* and *winter*). Without phoneme-level awareness as well as access (indexed by performance in rapid automatized naming tasks; see chapter 7, page 117), there are no reliable anchoring points for the specific letter sequences in words to become "bonded" to the spoken pronunciations.

5. Phonological awareness skills can be transferred from a student's first language (L1) to the student's second language (L2). English learners already have phonological awareness skills in their first language, and teachers can capitalize on that knowledge to improve phonological awareness and decoding in English because that knowledge is transferrable. For example, Yang Cathy Luo, Xi Chen, and Esther Geva (2014) show that phonological awareness in Chinese (L1) was predictive of reading in English (L2). Elsa Cárdenas-Hagan (2020) offers several examples of sounds that are common between language pairs (Spanish and English) that teachers can purposely incorporate in their teaching.

6. Explicit and systematic instruction in phonological awareness, along with direct instruction in phonics, can prevent and remediate reading difficulties (Al Otaiba et al., 2016; Shapiro & Solity, 2008). For example, Donna M. Scanlon, Frank R. Vellutino, Sheila G. Small, Diane P. Fanuele, and Joan M. Sweeney (2005) show that the number of students who experienced reading difficulties in grade 1 could be substantially reduced through the provision of a rather limited kindergarten intervention program (thirty minutes twice per week for twenty-five weeks) focusing on phonological awareness skills. Their study also finds that students who experienced reading difficulties, despite having the supplemental intervention in kindergarten, were much less likely to demonstrate severe reading difficulties at the end of grade 1 than were students who did not participate in the kindergarten intervention.

7. Phonological awareness appears to be the "gatekeeper" to who may benefit from phonics intervention. For example, Robert Savage and colleagues (2020) show that grade 2 students with reading difficulties who responded favorably to phonics intervention had started the intervention program with higher phonological awareness.

In view of the importance of phonological awareness in literacy acquisition, it is crucial to teach it. In the next section, we discuss how to assess the level of phonological awareness in students to gauge how to teach it.

## How to Assess Phonological Awareness

Formal and informal assessments of phonological awareness are an integral part of instruction (see chapter 1, page 9). Whatever instrument you choose to assess your students' phonological awareness, you should use the data generated from the assessment to guide your instruction. This is particularly important in the case of students with decoding problems, as they most often experience difficulties in phonological awareness. Assessing them in phonological awareness will help you determine (1) if they experience difficulties in phonological awareness and (2) in what specific phonological awareness subskill. You can then use this information to better target your classroom instruction or intervention. We recommend you use informal assessments of phonological awareness every two to three weeks to see if your students have mastered the different phonological awareness subskills you have taught them and formal assessments of phonological awareness three times a year (September, January, and May).

### Informal Assessments

Stephanie Al Otaiba, Marcia L. Kosanovich, and Joseph K. Torgeson (2012) provide a table with several phonological awareness assessments. Some of the informal assessments are the Yopp-Singer Test of Phoneme Segmentation (kindergarten to grade 1), the Fox in a Box (kindergarten to grade 2), and the Rosner Test of Auditory Analysis Skills (kindergarten to grade 3).

The Phonological Awareness Screening Test (accessible online at thepasttest.com), developed by David Kilpatrick, has four alternate forms. The test assesses students' knowledge of basic syllable levels, onset-rime levels, basic phoneme levels, and advanced phoneme levels. Information on how to effectively use the test can also be found in chapter 11 of Kilpatrick's (2015) manual, called "Equipped for Reading Success".

You may also want to check out these websites, as they also have freely accessible phonological awareness measures along with instructions on how to administer them.

- **Abecedarian (Wren & Watts, 2002):** www.pathstoliteracy.org/wp-content/uploads/2022/06/abecedarian.pdf
- **Really Great Reading:** www.reallygreatreading.com/diagnostics
- **DIBELS (University of Oregon):** www.dibels.uoregon.edu/materials/dibels
- **Heggerty:** www.heggerty.org/assessments

### Formal Assessments

In this section we describe five formal (or norm-referenced) assessments. The purpose of norm-referenced assessments is to provide a standard score or a percentile rank that allows us to compare a student's performance to the performances of other students of the same age or grade level based on a large national sample that is assumed to represent the demographics of the target population. Here are a few we recommend.

#### Comprehensive Test of Phonological Processing, Second Edition (CTOPP-2)

This battery of tasks includes a set of phonological awareness measures that can be administered to individuals four to twenty-four years of age (Wagner et al., 2013). The phonological awareness tasks include phoneme matching, elision (saying what is left in a word after deleting one of its sounds), blending words, phoneme isolation, blending nonwords, and segmenting nonwords. For ages four to six, a composite score can be calculated from students' scores in elision, blending words, and sound matching. In turn, for ages seven to twenty-four, a composite score can be calculated from elision, blending words, and phoneme isolation. An alternate composite score for phonological awareness can also be formed by combining the scaled scores in blending nonwords and segmenting nonwords. A big advantage of the CTOPP-2 is that it provides norms for older students, which means that it can be used even in upper elementary grades when we suspect that a student might be experiencing phonological awareness deficits and could benefit from phonological awareness intervention.

#### Test of Phonological Awareness, Second Edition: PLUS (TOPA-2+)

The TOPA-2+ is either group administered or individually administered and is appropriate for students ages five through eight years (Torgesen & Bryant, 2004). The TOPA-2+ has two versions, a Kindergarten version and an Early Elementary version, that measure young students' ability to (1) isolate individual phonemes in spoken words and (2) understand the relationships between letters and phonemes in English. Items on the Kindergarten version present a target word and ask students to choose which of three other words begins with the same sound, and then which of four other words begins with a different sound. Items on the Early Elementary version are similar in format, but require students to identify final sounds, which is more difficult.

#### Test of Preschool Early Literacy (TOPEL)

The TOPEL is individually administered and is appropriate for ages three to five years (Lonigan, Wagner, Torgesen, & Rashotte, 2007). Beyond print knowledge and vocabulary, the TOPEL measures phonological awareness. In the first twelve items of the phonological awareness task, the student is asked to say a word and then say what is left in the word after deleting specific sounds (elision). In the remaining fifteen items, the student is asked to listen to separate sounds and combine them to form a word (blending).

### York Assessment of Reading for Comprehension (YARC)

YARC-Early Reading (ages four to six) is a battery of tests including two measures of phonological awareness (sound isolation and sound deletion; Snowling et al., 2012). In sound isolation, students are asked to identify the initial sound in words (six items; for example, "Say 'san.' What is the first sound in 'san'?") and the final sound in words (six items; for example, "Say 'duck.' What is the last sound in 'duck'?"). In sound deletion, students are asked to say a word and then say what is left in the word after deleting one of its sounds (for example, "Say 'sheep.' Now say 'sheep' without the /p/").

### Test of Early Language and Literacy (TELL)

The TELL (Phillips & Hayward, 2016) is a diagnostic assessment of language and literacy skills for students three to eight years of age. TELL comprises eight sections, which are administered individually to students. The Phonological Awareness section comprises six tasks: (1) blending syllables in words, (2) blending sounds in words, (3) identifying sounds at the beginning of words, (4) identifying sounds at the end of words, (5) segmenting syllables in words, and (6) segmenting sounds in words. The tasks administered are age dependent, and the total scores equal the number of correct items in each task. Standard scores and percentile ranks can be viewed relative to the child's age group and, if completed as part of the oral language or literacy test battery, will form part of the child's Oral Language and Literacy composite scores. Testing time varies based on the number of phonological awareness tasks administered and the tester's familiarity with the tasks.

> **Teaching of phonological awareness should be very frequent (ideally, daily), at least at the very beginning of learning to read.**

## How to Teach Phonological Awareness

We are not aware of any studies that have examined what frequency in teaching phonological awareness produces the best results. However, it would be safe to say that its teaching should be very frequent (ideally, daily), at least at the very beginning of learning to read (grades K–1). By the end of grade 2, most students should master most phonological awareness skills, and instruction should continue only if students continue to experience difficulties in word reading. In this case, it is recommended that you group together the students who experience reading difficulties and provide instruction to them in a pullout setting.

A phonological awareness lesson should last five to ten minutes to keep it brief and engaging. This estimate seems to be in line with the findings of a recent meta-analysis showing that the effects of phonological awareness instruction increased with increasing dosage up to ten hours of instruction, after which the effects started to decline (Erbeli et al., 2024). With that said, factors such as class size and student level will impact the lesson length. You need to provide enough practice opportunities for students, particularly the struggling ones, to engage with the material and master the targeted concept.

## Scope and Sequence in Phonological Awareness

Although there are lots of resources on how to teach phonological awareness, there are not many scope and sequences in teaching phonological awareness, and, whenever this is done, they are usually based on what phonological awareness skill is expected to be mastered by a specific age. For example, teachers are asked to teach rhyming and alliteration at the beginning of kindergarten followed by blending of onset and rime, then syllable deletion, and so on. Unfortunately, from our experience, this lack of precision in what to teach every day is often preventing teachers from teaching phonological awareness altogether. For the purpose of this book, we present an example of a scope and sequence from the literacy curriculum organization Heggerty (2022), shown in figure 5.3 (page 100), that provides information on what to teach every day for thirty-five weeks. We wish to highlight three things from this scope and sequence: It is a daily activity, it lasts throughout the year, and you practice multiple phonological awareness skills at the same time. In other words, you do not finish teaching one skill (like rhyming) before you teach another (like blending).

## The Difficulty Level of a Phonological Awareness Activity

Hugh W. Catts, Kim A. Wilcox, Carla Wood-Jackson, Linda S. Larrivee, and Victoria G. Scott (1997; see also Al Otaiba et al., 2016; Phillips, Clancy-Menchetti, & Lonigan, 2008) offer six guiding principles about what makes a phonological awareness activity easier or more difficult and subsequently impacts the success in teaching it.

1. **The size of the spoken sound:** The bigger the size of the sound unit to work with, the easier it is to manipulate. This is also following the developmental trajectory of phonological awareness as larger sound units (such as whole words, onset, and rime) are mastered earlier by students than smaller sound units (such as individual sounds). For example, it is easier to blend *pop* and *corn* to make *popcorn* than to blend /k/, /or/, and /n/ to make *corn*.

2. **The complexity of the linguistic skill required:** It is already known that some phonological awareness tasks are taxing working memory more than others. For example, spoonerism, the task in which individuals are asked to swap the first sound in a pair of words and then say what the newly created words are (such as *basket: lemon* will become *lasket: bemon*) is much harder than determining if *cat* and *hat* rhyme.

3. **The number of units in a word:** In blending or deletion tasks, it is easier to blend or delete a two-phoneme word such as *up* than a four-phoneme word such as *flap*. This probably has to do also with the amount of information someone has to retain in short-term memory.

**Figure 5.3: Kindergarten scope and sequence sample**

| Week | Scope and sequence progression (Weeks 1–35) |
|---|---|
| **Rhyme** | Rhyme Repetition (1–2) · Rhyme Recognition (3–12) · Rhyme Production (13–17) |
| **Initial Phoneme Isolation** | Isolate Initial Components (3–4) · Isolate Initial Components: Series of Words (5–7) · Isolate Initial Components and Short Vowels (8–11) · Isolate Initial Components, Short Vowels, and Long Vowels (12–16) · Isolate Initial Digraphs (17–18) · Isolate Initial Phoneme of a Blend (19–21) |
| **Blend** | Compound Words (1–3) · Syllables (4–6) · Body-Coda (7–8) · Onset-Rime (9–10) · Blending Two Phonemes (11–12) · Blending Three Phonemes (13–22) · Blending Three Phonemes: Digraphs (23–24) · Blending Four Phonemes: Blends (25–30) · Blending Three or Four Phonemes (31–35) |
| **Phoneme Isolation: Final or Medial Sounds** | Find Phoneme Isolation (5–8) · Find Phoneme Isolation: Series of Words (9–11) · Medial Phoneme Isolation: Short Vowels (12–15) · Medial Phoneme Isolation: Long Vowels (16–18) · Medial Phoneme Isolation: Short and Long Vowels (19–21) · Find Phoneme Isolation: Digraphs (22–24) · Find Phoneme Isolation: Consonants and Digraphs (25–26) · Medial Phoneme Isolation (27–35) |
| **Segment** | Compound Words (1–5) · Syllables (5–7) · Onset-Rime (8–10) · Segment Words Into Two Phonemes (11–12) · Segment Words Into Three Phonemes (13–22) · Segment Words Into Three Phonemes With Digraphs (23–24) · Segment Words Into Four Phonemes: Blends (25–29) · Segment Words Into Three or Four Phonemes (30–35) |
| **Add** | Compound Words (1–4) · Syllables (5–7) · Add Initial Phoneme (13–22) · Add Initial Phoneme: Diagraphs (23–24) · Add Initial Phoneme: Mixed Rimes (25–27) · Add Final Phoneme of a Blend (28–33) |
| **Delete** | Compound Words (1–4) · Syllables (5–7) · Delete Initial Phoneme (13–22) · Delete Initial Phoneme: Diagraphs (23–24) · Delete Initial Phoneme: Mixed Rimes (25–27) · Delete Final Phoneme (28–35) |
| **Substitute** | Compound Words (1–4) · Syllables (5–7) · Substitute Initial Phoneme (13–22) · Substitute Initial Phoneme: Diagraphs (23–24) · Substitute Initial Phoneme: Mixed Rimes (25–27) · Substitute Final Phoneme (28–30) · Substitute Vowel/Medial Phoneme (31–35) |

**Early Literacy Skills**

| Skill | Scope and sequence progression (Weeks 1–35) |
|---|---|
| **Alphabet Knowledge** | Twenty-Six Letters and Sounds: Alphabetical Order (1–6) · Twenty-Six Letters and Sounds: Random Order (7–11) · Letters and Sounds: Random Order/As Needed (12–17) · Multiple Sounds of Consonants and Vowels (18–22) · Consonant Digraphs (23–24) · L Blends / L, S Blends / S Blends / R Blends / L, S, R Blends (25–29) · Review of Consonants, Digraphs, Vowels, and Blends (30–35) |
| **Phoneme-Grapheme Connection** | Map Initial Phonemes (1–4) · Map Final Phonemes (5–8) · Map Medial Phonemes (9–17) · Connect Phonemes to Graphemes (18–35) |
| **Language Awareness** | Sentence Repetition: Counting Words (1–3) · Sentence Completion: Counting Words (4–6) · Nursery Rhymes (7–17) |

*Source: Heggerty, 2022. Used with permission.*

**Figure 5.3: Kindergarten scope and sequence sample.**

4. **The position of a sound in a word:** Research has shown that performance is higher when individuals are asked to identify or delete the initial sound in words (Brady, 2020). This is followed by the final sound. The most difficult is the middle sound, which is usually a vowel. Hearing the sounds within a blend (like hearing /r/ in *strain*) is the most challenging.

5. **Blend and segment continuous sounds before stop sounds:** It is easier to blend continuous sounds like /m/, /s/, /f/, /l/, /r/, /n/, /v/, and /z/ than stop sounds like /p/, /t/, /k/, /b/, /d/, /g/, and /j/. Try, for example, to blend slowly the sounds in *sun*. You can say sss-uuu-nnn. You cannot do the same in *tap*. If you choose to use stop consonants, make sure you pronounce the consonants correctly without adding /uh/ to them (a frequent mistake). For example, do not say, "What word do /tuh/, /a/, and /puh/ make?" because the student won't hear *tap*.

6. **Make the sounds, words, and process more concrete:** You may wonder why some teachers use colored cubes or chips to represent sounds. This is particularly true of tasks using Elkonin boxes, in which students are asked to say the sound while moving a chip into the respective box. This is because the use of manipulatives reduces the memory load and allows students to perform the activity without additional requirements.

We would like to add that production tasks are always harder than identification tasks. For example, it is easier for students to pick which of the three pictures does not rhyme with the other two than to give them a word (for example, *lake*) and ask them to provide a word that rhymes with it.

### Sample Lesson Plans

In appendix A (page 171), we provide a sample lesson plan along with materials for each of the main phonological awareness subskills. This is not meant to be a comprehensive program of teaching phonological awareness but rather a collection of ideas on how to teach each of the phonological awareness subskills.

- Syllable awareness (see page 172)

- Onset and rime awareness (see page 173)

- Phoneme isolation 1 (see page 177)

- Phoneme isolation 2 (see page 181)

- Phoneme blending (see page 185)

- Phoneme deletion (see page 190)

- Phoneme segmentation (see page 194)

- Phoneme substitution (see page 200)

Research supports using successive (or continuous) blending with students who struggle moving from isolating phonemes to blending phonemes to decoding of words. We represented the concrete connection in the sample lesson with an arrow. This encourages students to slide through the sounds "quickly," helping to bridge the isolation-to-blending increment. The successive blending strategy also leads to better consolidation of mapping sounds and builds fluency. One way to stretch sounds or quickly put them together to blend is to use a slinky.

## Conclusion

It would not be an exaggeration to say that one of the literacy skills for which there is very little disagreement among researchers regarding its importance for literacy is phonological awareness. Researchers have been examining the role of phonological awareness in reading acquisition since the 1970s, and they concur that it is critical in developing good decoding skills, particularly before students receive any formal literacy instruction. Students with decoding difficulties often have deficits in phonological awareness, and intervention programs focusing on phonological awareness have produced significant effects on students' early literacy skills. Although a precise estimate of the frequency and length of phonological awareness lessons is still a subject of debate, we recommend that teachers of early grades (kindergarten to grade 2) teach it every day.

Because phonological awareness has been extensively researched, we have several assessment tools (both formal and informal) to measure it. The scores from these assessments should guide your classroom instruction and Tier 2 intervention. Solid phonological awareness skills, along with good letter knowledge, will provide a solid foundation for phonics instruction covered in the next chapter.

# Key Readings and Resources

- Al Otaiba, S., Allor, J., Werfel, K. L., & Clemens, N. (2016). Critical components of phonemic awareness instruction and intervention: Recommendations for teacher training and for future research. In R. Schiff & R. M. Joshi (Eds.), *Interventions in learning disabilities* (pp. 9-27). New York: Springer.

- Al Otaiba, S., Kosanovich, M. L., & Torgesen, J. K. (2012). Assessment and instruction for phonemic awareness and word recognition skills. In A. G. Kahmi & H. W. Catts (Eds.), *Language and reading disabilities* (3rd ed., pp. 112-145). Harlow, Essex, England: Pearson.

- Anthony, J. L., & Francis, D. J. (2005). Development of phonological awareness. *Current Directions in Psychological Science*, 14(5), 255-259.

- Kilpatrick, D. A. (2015). *Essentials of assessing, preventing and overcoming reading difficulties*. Hoboken, NJ: Wiley.

- Moats, L. C. (2010). *Speech to print: Language essentials for teachers*. Baltimore: Brookes.

- Piasta, S. B., & Hudson, A. K. (2022). Key knowledge to support phonological awareness and phonics instruction. *The Reading Teacher*, 76(2), 201-210. https://doi.org/10.1002/trtr.2093

- Stalega, M. V., Kearns, D. M., Bourget, J., Bayer, N., & Hebert, M. (2024). Is phonological-only instruction helpful for reading?: A meta-analysis. *Scientific Studies of Reading*, 28(6), 614-635. https://doi.org/10.1080/10888438.2024.2340708

Here are a few websites that include useful information and material for teaching phonological awareness.

- **Florida Center for Reading Research (fcrr.org/student-center-activities):** This resource offers teachers vocabulary activities for students in kindergarten to grade 5. Each activity is accompanied by a lesson plan outlining the lesson's objectives, required materials, and step-by-step implementation instructions. All necessary materials are included within the resource, eliminating the need for teachers to develop additional materials.

- **Heggerty (www.heggerty.org):** This site offers webinars, sample lesson plans, lesson videos, and other helpful tools that can support teachers.

- **ABRACADABRA Interactive Games (abralite.concordia.ca):** Developed by Dr. Robert Savage, this resource features a series of interactive exercises designed to support the teaching of various literacy skills, including phonological awareness. Accessible in both English and French, many teachers use activities from this site to complement their in-class instruction or to offer additional support at home

- **Reading A-Z (www.readinga-z.com):** This site includes a variety of lessons and supplementary resources for teaching phonological awareness in kindergarten and grade 1. Teachers can access lesson guides along with accompanying activities to complement classroom instruction.

- **Sightwords: Phonological awareness activities including a proposed scope and sequence (sightwords.com/phonemic-awareness/curriculum):** In this site, authors provide examples of activities you can do with your students including a scope and sequence for early grades.

CHAPTER 6

# Phonics

When students begin to learn to read, they are familiar with a substantial number of spoken words, but they cannot recognize these words in printed form (Adams, 1990; Beck & McKeown, 1991). After some formal reading instruction and print exposure, students begin to realize that letters correspond to sounds. For example, the letter *m* at the beginning of the word *map* is pronounced /m/. Students are able to use this basic information about these letter-sound correspondences to help them sound out other words (such as *man*). Words that can be sounded out successfully using the letter-sound correspondences are referred to as "regular" words (for example, *pet*, *hat*, and *film*). As students' knowledge of phonics rules grows, they can sound out longer and more complex words.

A large body of research shows that the most effective way to teach a student to read independently is to cover the most common letter-sound correspondences explicitly and systematically (Brady, 2011; Castles et al., 2018; Foorman et al., 2016; National Reading Panel, 2000; Stalega et al., 2024; Taylor, Davis, & Rastle, 2017). Sounding out using letter-sound correspondences is a good strategy for reading words, but it is also a slow process. Every time a student sounds out a word correctly, they gain valuable practice with that word. Quite quickly, students not only learn to sound out the word, but they also learn to recognize that word as a whole. This practice builds automaticity so when they see the word again, the pronunciation of the entire word is activated and deciphering each grapheme is no longer necessary. This is called whole-word recognition or sight word reading.

However, about 25 percent of monosyllabic words in English cannot be read accurately using only letter-sound correspondence rules. These are known as "irregular" words (such as *give*, *come*, and *iron*). Different cognitive processes are needed for students to be successful in recognizing these words as whole units (Kilpatrick, 2015; Steacy et al., 2019; see also Colenbrander, Wang, Arrow, & Castles, 2020, for a review). In this chapter, we focus on phonics; we define it, describe how to assess it, and discuss how to teach it to a whole classroom.

## The Meaning of Phonics

Phonics refers to the systematic and explicit teaching of letter-sound correspondences and how to use them to decode and spell words. Phonics is frequently confused with phonological awareness (see chapter 5, page 91), which is a cognitive skill referring to students' ability to identify and manipulate speech sounds.

Here is a tip to help you remember the difference: Phonological awareness can be taught with your eyes closed (you only need to hear the words and act on them by deleting, adding, or substituting a sound). In phonics, you need to see the letters (or letter combinations) to be able to map them to their sounds and then blend the sounds together to read the word.

> **Early reading instruction must have a well-developed systematic and explicit phonics component.**

## Why We Should Teach Phonics

Phonics instruction is one of the most researched aspects in education. Numerous reviews of scientific studies of reading have recommended that early reading instruction must have a well-developed systematic and explicit phonics component (Hattie, 2009; National Reading Panel, 2000). Research has also shown that students who struggle to learn to read are most likely to benefit from highly systematic and explicit phonics instruction (Savage et al., 2020). The following are four reasons why you should teach phonics.

1. English is a morphophonemic orthography in which spellings have evolved to represent both the sounds and the meaning (Venezky, 1967; see also Bowers & Bowers, 2018). It is phonemic because the *letters* (graphemes) used in English correspond to *sounds* (phonemes). English has twenty-six letters and forty-four phonemes (see table 6.1), and this means that some letters need to be combined (see *sh*, *ch*, and *th*) to represent some of the phonemes. At the same time, it is morphemic, which means that spelling has evolved to preserve the meaning of the words (for example, there is a *g* in *sign*, even though you do not hear it, to signal its connection to words like *signal*, *significant*, and *signature*).

2. In 2000, after reviewing several published studies on teaching reading in English, the National Reading Panel identified phonics as one of the five most effective areas of instruction (the other four are phonological awareness, reading fluency, vocabulary, and reading comprehension).

3. Learning and applying phonics skills to decode words functions as a "self-teaching mechanism" (Share, 1995). This means that teaching students phonics provides them with a powerful strategy that they can use in the future when they encounter new words.

4. Several intervention studies (including meta-analyses) have shown that phonics produces better results than alternative methods that do not target letter-sound correspondences (Ehri, Nunes, Stahl, & Willows, 2001; Galuschka et al., 2014; Hatcher, Hulme, & Snowling, 2004; Savage & Cloutier, 2017; Stalega et al., 2024). For example, in their meta-analysis, Katharina Galuschka and colleagues (2014) find that phonics is the only method that has a significant effect on word reading and spelling.

Teachers must understand what level of phonics comprehension students have already reached to be able to teach students phonics. The following section provides several methods to assess a student's phonics understanding.

## How to Assess Phonics

Whatever instrument you choose to assess your students' phonics knowledge, you should use the data generated from the assessment to guide your instruction. It is not enough to assess your students at the beginning and the end of the school year. We recommend you use informal assessments of phonics every two to three weeks (this will allow you to chart the progress of your students) and formal assessments of phonics three times a year (beginning, middle, and end of each grade level). This will allow you to check whether they meet acceptable outcomes at each measurement point and to identify students in need of further support.

### Informal Assessments

In the following, we provide a quick screener of students' knowledge of letter-sound correspondences, and how you can use it.

1. Print each letter (or letter combination) on a card and show it to your student in the same order they are listed in figure 6.1 (page 109).

**Table 6.1: The Phonemes (Sounds) of English**

| Consonant Sounds | | | Vowel Sounds | | |
|---|---|---|---|---|---|
| IPA | Phoneme | Word | IPA | Phoneme | Word |
| p | /p/ | **p**an | iː | /ē/ | fr**ee** |
| b | /b/ | **b**ath | ɪ | /ĭ/ | l**i**d |
| t | /t/ | **t**ap | e | /ĕ/ | v**e**t |
| d | /d/ | **d**ig | æ | /ă/ | p**a**t |
| k | /k/ | **k**ite | ɑː | /ŏ/ | f**a**ther |
| g | /g/ | **g**ate | ɑː | /ŏ/ | h**o**t |
| f | /f/ | **f**ish | ɑː | /aw/ | dr**aw** |
| v | /v/ | **v**ase | ʊ | /ʊ/ | f**oo**t |
| θ | /th/ (voiceless) | **th**ink | ʃuː | /oo/ | bl**ue** |
| ð | /th/ (voiced) | **th**ey | ʌ | /ŭ/ | d**u**ck |
| s | /s/ | **s**oon | ɜː | /er/ | tw**ir**l |
| z | /z/ | **z**oom | ə | ə | **a**bove |
| ʃ | /sh/ | **sh**ip | eɪ | /ā/ | spr**ay** |
| ʒ | /ʒ/ | mea**s**ure | oʊ | /ō/ | n**o**se |
| tʃ | /ch/ | **ch**est | aɪ | /ī/ | **high** |
| dʒ | /j/ | **j**ump | aʊ | /ow/ | n**ow** |
| m | /m/ | **m**ouse | ɔɪ | /oi/ | b**oy** |
| n | /n/ | **n**est | ɪr | /ear/ | **here** |
| ŋ | /ŋ/ | si**ng** | ðer | /air/ | **there** |
| l | /l/ | **l**ast | jʊr | /yoor/ | **pure** |
| r | /r/ | **r**ack | | | |
| j | /y/ | **y**es | | | |
| w | /w/ | **w**atch | | | |
| h | /h/ | **h**ome | | | |

*Note. IPA = International Phonetic Alphabet.*

2. Sit across from your student and show them the cards, one at a time and in the specific order they are listed in figure 6.1.

3. Ask your student to tell you what sound each letter (or letter combination) makes.

4. If the answer is correct, put a checkmark (✓) in the last column of the figure. If the answer is incorrect, put an X.

5. Discontinue after six consecutive errors.

6. To find the total score, count how many correct answers the student has provided.

Typically, phonics knowledge is assessed with nonsense word reading tasks (sometimes it is called nonword reading or pseudoword reading). Nonsense words are pronounceable letter strings that are not English words (such as *ib*, *bave*, and *blork*). Because these words do not exist in English, this allows teachers to examine how well their students apply their phonics knowledge to read them. Performance in nonsense word reading has been found to correlate strongly with real-word reading. This should not surprise you, as real words that students encounter in text for the first time can be considered "nonsense" words (they have not seen them before, and they approach them the same way they approach nonwords). A popular informal assessment of phonics is DIBELS Nonsense Word Fluency (University of Oregon, 2021). In figure 6.2 (page 110), you will find an assessment with seventy-five nonwords and a chart that you can use for progress-monitoring purposes.

> Typically, phonics knowledge is assessed with nonsense word reading tasks.

### Formal Assessments

The following is a list of formal assessments of phonics. Some of them may require advanced assessment skills, and teachers who do not have these qualifications should not use these assessments to assess their students. We describe them here because from our experience there is always a teacher at each school who has these qualification skills and can help you test certain students who may need this kind of testing.

- **Woodcock-Johnson IV Tests of Achievement** (Schrank, McGrew, Mather, Wendling, & Dailey, 2014) and **Wechsler Individual Achievement Test, Third Edition** (WIAT-III; Wechsler, 2009; this also has Canadian norms) are norm-referenced psychometric batteries that include a nonsense reading task. The task is individually administered (it takes about six to eight minutes per student), and the score is how many nonwords a student has read correctly.

- **Phonemic Decoding Efficiency from the Test of Word Reading Efficiency, Second Edition** (Torgesen, Wagner, & Rashotte, 2012), is also a popular norm-referenced assessment of nonsense word reading. Students are tested individually and are given forty-five seconds to read as many nonsense words as possible. In all of these tasks, the raw score a student obtains is converted to a standard score, a percentile rank, or a

| Starting Point | | Grapheme | X or ✓ | | Starting Point | | Grapheme | X or ✓ |
|---|---|---|---|---|---|---|---|---|
| K and grade 1 | 1 | a | | | | 39 | kn | |
| | 2 | t | | | | 40 | gn | |
| | 3 | s | | | | 41 | mb | |
| | 4 | p | | | | 42 | le | |
| | 5 | i | | | | 43 | -ed | |
| | 6 | n | | | | 44 | ea | |
| | 7 | r | | | | 45 | ee | |
| | 8 | l | | | | 46 | ey | |
| | 9 | e | | | | 47 | ie | |
| | 10 | d | | | | 48 | ow | |
| | 11 | f | | | | 49 | ou | |
| | 12 | m | | | | 50 | ai | |
| | 13 | o | | | | 51 | ay | |
| | 14 | c | | | | 52 | oo | |
| | 15 | g | | | | 53 | or | |
| | 16 | b | | | | 54 | oa | |
| | 17 | u | | | | 55 | oe | |
| | 18 | v | | | | 56 | aw | |
| | 19 | k | | | | 57 | au | |
| | 20 | h | | | | 58 | al | |
| | 21 | w | | | | 59 | oi | |
| | 22 | j | | | | 60 | oy | |
| | 23 | z | | | | 61 | tch | |
| | 24 | y | | | | 62 | igh | |
| | 25 | x | | | | 63 | ew | |
| | 26 | qu | | | | 64 | ue | |
| | 27 | ng | | | | 65 | ui | |
| | 28 | sh | | | | 66 | air | |
| | 29 | ch | | | | 67 | are | |
| Grade 2 start here | 30 | th | | | | 68 | ear | |
| | 31 | ck | | | | 69 | eer | |
| | 32 | ar | | | | 70 | ire | |
| | 33 | or | | | | 71 | ure | |
| | 34 | er | | | | 72 | ore | |
| | 35 | ir | | | | 73 | wr | |
| | 36 | ur | | | | 74 | gh | |
| | 37 | nk | | | | 75 | ph | |
| | 38 | wh | | | | **Total score =** | | |

*Source:* Teacher Tool 1B from The Phonics Companion Quick Screener *by George Georgiou and Kristy Dunn (2023, pp. 9–13).* © 2023. *Reprinted with permission by Pearson Canada, Inc.*

**Figure 6.1: Test of letter-sound correspondences knowledge.**

## Progress Monitoring Nonsense Word Fluency (NWF) K.17

| | | | | | CLS | WRC |
|---|---|---|---|---|---|---|
| rin /r/ /i/ /n/ | tob /t/ /o/ /b/ | det /d/ /e/ /t/ | sem /s/ /e/ /m/ | fon /f/ /o/ /n/ | ‾15 | ‾5 |
| hom /h/ /o/ /m/ | lom /l/ /o/ /m/ | nem /n/ /e/ /m/ | het /h/ /e/ /t/ | sig /s/ /i/ /g/ | ‾15 | ‾5 |
| nop /n/ /o/ /p/ | hab /h/ /a/ /b/ | sim /s/ /i/ /m/ | rom /r/ /o/ /m/ | rab /r/ /a/ /b/ | ‾15 | ‾5 |
| seb /s/ /e/ /b/ | nim /n/ /i/ /m/ | som /s/ /o/ /m/ | hig /h/ /i/ /g/ | rit /r/ /i/ /t/ | ‾15 | ‾5 |
| ped /p/ /e/ /d/ | rop /r/ /o/ /p/ | hon /h/ /o/ /n/ | tep /t/ /e/ /p/ | nup /n/ /u/ /p/ | ‾15 | ‾5 |
| fim /f/ /i/ /m/ | wom /w/ /o/ /m/ | pim /p/ /i/ /m/ | lod /l/ /o/ /d/ | dep /d/ /e/ /p/ | ‾15 | ‾5 |
| rup /r/ /u/ /p/ | yed /y/ /e/ /d/ | lib /l/ /i/ /b/ | mim /m/ /i/ /m/ | hup /h/ /u/ /p/ | ‾15 | ‾5 |
| tud /t/ /u/ /d/ | teb /t/ /e/ /b/ | mem /m/ /e/ /m/ | hib /h/ /i/ /b/ | fom /f/ /o/ /m/ | ‾15 | ‾5 |
| dag /d/ /a/ /g/ | hud /h/ /u/ /d/ | pom /p/ /o/ /m/ | sud /s/ /u/ /d/ | pem /p/ /e/ /m/ | ‾15 | ‾5 |
| heg /h/ /e/ /g/ | mig /m/ /i/ /g/ | mep /m/ /e/ /p/ | gid /(g/j)/ /i/ /d/ | mun /m/ /u/ /n/ | ‾15 | ‾5 |
| yig /y/ /i/ /g/ | vid /v/ /i/ /d/ | yot /y/ /o/ /t/ | pag /p/ /a/ /g/ | vad /v/ /a/ /d/ | ‾15 | ‾5 |
| vot /v/ /o/ /t/ | gup /g/ /u/ /p/ | yut /y/ /u/ /t/ | wim /w/ /i/ /m/ | mub /m/ /u/ /b/ | ‾15 | ‾5 |
| mib /m/ /i/ /b/ | lub /l/ /u/ /b/ | fup /f/ /u/ /p/ | bab /b/ /a/ /b/ | geg /(g/j)/ /e/ /g/ | ‾15 | ‾6 |
| fub /f/ /u/ /b/ | meb /m/ /e/ /b/ | wab /w/ /a/ /b/ | wam /w/ /a/ /m/ | vem /v/ /e/ /m/ | ‾15 | ‾5 |
| reb /r/ /e/ /b/ | fip /f/ /i/ /p/ | mog /m/ /o/ /g/ | wap /w/ /a/ /p/ | bem /b/ /e/ /m/ | ‾15 | ‾5 |

Total Correct _____ _____

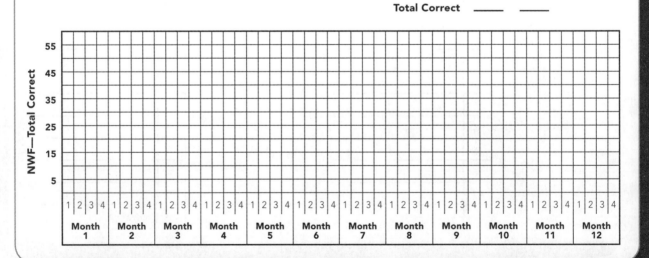

Figure 6.2: Nonsense word fluency assessment.

*Visit **go.SolutionTree.com/literacy** for a free reproducible version of this figure.*

grade equivalent following instructions in the respective manuals that tells teachers how well the student performs compared to a normative sample of same-age or same-grade-level students.

## How to Teach Phonics

There are very few guidelines on how many letter-sound correspondences and at what pace they should be taught at each grade level. According to some researchers, introducing too many letters at a time imposes a heavy paired associate learning (PAL) demand that may confuse and frustrate young learners (Hulme, Goetz, Gooch, Adams, & Snowling, 2007). On the other hand, introducing letters at a slow pace does not allow students to distinguish between many visually similar letters and limits decoding practice opportunities when students know only a small set of letters.

### Scope and Sequence in Phonics

Given that instruction should be provided in a systematic way in order to be as effective as possible, this means that teachers should have a plan that tells them what letter-sound correspondences to teach and when to teach them. There are a few scope and sequences for teaching phonics available in the literature (see Kearns, n.d.; Larsen, Schauber, Kohnen, Nickels, & McArthur, 2020; Moats & Tolman, 2017; Vousden, Ellefson, Solity, & Chater, 2011; Young, 2016). Most have been developed following a specific criterion (such as the frequency of the letter-sound correspondence in the corpus of English words in students' books or in literature in general). For example, Kearns (n.d.) provides a list of 137 letter-sound correspondences ordered by frequency (based on English words in texts for grades 1 to 5). Given that the frequency is determined based on texts up to grade 5, many of the words provided to exemplify (and subsequently practice) the letter-sound correspondences are not appropriate for students in grades K–2—the grades that are most likely to receive phonics instruction.

George Georgiou and Kristy Dunn (2023) developed a scope and sequence that we present in table 6.2 (page 112). The scope and sequence adheres to two principles: (1) the frequency of the letter-sound correspondences found in students' books and (2) sound instructional pedagogy. In regard to the latter, Georgiou and Dunn (2023) incorporate teachers' feedback on what groups of letter-sound correspondences go together (the *r*-controlled vowels) even though they do not necessarily follow each other in frequency. To our knowledge, no study has contrasted the effect of different scope and sequences in students' word recognition. Most scope and sequences appear to agree on what letter-sound correspondences should be taught in the first thirty lessons (even though their ranking may be slightly different in different resources).

112 | BETTER TOGETHER

**Table 6.2: Scope and Sequence**

| Lesson | Grapheme | Phoneme | Pronounced as in: | Lesson | Grapheme | Phoneme | Pronounced as in: |
|---|---|---|---|---|---|---|---|
| 1 | a | /ă/ | at | 37 | or | /or/ | for |
| 2 | t | /t/ | tap | 38 | er | /er/ | her |
| 3 | s | /s/ | sat | 39 | ir | /er/ | bird |
| 4 | p | /p/ | pat | 40 | ur | /er/ | turn |
| 5 | i | /ĭ/ | tip | 41 | i | /ī/ | kind |
| 6 | n | /n/ | nap | 42 | a | /ā/ | later |
| 7 | r | /r/ | ran | 43 | o | /ō/ | cold |
| 8 | l | /l/ | lap | 44 | e | /ē/ | we |
| 9 | e | /ĕ/ | set | 45 | c | /s/ | face |
| 10 | d | /d/ | did | 46 | g | /j/ | page |
| 11 | f | /f/ | fast | 47 | nk | /ŋk/ | sink |
| 12 | m | /m/ | man | 48 | -dge | /j/ | edge |
| 13 | o | /ŏ/ | on | 49 | a_e | /ā/ | same |
| 14 | c | /k/ | can | 50 | i_e | /ī/ | like |
| 15 | g | /g/ | get | 51 | o_e | /ō/ | home |
| 16 | b | /b/ | big | 52 | u_e | /ū/ | cute |
| 17 | u | /ŭ/ | up | 53 | wh | /w/ | when |
| 18 | v | /v/ | vet | 54 | kn | /n/ | knife |
| 19 | k | /k/ | kit | 55 | gn | /n/ | sign |
| 20 | h | /h/ | had | 56 | mb | /m/ | lamb |
| 21 | w | /w/ | wig | 57 | le | /əl/ | little |
| 22 | j | /j/ | jump | 58 | -ed | /d/ | filled |
| 23 | z | /z/ | zip | 59 | -ed | /t/ | boxed |
| 24 | y | /y/ | yes | 60 | -ed | /id/ | painted |
| 25 | x | /ks/ | six | 61 | ea | /ē/ | bead |
| 26 | qu | /kw/ | quit | 62 | ee | /ē/ | seen |
| 27 | ng | /ŋ/ | sing | 63 | ey | /ē/ | key |
| 28 | s | /z/ | pins | 64 | ie | /ē/ | field |
| 29 | sh | /sh/ | wish | 65 | ow | /ow/ | town |
| 30 | ch | /ch/ | much | 66 | ou | /ow/ | sound |
| 31 | th | /th/ | with | 67 | ai | /ā/ | rain |
| 32 | ck | /k/ | back | 68 | ay | /ā/ | play |
| 33 | -ff | /f/ | off | 69 | oo | /oo/ | soon |
| 34 | -ll | /l/ | still | 70 | or | /er/ | work |
| 35 | -ss | /s/ | dress | 71 | y | /ī/ | try |
| 36 | ar | /ar/ | hard | 72 | a | /ŏ/ | wash |

| Lesson | Grapheme | Phoneme | Pronounced as in: | Lesson | Grapheme | Phoneme | Pronounced as in: |
|---|---|---|---|---|---|---|---|
| 73 | ow | /ō/ | know | 97 | ou | /oo/ | you |
| 74 | oa | /ō/ | coat | 98 | o | /oo/ | into |
| 75 | oe | /ō/ | toe | 99 | ue | /oo/ | true |
| 76 | oo | /ʊ/ | good | 100 | ui | /oo/ | fruit |
| 77 | i_e | /ĭ/ | give | 101 | air | /ā//r/ | pair |
| 78 | aw | /ŏ/ | draw | 102 | are | /ā//r/ | share |
| 79 | au | /ŏ/ | cause | 103 | ear | /ē//r/ | hear |
| 80 | al | /ŏ/ | walk | 104 | eer | /ē//r/ | deer |
| 81 | y | /ĭ/ | gym | 105 | ire | /ī//r/ | fire |
| 82 | ch | /k/ | school | 106 | ure | /ʊ//r/ | cure |
| 83 | u | /ʊ/ | put | 107 | ore | /or/ | store |
| 84 | t | /d/ | city | 108 | t | /ch/ | picture |
| 85 | oi | /oi/ | point | 109 | wr | /r/ | write |
| 86 | oy | /oi/ | boy | 110 | gh | /f/ | laugh |
| 87 | ea | /ĕ/ | head | 111 | ph | /f/ | phone |
| 88 | tch | /ch/ | match | 112 | ou | /ŭ/ | young |
| 89 | igh | /ī/ | night | 113 | c | /sh/ | musician |
| 90 | ie | /ī/ | lie | 114 | s | /zh/ | measure |
| 91 | y_e | /ī/ | type | 115 | t | /sh/ | motion |
| 92 | y | /ē/ | body | 116 | s | /sh/ | tension |
| 93 | th | /th/ | that | 117 | ea_e | /ē/ | leave |
| 94 | ar | /or/ | warm | 118 | oo_e | /oo/ | choose |
| 95 | ew | /oo/ | flew | 119 | ee_e | /ē/ | sleeve |
| 96 | u_e | /oo/ | flute | 120 | ar_e | /ar/ | large |

*Source: Table 1 from* The Phonics Companion Quick Screener *by George Georgiou and Kristy Dunn (2023, pp. 9–13). © 2023. Reprinted with permission by Pearson Canada, Inc.*

The scope and sequence that you see in table 6.2 includes 120 letter-sound correspondences. In the first column you can see the order of each letter-sound correspondence. In the second column, we present the letter-sound correspondences in descending order. Beside each letter-sound correspondence we present the phoneme that each letter (or letter combination) corresponds to (third column). Finally, in the last column, we present a target word so teachers know what sound we have in mind for that specific letter.

### Phonics Instruction by Grade

Preliminary evidence suggests that introducing letters at a faster pace (two to four per week), with cycles of review, affords slower learners time to develop automatized sound retrieval for all letters and, at the same time, allows faster learners to apply their letter-sound knowledge sooner to decode and spell words (Jones & Reutzel, 2012; Vadasy & Sanders, 2021). This has also been our own experience with the pace of teaching new letter-sound correspondences to students in Alberta (Canada). Every lesson should last about thirty minutes and can be delivered either as a block or in three interleaved sessions of ten minutes each (ten minutes early in the morning, ten minutes before lunch, and ten minutes before students are dismissed). There is some evidence to suggest that distributed learning (sometimes called "spaced" learning) aids memory of words and letter-sound correspondences. Based on the aforementioned evidence, what we think is reasonable, and the phonics standards in different English-speaking countries like the United States, Canada, and Australia, we recommend the following.

- **Kindergarten:** Teach the first thirty letter-sound correspondences at a pace of one per week.

- **Grade 1:** Teach the next sixty letter-sound correspondences at a pace of two per week.

- **Grade 2:** Teach the next thirty letter-sound correspondences during the first semester of grade 2 at a pace of two per week.

- **Grade 3 and above:** Cover any letter-sound correspondences from the list of 120 that your students do not know, after you assess them with a phonics screener.

### Prerequisite Skills for Phonics Learning

Phonics relies on two important skills that need to be in place (ideally before the end of kindergarten) for phonics instruction to be effective.

1. **Adequate letter knowledge:** If students do not know the letters (both lowercase and uppercase), they cannot retrieve their sounds from long-term memory to allow for blending to take place.

2. **Adequate phonological awareness:** If students do not have the skills to effectively process spoken words (particularly phoneme blending, phoneme segmentation, and phoneme substitution), they cannot blend the sounds to read words. Our research with struggling grade 2 readers has shown that students with better phonological awareness skills responded better to phonics instruction than students with low phonological awareness skills (Savage et al., 2020).

### Sample Lesson Plans

In appendix B (page 205), we include two sample lesson plans along with materials on how to teach phonics. This is not meant to be a comprehensive program of teaching phonics but rather is a collection of ideas on how to teach each of the phonics subskills.

- Sorting Words (see page 206)
- Mapping Letter to Sound (see appendix B, "Tap, Map, Blend," on page 214)

Note that shared book reading is an important component of phonics instruction as it allows students to see the words they practiced earlier in isolation now embedded in text. The text they practice with should be decodable. This means that the majority of the words in the text are regular (or they can be read accurately by applying the grapheme-phoneme correspondence rules). Of course, different phonics programs come with their own decodable texts. Some are fancier than others (and more expensive), but the point of this component of phonics instruction is to give students more practice with the words they sounded out earlier. Thus, teachers could use any kind of decodable text they want, including writing their own sentences. We say this because we often hear from teachers that they cannot afford to pay for a specific collection of decodable books, and they avoid engaging their students in shared book reading.

## Conclusion

In alphabetic orthographies like English, letters (graphemes) correspond to sounds (phonemes). This means that students do not have to memorize a large number of words in order to read accurately and fluently. Instead, they need to learn a finite number of letter-sound correspondences (phonics) that will allow them to "attack" any word they encounter in print. Even though the number of letter-sound correspondences students must learn remains a subject of debate, a wealth of evidence suggests that phonics is quintessential in learning to read English, particularly for students with early reading difficulties (Galuschka et al., 2014; Vousden et al., 2011).

Beyond explaining why phonics is important in learning to read English, in this chapter, we also provided you a scope and sequence for teaching phonics (Georgiou & Dunn, 2023), a quick screener of the letter-sound correspondences, and sample lessons on how to teach phonics. Both of these lessons end with shared book reading using a decodable text as it is critical for students to practice reading the words in text and not only in isolation. It is important to note here that using phonics to decode a word should gradually become a backup strategy. If phonics is applied in reading every word in text, this will most certainly make reading laborious and lead to problems with prosody (expression). We address the issues of reading speed and prosody in the next chapter.

**Shared book reading is an important component of phonics instruction.**

# Key Readings and Resources

- Castles, A., Rastle, K., & Nation, K. (2018). Ending the reading wars: Reading acquisition from novice to expert. *Psychological Science in the Public Interest*, *19*(1), 5-51.

- Colenbrander, D., Wang, H.-C., Arrow, C., & Castles, A. (2020). Teaching irregular words: What we know, what we don't know, and where can we go from here. *The Educational and Developmental Psychologist*, *37*(2), 97-104. https://doi.org/10.1017/edp.2020.11

- Ehri, L. C., Nunes, S. R., Stahl, S. A., & Willows, D. M. (2001). Systematic phonics instruction helps students learn to read: Evidence from the National Reading Panel's meta-analysis. *Review of Educational Research*, *71*(3), 393-447.

- Mesmer, H. A. E., & Griffith, P. L. (2005). Everybody's selling it—but just what is explicit, systematic phonics instruction? *The Reading Teacher*, *59*(4), 366-376. https://doi.org/10.1598/RT

- Moats, L. C. (2010). *Speech to print: Language essentials for teachers*. Baltimore: Brookes.

- Share, D. L. (1999). Phonological recoding and orthographic learning: A direct test of the self-teaching hypothesis. *Journal of Experimental Student Psychology*, *72*(2), 95-129. https://doi.org/10.1006/jecp.1998.2481

- Torgerson, C., Brooks, G., Gascoine, L., & Higgins, S. (2019). Phonics: Reading policy and the evidence of effectiveness from a systematic "tertiary" review. *Research Papers in Education*, *34*(2), 208-238. https://doi.org/10.1080/02671522.2017.1420816

- Ziegler, J., Gioia, P., & Deauvieau, J. (2024). *Strict phonics beats mixed phonics: Effective teaching improves reading acquisition and reduces social inequalities*. Accessed at https://amu.hal.science/hal-04769557v1 on February 22, 2025.

Here are a few websites that include useful information and material for teaching phonics:

- **Florida Center for Reading Research (fcrr.org/student-center-activities):** This resource offers teachers vocabulary activities for students in kindergarten to grade 5. Each activity is accompanied by a lesson plan outlining the lesson's objectives, required materials, and step-by-step implementation instructions. All necessary materials are included within the resource, eliminating the need for teachers to develop additional materials.

- **Kiz Phonics (www.kizphonics.com/phonics-program):** Kiz Phonics includes games for teaching K-2 phonics concepts. Animated games and videos help students develop skills in reviewing a variety of grapheme phoneme correspondences, including short vowels, vowel digraphs, and consonant blends.

- **Turtle Diary, Phonics (www.turtlediary.com):** This site includes online games and printable worksheets for learning phonics. Letter-sound correspondences are taught through video examples with a demonstration of the speech sound. Turtle Diary covers a variety of grapheme-phoneme correspondences, including single consonants, long and short vowels, vowel diagraphs, and diphthongs.

CHAPTER 7

# Fluency

The image of a student who can read accurately but slowly is very familiar to most teachers. In fact, the National Assessment of Educational Progress (NAEP) has consistently shown that two-thirds of students in the United States are unable to read with proficiency in grades 4 and 8 (Hussar, et al., 2020). Just like reading is not natural and must be taught explicitly and systematically, reading fluency is not the natural progression of reading accuracy (Breznitz, 2006; Wolf & Katzir-Cohen, 2001). Students do not simply grow to become fluent readers after reaching a certain level of reading accuracy. And even when they are able to recognize many words automatically (without conscious effort), they may still not be reading with proper expression.

Teaching reading fluency does not mean teaching students to read lists of words faster and faster (International Literacy Association, 2018). Instruction that focuses on making students read faster does not necessarily lead to better reading outcomes. As pointed out by a prominent figure in the field (Rasinski, 2012), because the standards for reading rate have been increasing year after year, fluency instruction has become exceedingly focused on increasing students' speed, regardless of whether students comprehend what they read. Consequently, reading fluency has become a speed-reading contest and divorced itself from the essence of reading comprehension.

Reading fluency should be the bridge between decoding and reading comprehension (Pikulski & Chard, 2005). When students do not read fluently, they use significantly more cognitive resources to process words and sentences. This leads to poorer reading comprehension, less motivation, and lower achievement across many other subject areas. It is therefore essential that teachers working with developing readers understand what reading fluency is, how it can be assessed, and how it can be improved through the implementation of quality instruction.

## The Meaning of Reading Fluency

Several definitions of reading fluency exist in the literature. Some definitions focus more on decoding and speed, whereas others emphasize the role of comprehension. Here, we cite three popular definitions.

- "Fluency [is] the ability to read text quickly, accurately, and with proper expression" (National Reading Panel, 2000, pp. 3–5).

- "Reading fluency refers to efficient, effective word recognition skills that permit a reader to construct the meaning of a text. Fluency is manifested in accurate, rapid, expressive oral reading and is applied during, and makes possible, silent reading comprehension" (Pikulski & Chard, 2005).

- "Reading fluency is the product of the initial development of accuracy and the subsequent development of automaticity in underlying sublexical processes, lexical processes, and their integration in single word reading and connected text. These include perceptual, phonological, orthographic, and morphological processes at the letter, letter-pattern, and word levels, as well as semantic and syntactic processes at the word level and connected-text level. After it is fully developed, reading fluency refers to a level of accuracy and rate where decoding is relatively effortless; where oral reading is smooth and accurate with correct prosody; and where attention can be allocated to comprehension" (Wolf & Katzir-Cohen, 2001).

Despite the fact that researchers have defined reading fluency differently, most definitions of fluency include three components: *accuracy*, *rate*, and *prosody*. The following sections describe each component in further detail.

> **Most definitions of fluency include three components: *accuracy*, *rate*, and *prosody*.**

### Accuracy

Accuracy means that students recognize the words they have in front of them accurately. Unless students read the words in a text accurately, they will not be able to understand what they read. To the best of our knowledge, no studies have specified what percentage of words must be read correctly before a student can adequately comprehend a text, but there is some consensus among researchers that comprehension will be impaired if a given text is read with less than 95 percent accuracy (for example, in a passage that has 100 words, the student must read 95 of them accurately).

### Rate

Strictly speaking, reading rate is the speed with which students read a given passage. We do not want our students to be reading text either way too slow or way too fast. Too slow or too fast won't help students comprehend what they read. Their reading should be smooth and resemble conversational language. To be reading at an appropriate rate, students should recognize many words automatically (without sounding them out). Automaticity refers only to accurate and speedy word recognition (word recognition without our conscious effort), not to prosody. This is an important point because often reading fluency is mistakenly considered to be synonymous with reading rate.

### Prosody

Prosody has been called the "rhythm and melody of spoken language" (Beckman, 1996, p. 21) and the "organizational structure of speech" (Speer & Ito, 2009, p. 90). It includes different elements such as pitch (intonation), stress patterns (syllable prominence), and duration. To read with good prosody, readers must be able to break the text into meaningful "chunks" in accordance with the syntactic structure of the text. Let's have a look at the following picture from a billboard outside of an elementary school (see figure 7.1). Try to read it line by line.

Kindness. It costs [so kindness can be expensive] nothing and means everything.

Instead of: Kindness [short pause]. *It costs nothing and means everything.*

Where we pause and what words we emphasize in a sentence play an important role in our comprehension.

Figure 7.1: Marquee in front of a school.

## Why We Should Teach Reading Fluency

Lesly Wade-Woolley, one of the leading researchers in reading fluency, offers in one of her presentations to teachers a powerful example to help teachers remember why we need reading fluency. She argues that reading is like our bank account that, most often, has limited funds. Different goods cost different amounts of money (cognitive resources). Getting words off the page (known as *decoding*) and reading comprehension can both cost money, and we know that comprehension processes will always cost us some money. Assuming there is no efficient decoding and we have to pay for it, there will be very little money left in our savings account for the comprehension processes that always come at a cost. On the other hand, if our decoding becomes free (with experience and practice), then there will be more money left in our savings account for the expensive comprehension processes.

This example complements what David LaBerge and S. Jay Samuels (1974) say in their seminal paper that if students spend all their cognitive resources in the accurate reading of words, they will not have any cognitive resources left for higher-level cognitive tasks such as reading comprehension. In summary, there are four main reasons why we should teach reading fluency.

1. Fluency at the letter level helps support the development of high-quality orthographic representations of words. As pointed out by Patricia G. Bowers and Maryanne Wolf (1993), if students do not retrieve the names of letters quickly enough from their long-term memory, this will prevent

the unitization process and will eventually harm the development of whole-word orthographic representations.

2. Fluency at the word level allows students to allocate their cognitive resources to higher-level skills such as comprehension (LaBerge & Samuels, 1974). Because fluent readers do not have to pay attention to decoding, they can focus on what the text means.

3. Assuming reading is laborious and inaccurate, students will not likely enjoy reading and may even start to avoid reading (van Bergen et al., 2023). Fluency helps alleviate this struggle and encourages students to develop reading motivation.

4. Fluency helps students become better prepared for the demands of reading in upper grades (Bigozzi, Tarchi, Vagnoli, Valente, & Pinto, 2017). In upper grades, students are expected to do a lot of independent reading, and texts are usually long and contain polysyllabic words. If students are reading these texts word by word, it will take them significantly longer to finish their schoolwork and negatively impact their reading comprehension.

## Prerequisite Skills for Fluency

To develop reading fluency, students must have accurate decoding and large sight vocabulary. As some researchers pointed out (Hasbrouck & Hougen, 2020; Rasinski, Reutzel, Chard, & Linan-Thompson, 2011), we cannot measure reading fluency if accuracy is not at the "independent level" (reading a grade-level passage with at least 95 percent accuracy). This is the reason why we can't really speak about reading fluency at the beginning of learning to read since students are still learning how to accurately decode words. As mentioned earlier, to read at an appropriate rate, students should have a large number of sight words in their lexicon to retrieve quickly when they see them in print. The number of words they do not know, and will have to sound out, determines how quickly they can finish reading a passage. That is the reason why some researchers like Kilpatrick (2015) consider assessments of word reading fluency like the Test of Word Reading Efficiency, Second Edition (Torgesen et al., 2012), as effective measures of one's sight vocabulary.

Similar to other pillars of literacy instruction, reading fluency develops over time and with practice. According to Roxanne F. Hudson, Paige C. Pullen, Holly B. Lane, and Joseph K. Torgesen (2009; see also Y. Kim, 2015), students develop first their decoding fluency before developing their text-reading fluency. Decoding fluency requires the development of phoneme blending fluency and letter-sound fluency. To decode a word faster, students should be able to retrieve the sounds of the letters in a word and then blend the sounds quickly. Decoding fluency also requires phonogram fluency. Phonograms are letter groups within a word that share a pattern across words (-*ice* as in *nice*, *mice*, and *dice*). Without knowledge of patterns across words, readers will not be able to move to more efficient decoding (Kilpatrick, 2015). After students master decoding fluency, they move to a more advanced stage of text reading fluency that includes sight word efficiency and decoding fluency (for the words in a text that students may have not seen before and will need to decode). Once prerequisite skills are confirmed and developed in students, teachers must be able to assess students' level of fluency.

## How to Assess Reading Fluency

If we want to help students become fluent readers, we should start by identifying which students are sufficiently fluent and which ones are struggling and need additional support or intensive intervention. This is done with the implementation of reliable and valid assessments of reading fluency. Thus, in this section, we will review formal and informal assessments of reading fluency. Given that reading fluency involves reading accurately, at an appropriate rate, and with prosody, we will present assessments of these aspects.

### Informal Assessments

Recognizing the need for a reading assessment that was valid and time efficient, Stanley L. Deno (1985) of the University of Minnesota developed an approach referred to as curriculum-based measurement (CBM) in reading. Because this approach is clearly focused on reading fluency, it has also been called an oral reading fluency (ORF) assessment. ORF requires students to read aloud from an unpracticed passage or list of letters or words for a minute while an examiner records any errors (words read incorrectly, omitted, read out of order, or provided to the student by the examiner after a three-second pause). This involves the following four steps.

1. The teacher selects an appropriate passage at the student's grade level (*not* the student's reading level).

2. The student reads the passage aloud and is asked to stop after a minute.

3. The teacher counts the number of words read correctly (accurate words) within the one-minute time limit. If the student read twenty-five words, of which five were read incorrectly, then their score is twenty.

4. Compare the score either to an established benchmark that indicates proficiency at that specific grade level or to a specific goal you have set for that student.

If a student scores at or above the benchmark level, they are considered low risk (as in on par with the expected reading skill development). Students are considered possibly at risk if they score slightly below the benchmark level and at risk if they score significantly below the benchmark level (see table 7.1, page 122, for an example). Obviously, the natural follow-up question is what the benchmark level for each grade is. Literacy specialists Jan Hasbrouck and Gerald Tindal published national norms for ORF in 2017 that span grades 1 to 6. They also published norms for grades 7 and 8 in 2006 (Hasbrouck & Tindal, 2006). When a teacher assesses their student on an unpracticed grade-level passage, they can then compare their score to these norms and estimate whether that student is at risk or not. These norms can be seen in table 7.1. Note that this table provides norms not only per grade level but also for the time of the year the test is administered (fall, winter, or spring).

According to Hasbrouck and Tindal (2017), students scoring ten or more words below the 50th percentile using the average score of two unpracticed readings from grade-level materials need a fluency-building program. Let's look at the following two examples.

### Example A

Andrew was in the third grade when he was assessed by his teacher in May. His score in reading the first passage was 120 words correct per minute (WCPM). His score in reading the second passage was 116 WCPM.

1. Calculate Andrew's ORF score by averaging the two scores, (120 + 116) / 2 = 118.

2. Check the score corresponding to the 50th percentile in the spring of grade 3 (since Andrew is in grade 3 and he was tested in May). That score is 112.

3. Compare Andrew's score (118) to the score corresponding to the 50th percentile (112). Since 118 is higher than 112, we can conclude that Andrew is reading at grade-level expectations and does not need any additional support.

### Example B

Vanessa was in the sixth grade when she was assessed by her teacher in September. Her score in reading the first passage was 108 WCPM. Her score in reading the second passage was 116 WCPM.

1. Calculate Vanessa's ORF score by averaging the two scores,
(108 + 116) / 2 = 112.

**Table 7.1: Fluency Norms by Grade**

| Grade | Percentile | Fall WCPM* | Winter WCPM | Spring WCPM |
|---|---|---|---|---|
| 1 | 90 | | 97 | 116 |
| | 75 | | 59 | 91 |
| | 50 | | 29 | 60 |
| | 25 | | 16 | 34 |
| | 10 | | 9 | 18 |
| 2 | 90 | 111 | 131 | 148 |
| | 75 | 84 | 109 | 124 |
| | 50 | 50 | 84 | 100 |
| | 25 | 36 | 59 | 72 |
| | 10 | 23 | 35 | 43 |
| 3 | 90 | 134 | 161 | 166 |
| | 75 | 104 | 137 | 139 |
| | 50 | 83 | 97 | 112 |
| | 25 | 59 | 79 | 91 |
| | 10 | 40 | 62 | 63 |
| 4 | 90 | 153 | 168 | 184 |
| | 75 | 125 | 143 | 160 |
| | 50 | 94 | 120 | 133 |
| | 25 | 75 | 95 | 105 |
| | 10 | 60 | 71 | 83 |
| 5 | 90 | 179 | 183 | 195 |
| | 75 | 153 | 160 | 169 |
| | 50 | 121 | 133 | 146 |
| | 25 | 87 | 109 | 119 |
| | 10 | 64 | 84 | 102 |
| 6 | 90 | 185 | 195 | 204 |
| | 75 | 159 | 166 | 173 |
| | 50 | 132 | 145 | 146 |
| | 25 | 112 | 116 | 122 |
| | 10 | 89 | 91 | 91 |

* WCPM = words correct per minute.

*Source: Hasbrouck & Tindal (2006). Courtesy of Behavioral Research and Teaching, University of Oregon. Used with permission.*

2. Check the score corresponding to the 50th percentile in the fall of grade 6 (since Vanessa is in grade 6 and she was tested in September). That score is 132.

3. Compare Vanessa's score (112) to the score corresponding to the 50th percentile (132). Since 112 is more than 10 points lower than 132, we can conclude that Vanessa is reading below grade level and needs additional support.

It should be made clear here that ORF is a *screening* tool, not a diagnostic tool. It can only tell us if the student has a problem in reading fluency or not. It does not tell us what the cause of the problem is or how to address the problem. If the student is identified through ORF as being at risk, then we as teachers should use a diagnostic tool to determine the root of the problem and subsequently select an intervention program that targets that specific problem.

Another informal measure of reading fluency is the DIBELS-8 Oral Reading Fluency Test (University of Oregon, 2021). In this task, students are asked to read as much text as possible within a one-minute time limit. Teachers mark down how many words students read correctly in one minute.

ORF tasks are appealing to teachers because you can get a snapshot of your students' reading fluency in a short period of time (for example, one minute). However, there is also a trade-off for this convenience. First, these are onetime point assessments, and it would be prudent to obtain additional information about a student's reading ability before you make any instructional decisions. If, for example, the day that you administered the assessments the student was sick, their performance may be low, not because they are reading at that level, but because they were not feeling well enough that day to perform at an optimal level. In addition, most of these tasks are criterion referenced. Criterion-referenced tests compare a student's knowledge and skills against a predetermined standard or cutoff score. The performance of other students in a given task does not affect a specific student's score in that task. In contrast, norm-referenced assessments compare the performance of a student against the performance of their peers. We used different norm-referenced tasks in our own research and practice in several schools in the United States and Canada, and they work very well for screening for reading difficulties, as well as for progress monitoring. Please note that the following list of formal assessments is not exhaustive, and it should not be taken to mean that these are the only norm-referenced assessments of reading fluency.

### Formal Assessments

In the following sections, we describe formal assessments of reading fluency. Because some of these assessments require students to read words and others to read sentences or text, we describe them as follows according to their requirements.

## Word-Level Fluency Assessments

- **Test of Word Reading Efficiency, Second Edition (TOWRE-2; Torgesen et al., 2012):** The TOWRE-2 is a popular word-reading efficiency task that comprises two subtests: one with real words called Sight Word Efficiency (SWE) and one with pseudowords called Phonemic Decoding Efficiency (PDE). Both tasks have four alternate forms, and the scores from both tasks can be combined to give you a standard score on fluency (in the manual it is called Index). In SWE, students are presented with a page that has four columns of twenty-seven words arranged in terms of increasing difficulty. The students are given forty-five seconds to read as many words as possible. The score is the total number of words read correctly in forty-five seconds. For example, if a student attempts sixty-two words and makes eight errors, then their score will be fifty-four. In PDE, students are asked to read sixty-six pseudowords (such as *ip*, *vasp*, and *plofent*) arranged in three columns of twenty-two. Similar to SWE, the student's score is calculated by subtracting any errors from the total number of pseudowords attempted in forty-five seconds. Importantly, the authors of the TOWRE-2 include a table that tells teachers the acceptable pronunciation of each pseudoword. Because students pronounce the nonwords quickly, you may want to record their responses with a voice recorder (your cell phone) and listen to their recording later on to determine the accuracy of their reading. The raw scores in SWE and PDE are converted to a scaled score following the procedures in the manual, and the scaled scores are combined to give you a standard score. Importantly, the norms for the TOWRE-2 go for ages 6.0 to 24.11, and the same task (SWE and PDE cards) is used in different grade levels. This obviously makes it cost-effective for a school that wants to use it with all their grade levels.

- **Test of Silent Word Reading Fluency, Second Edition (TOSWRF-2; Mather, Hammill, Allen, & Roberts, 2014):** In the TOSWRF-2, students are presented with strings of words with no spaces in between them (like onatgetruncarisfunbluebiglikeback) and are given three minutes to separate the words by putting a slash mark where the space should be (on/at/get/run/car/is/fun/blue/big/like/back/). The score is the total number of words correctly separated. The TOSWRF-2 has three alternate forms and allows researchers and practitioners to calculate standard scores and percentile ranks for their students. With the time for instructions, this task may take you up to five or six minutes to administer. Similar to the TOWRE-2, the same task can be given to students ages 6.0 to 24.0. For students in grades 1 and 2 or students with fine motor challenges, you may consider enlarging the page, as it is hard for these students to put their slash mark in between words that are printed in such a small font size.

## Sentence-Level Fluency Assessments

- **Test of Silent Reading Efficiency and Comprehension (TOSREC; Wagner, Torgesen, Rashotte, & Pearson, 2010):** In the TOSREC, students are asked to silently read simple sentences (for example, *Ice is hot*) and circle *Y* (Yes) if the meaning of the sentence is true or *N* (No) if the meaning of the sentence is false. The *Y* and *N* are printed at the end of each sentence. Students are given three minutes to read as many of the sixty sentences as possible, and their score is calculated by subtracting the number of incorrect responses from the number of correct (this is done to correct for guessing). Even though the test also has four parallel forms, schools need to know that there is a different package per grade level.

- **Reading Fluency (Woodcock-Johnson III Tests of Achievement; Woodcock, McGrew, & Mather, 2001):** The Reading Fluency task is almost identical to the TOSREC. It requires students to read as fast as possible ninety-eight sentences and circle *Yes* or *No* at the end of each sentence within a three-minute time limit. The only difference is that the same task is used for all ages (there are no separate kits per grade level as in the TOSREC).

## Text-Level Fluency Assessments

- **Gray Oral Reading Test, Fifth Edition (GORT-5):** The GORT-5 (Wiederholt & Bryant, 2012) includes two equivalent forms, both of which contain sixteen developmentally sequenced passages that students are asked to read aloud as fast and as accurately as possible. The time and accuracy to read each whole passage is noted, and then the score on fluency is determined on the basis of the time and number of errors. Note that the GORT-5 also has five multiple-choice questions following each passage to assess comprehension. Some researchers have argued that students can correctly answer these questions beyond chance level without needing to read the passage (they call it passageless comprehension) and questioned the validity of this measure (Keenan & Betjemann, 2006). However, the passage fluency can still be used, and this is why we present it here. Similar to the TOWRE-2, the GORT-5 can be used with all grade levels, and standard scores can be calculated for ages 6.0 to 23.11.

- **Nelson-Denny Reading Test (Fishco, 2019):** This task has two equivalent forms (I and J) and is appropriate for students ages fourteen all the way to second and fourth year at the university level. Even though this task will be presented in more detail in chapter 8 (page 133), we mention it here as well because teachers and practitioners can also obtain a reading rate score by administering this task. The reading rate score can be obtained by asking students to record in the margin the number that corresponds to the last sentence they were reading in passage one of the comprehension subtest after exactly one minute. Students are asked to read at their normal reading

## BETTER TOGETHER

rate, neither faster nor slower than usual. Similar to other silent reading tasks (TOSREC), we do not know whether the words the students read are read accurately or not.

### Prosody Assessments

Despite the efforts made over the last decade to automatize the scoring of students' prosody, no software is yet available for teachers to use. Instead, teachers and researchers are encouraged to use rubrics. Two of the most popular are (1) NAEP's rubric and (2) the Multidimensional Fluency Scale by Jerry Zutell and Timothy V. Rasinski (1991). The former is a more holistic measure that lumps various aspects of prosody together (see figure 7.2). Teachers are asked to listen to the student while reading a text and then decide what level the student's reading belongs to.

| | | |
|---|---|---|
| **Fluent** | Level 4 | Reads primarily in larger meaningful phrase groups, and most of the story is read with expressive interpretation. |
| | Level 3 | Reads primarily in three- or four-word phrase groups with little or no expressive interpretation. |
| **Nonfluent** | Level 2 | Reads primarily in two-word phrases with the word groupings being rather awkward and unrelated to the larger context of the sentence or passage. |
| | Level 1 | Reads primarily word by word. |

*Source: Adapted from Pinnell et al., 1995.*

**Figure 7.2: NAEP's prosody scale.**

The Multidimensional Fluency Scale is more analytic than NAEP's rubric and requires teachers to evaluate different aspects of prosody using a four-point scale (the Multidimensional Fluency Scale is available to view on p.19 of the United States Department of Education, Education Resources Information Center's [ERIC] report, titled "Assessing Reading Fluency", which can be accessed online). The scale measures students in four categories: expression and volume, phrasing, smoothness, and pace. Scores below ten overall indicate that the student needs additional instruction in fluency. See the following list for descriptions of what an exceptional reader (scoring four out of four in each category) looks like according to the Multidimentional Fluency Scale (Zutell & Rasinski, 1991).

- **Expression and volume:** Reads with varied volume and expression. The reader sounds like they are talking to a friend with their voice matching the interpretation of the passage.

- **Phrasing:** Reads with good phrasing, adhering to punctuation, stress, and intonation.

- **Smoothness:** Reads smoothly with some breaks, but self-corrects with difficult words or sentence structures.

- **Pace:** Reads at a conversational pace throughout the reading.

### Rapid Automatized Naming (RAN)

A concept that is frequently confused with reading fluency is that of rapid automatized naming (RAN). The RAN tasks require students to name as fast as possible an array (such as a five-by-ten grid) of highly familiar visual stimuli such as colors, objects, digits, and letters (see figure 7.3, page 128, for an example). Measures of RAN can be found in different batteries such as the CTOPP-2 (Wagner et al., 2013) or the RAN/RAS (rapid alternating stimulus) battery by Maryanne Wolf and Martha B. Denckla (2005). Research has shown that RAN is a strong correlate of reading fluency (Georgiou, Aro, Liao, & Parrila, 2016) and a core deficit in students with reading disabilities (Wolf & Bowers, 1999). Because RAN tasks assume a level of automaticity in naming these stimuli (that is, students should know the names of the stimuli so the task accuracy is not a problem), RAN Colors and Objects are more appropriate for kindergarten, and RAN Digits and Letters are more appropriate from grade 1 onward. The score in the RAN tasks is usually the time to name all the stimuli in an array. However, some researchers have also reported other scores such as the number of items per second or time per item. Even though the RAN tasks are strongly related to reading fluency and predictive of reading difficulties, they should not be used as measures of reading fluency.

## How to Teach Reading Fluency

Given that reading fluency develops with a lot of practice, by reading various types of text (known as wide reading), and after hearing models of fluent reading (teacher), it is rather obvious that it must be practiced every day. To help us better understand what a week of reading fluency activities looks like, Timothy V. Rasinski and his colleagues propose a weekly plan (Rasinski, n.d.). On Mondays, students are invited to choose a text (script, poem, song, or monologue) that they will perform at the end of the week. Students can work either individually or as a group. Here's how the weekly routine usually works.

- **Monday:** The teacher models the reading of the texts while students follow along silently. They discuss the meaning of the texts, as well as how the teacher reads the texts orally. Students choose their texts for the assignment (Friday's performance).

- **Tuesday:** Teacher and students read texts together orally and discuss ways to convey meaning through oral reading.

- **Wednesday:** Students work in small groups or with partners to continue rehearsing their assigned texts. The teacher floats from group to group, providing encouragement and informative feedback.

| 2 | 5 | 9 | 4 | 7 | 5 | 9 | 2 | 4 | 7 |
| 4 | 9 | 7 | 5 | 2 | 7 | 2 | 9 | 5 | 4 |
| 9 | 2 | 4 | 7 | 5 | 9 | 4 | 5 | 7 | 2 |
| 5 | 7 | 2 | 9 | 4 | 2 | 7 | 4 | 9 | 5 |
| 7 | 4 | 5 | 2 | 9 | 4 | 5 | 7 | 2 | 9 |

**Figure 7.3: An example of a RAN Digits task.**

- **Thursday:** Dress rehearsal. Students practice performing all the assigned texts for themselves and their teacher.

- **Friday:** Students perform their assigned texts for invited guests, like the school principal, educational assistants, family members, and others.

There are two popular instructional approaches that aim to help students with their reading fluency: assisted reading and repeated reading. Irrespective of what instructional approach teachers may use, the goal remains the same: teaching of all three components of reading fluency (accuracy, rate, and prosody). Because these components are interrelated, when we work on one of these components, it is as if we also work on the other. For example, to the extent we succeed in improving students' reading rate, this will translate to improvements in prosody as well because students can now pay attention to the phrasing and meaning of the text rather than to the decoding of each word in the text.

> **There are two popular instructional approaches that aim to help students with their reading fluency: assisted reading and repeated reading.**

### Assisted Reading

According to Melanie R. Kuhn and Steven A. Stahl (2003), assisted reading is a set of instructional methods that provides support to students through the use of models of fluent reading. It is very important to give students varied opportunities for hearing text. This can take several forms such as teacher-assisted reading, peer-assisted reading, and audio-assisted reading. In teacher-assisted reading, the teacher reads a certain text with proper speed and expression, and the students follow along in their books. In peer-assisted reading, a fluent reader is usually paired with a less fluent reader, and they take turns reading a passage. This allows the less fluent reader to hear what fluent reading sounds like and receive feedback in a friendly environment. Finally, in audio-assisted reading, students will hear someone read a given text through a computer, and they follow along in their own book.

*Repeated Reading*

Several meta-analyses have concluded that repeated reading is an effective method to improve students' reading fluency (particularly for students with learning disabilities) with mean weighted effect sizes within the medium range ($d$ = 0.50 to 0.67) on reading outcomes usually measured by WCPM (Chard, Vaughn, & Tyler, 2002; Lee & Yoon, 2017; Stevens, Walker, & Vaughn, 2017). In repeated reading, students are required to read the same text a few times until a desirable goal is achieved, such as reading a certain number of WCPM. Similar to assisted reading, repeated reading can take different forms like choral reading, partner reading, and Reader's Theater. Table 7.2 describes several kinds of repeated reading.

Try the following repeated reading activity to get a sense of how to employ the method in the classroom.

1. Select a fragment or short text containing 50 to 200 words, depending on the student's skill and grade level. You can download grade-appropriate texts from Reading A–Z (www. readinga-z.com).

2. Ask the student to read the text aloud.

3. Record the number of words read correctly by the student. Share the outcome with the student and motivate the student to reread the text faster without making mistakes. Some teachers use a table with columns (see figure 7.4, page 130) in which students can mark the point they reached at each reading attempt.

**Table 7.2: Forms of Repeated Reading**

| Type | Description |
|---|---|
| **Choral Reading** | The teacher leads the entire class or group reading aloud in unison. |
| **Echo Reading** | The teacher reads a sentence, and then the class rereads it aloud. |
| **Partner Reading** | Pairs of readers alternate reading aloud by a set protocol. |
| **Whisper Reading** | Each student reads aloud (but not in unison) in a quiet voice. |
| **Reader's Theater** | A small group of students rehearses and then performs a script. |

4. Repeat the process for at least three repetitions; alternatively, continue reading until a predetermined fluency level is reached, such as ninety WCPM (Chard et al., 2002; Meyer & Felton, 1999).

*Complementary Strategies to Repeated Reading*

Research on the effects of repeated reading on reading fluency has shifted toward studying intervention strategies that enhance its effectiveness. Studies have shown that repeated reading yields better results when combined with additional strategies (Padeliadu & Giazitzidou, 2018). Some complementary and effective practices are described in the following sections.

**Prelistening to the Text**

Passage previewing or modeling, in combination with repeated reading, has shown significant differences in the gains made when compared to repeated reading without modeling, not just for beginning readers but also for students with learning

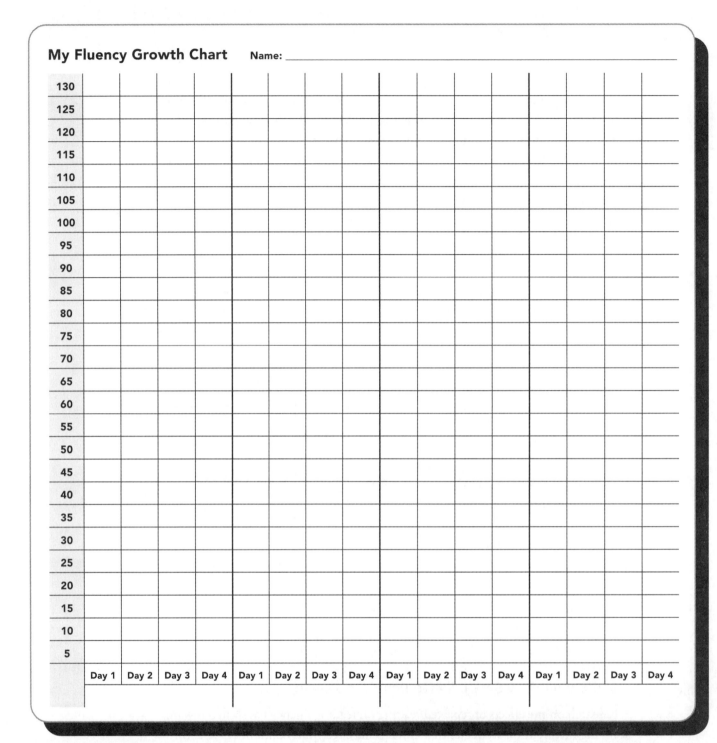

Figure 7.4: Fluency growth chart.

*Visit go.SolutionTree.com/literacy for a free reproducible version of this figure.*

disabilities (Lee & Yoon, 2017). Also, better results are obtained when reading is modeled by the teacher or instructor (Chard et al., 2002; Therrien, 2004). The way this works is that a teacher will first model reading the specific text, and then the student will practice reading it multiple times until a target is met.

### Reading Isolated Words First

Another effective practice for repeated reading intervention is to review potentially difficult or unknown words in isolation before the oral reading practice of the words in context (Coulter & Lambert, 2015). For example, in a text that includes the word *biodegradable*, the teacher may ask the student to use their strategies to decode that word before they engage in repeated reading.

### Providing Corrective Feedback

Providing feedback on decoding errors, either immediately after the error occurs or before proceeding with the next repetition, is another factor that enhances the effectiveness of the intervention. However, studies indicate that immediate corrective feedback yields the most significant results, improving both word reading and comprehension (Chard et al., 2002; Therrien, 2004). This is because the student can immediately learn the word that was initially read incorrectly and get multiple opportunities to read it correctly thereafter.

### Sample Lesson Plans

In appendix C (page 221), we include four sample lesson plans along with materials on how to teach different components of reading fluency. The first lesson plan aims to help with onset and rime word fluency, the second with sentence fluency, and the last two with prosody. This is not meant to be a comprehensive program of teaching reading fluency but rather is a collection of ideas on how to teach each of the fluency subskills.

- Onset and Rime Word Fluency (see page 222)
- Sentence Fluency (see page 228)
- Emphasize It! (see page 233)
- Punctuation Practice (see page 235)

## Conclusion

Reading fluency, a reading skill comprising accuracy, rate, and prosody, is crucial in reading comprehension. Students who devote their cognitive resources to decoding and whose reading is laborious will not have enough resources left for higher-order cognitive skills such as comprehension. In view of this, it should not surprise us that some measures of reading fluency (for example, TOSREC and CBM-Maze, which are described on pages 125 and 153, respectively) also include a comprehension component. Similar to phonological awareness and phonics, teaching of reading fluency should be explicit and systematic and start from the beginning of formal reading instruction. By prioritizing fluency instruction, we empower students to become confident, proficient readers who can engage deeply with a wide range of texts.

# Key Readings and Resources

- Begeny, J. C., Levy, R. A., & Field, S. A. (2018). Using small-group instruction to improve students' reading fluency: An evaluation of the existing research. *Journal of Applied School Psychology, 34*(1), 36-64.

- Hudson, R. F., Pullen, P. C., Lane, H. B., & Torgesen, J. K. (2009). The complex nature of reading fluency: A multidimensional view. *Reading & Writing Quarterly, 25*(1), 4-32.

- Kuhn, M. R., & Schwanenflugel, P. J. (2008). *Fluency in the classroom*. New York: Guilford Press.

- Kuhn, M. R., & Stahl, S. A. (2003). Fluency: A review of developmental and remedial practices. *Journal of Educational Psychology, 91*(1), 3-21.

- Rasinski, T. V. (2010). *The fluent reader: Oral and silent reading strategies for building word recognition, fluency, and comprehension* (2nd ed.). New York: Scholastic.

- Ritchley, K. D., & Speece, D. L. (2006). From letter names to word reading: The nascent role of sublexical fluency. *Contemporary Educational Psychology, 31*(3), 301-327.

- Wade-Woolley, L., Wood, C., Chan, J., & Weidman, S. (2021). Prosodic competence as the missing component of reading processes across languages: Theory, evidence and future research. *Scientific Studies of Reading, 26*(2), 165-181. https://doi.org/10.1080/10888438.2021.1995390

- Wolf, M., & Katzir-Cohen, T. (2001). Reading fluency and its intervention. *Scientific Studies of Reading, 5*, 211-239.

Here are a few websites that include useful information and material for teaching reading fluency:

- **Really Great Reading: Heart Word Magic (www.reallygreatreading.com/heart-word-magic):** Heart Word Magic is designed to help teach students high-frequency words and sight words (Heart Words). This resource offers animations to help students learn about Heart Words, along with activities for spelling practice.

- **Timothy V. Rasinski personal webpage (www.timrasinski.com/resources):** On this website, Timothy V. Rasinski (one of the leading figures in reading fluency) offers multiple downloadable materials, including research articles for those interested in learning more about current research in reading fluency.

CHAPTER 8

# Vocabulary

Some students are relatively accurate in reading words in text, but they experience difficulties understanding what the text is all about. This is a common phenomenon that is attributed to the fact that to comprehend what we read we need to not only accurately decode the words but also know their meaning. This taps into what we call vocabulary, the content of this chapter. Strong vocabulary is essential for reading comprehension, and academic vocabulary lays the foundation for success in secondary and postsecondary education. Indeed, there is evidence that vocabulary knowledge in early grades is predictive of students' reading achievement in high school (Dale, Paul, Rosholm, & Bleses, 2023; Lyster, Snowling, Hulme, & Lervåg, 2021). Despite the acknowledged importance of vocabulary in reading comprehension, evidence from different studies shows that relatively little time is devoted to vocabulary instruction in classrooms (Scott, Jamieson-Noel, & Asselin, 2003; Wright & Neuman, 2014). In this chapter, we contextualize the importance of teaching vocabulary in the classroom, specify how many and what kinds of words should be taught by grade level, and provide examples of viable methods for assessing vocabulary skills in students. Finally, we discuss the role of morphological awareness in vocabulary learning, and we review Structured Word Inquiry (Bowers, 2009), which is a method of teaching how the English spelling system works by examining the internal structure of words (such as how they are built).

## The Meaning of Vocabulary

Simply put, vocabulary is a storehouse of all the words we know either through our conversations or through our readings. Obviously, there are different degrees of knowing a word, and that is why one of the dimensions of vocabulary knowledge is vocabulary depth. Vocabulary depth is typically measured with definition tasks

(Wechsler, 2014) in which students are asked to define a given word (for example, "What is a *hat*?"). In this kind of task, students get to show how well they know a given word (they demonstrate the depth of their knowledge). Another dimension is *vocabulary breadth*, which is how many words an individual knows. Vocabulary breadth is typically measured with tasks that require students to point to a picture in a quadrant depicting the meaning of the word provided by the examiner (Peabody Picture Vocabulary Test, Fifth Edition [PPVT-5]; Dunn, 2018). Researchers have shown that both vocabulary depth and breadth are needed for comprehension (Binder, Cote, Lee, Bessette, & Vu, 2017; Ouellette, 2006).

> **Vocabulary knowledge is one of the strongest predictors of reading comprehension.**

In the literature, you may also come across the terms *expressive vocabulary* and *receptive vocabulary*. Expressive vocabulary refers to the words that an individual can use and produce in their spoken or written language to effectively communicate their thoughts, ideas, and feelings. In turn, receptive vocabulary refers to the words an individual can understand when reading or listening but may not necessarily use in their own speech or writing.

## Why We Should Teach Vocabulary

There are at least two reasons why we should teach vocabulary.

1. A larger vocabulary allows for better word recognition, particularly of irregular words. As students attempt to decode an unknown word, they are more likely to read it correctly if they already have that word in their oral vocabulary. For example, in the Mispronunciation Correction strategy (Savage et al., 2020), after we ask students to sound out an irregular word (like *said*), we ask them, "Is this a word you know?" The minute we ask this question, students almost immediately correct their pronunciation to the word *said*, which they have heard and used so many times in their everyday conversations.

2. Vocabulary knowledge is one of the strongest predictors of reading comprehension (Oakhill & Cain, 2012; Ouellette, 2006; Verhoeven & van Leeuwe, 2008). Students who do not know the meaning of words cannot comprehend what they read even if they decode the words in text correctly. In fact, vocabulary and reading comprehension are reciprocally related: Having a bigger vocabulary makes you a better reader; being a better reader makes it possible for you to read more; and reading more allows you to enhance your vocabulary. This reciprocal relationship tends to increase individual differences over time. On the positive side, better readers tend to read more, get bigger vocabularies, and become even better readers. On the negative side, poorer readers tend to read less, fail to develop large vocabularies, and find reading increasingly difficult as the vocabulary demands of the texts they must read increase.

Not only should we teach vocabulary as part of daily instruction, but it is important to know about the vocabulary gap, how many words we should teach, what words we should teach, and how to curate word lists for instruction.

### Why We Should Know About the Vocabulary Gap

Several research studies have shown that when students go to kindergarten, they have profound differences in their vocabulary knowledge (Colker, 2014; Dickinson et al., 2019; Reynolds et al., 2017). Our work on the home literacy environment (an umbrella term used to incorporate all the types of activities parents engage in with their children) has repeatedly shown that shared book reading and access to literacy materials (like books and educational programs) influence students' vocabulary knowledge and reading comprehension (Georgiou, Inoue, & Parrila, 2021; Inoue et al., 2020; Zhang, Inoue, Cao, Li, & Georgiou, 2023). Students who are exposed to more literacy materials and who are read to more frequently at home have a larger vocabulary in kindergarten than students who do not have any books at home and who are read to infrequently.

In one of the most cited studies on this topic, Betty Hart and Todd R. Risley (1995) find that by age three, students from affluent families had a working vocabulary of 1,116 words, compared to 749 words for students in working-class families, and 525 words for students on welfare. This study formed the basis of the "30-million-word gap" proposition, according to which students from a lower socioeconomic status heard 30 million fewer words than students from a higher socioeconomic status. Andrew Biemiller (2005) also finds that the bottom 25 percent of students begin kindergarten with 1,000 fewer root-word meanings than average students, and they also acquire about 1.6 root-word meanings per day as opposed to 2.4 root-word meanings by average students.

Even though these early studies indicate the presence of a significant vocabulary gap among students going to kindergarten, more recent evidence downplays that evidence. For example, Jill Gilkerson and colleagues (2017) collected data from 329 families using automated recorders that were tucked into students' clothing. Typically developing students between two and forty-eight months of age completed monthly, daylong recordings in their natural language environments over a span of approximately six to thirty-eight months. Gilkerson and colleagues (2017) did report some gaps in students' early language experiences, but they were not as pronounced as the original 30-million-word gap. Even though these findings suggest that the vocabulary gap may not be as pronounced, they still point to the fact that this early vocabulary gap will not close up in later grade years unless we provide both a rich language environment in our classes (for students to learn some vocabulary implicitly) and explicit vocabulary instruction.

### How Many Words We Should Teach

Given that the vocabulary gap is a sad reality and that we need to teach words explicitly in order for students with limited vocabularies to catch up, one of the most frequent questions we get is how many root words or word families teachers should explicitly teach per day. Researchers seem to agree that two words per day (or about ten per week) is probably enough (Beck, McKeown, & Kucan, 2002; Biemiller, 2005). However, assuming some students are way behind in vocabulary (like English learners), then you may consider teaching them more words per day (such as three to four words per day; Biemiller, 2003). We must clarify here that teaching vocabulary is not the exclusive job of language arts teachers. There is subject-specific vocabulary in social studies, science, mathematics, and other subjects. In fact, recent studies have shown that oral language skills (like vocabulary) are among the best predictors of mathematics problem solving (Bleses, Moos, Purpura, & Dale, 2023; Spencer, Fuchs, & Fuchs, 2020). The vocabulary taught in other subject areas also counts to the total number of words students learn. We say this in order to prevent a widespread misconception among teachers of other subject areas that teaching vocabulary is the job of language arts teachers. Teaching vocabulary is everyone's job.

### What Words We Should Teach

Because we emphasized the need for teachers to teach vocabulary explicitly in order to close the vocabulary gap as much as possible, the natural follow-up question is, What kind of words should we teach, and where can we find these words? There is no formula for selecting age-appropriate vocabulary for instruction. However, you can select what words to preteach by applying the following three general guidelines.

1. Select words that are unknown to most students (about 80 percent of the students in your class).

2. Select words that are critical for understanding the central themes and main ideas in the text.

3. Select words that students are likely to encounter in the future (such as in other books or subject areas) and are generally useful.

Tricia A. Zucker, Sonia Q. Cabell, and Danielle L. Pico (2021) propose an alternate way of choosing vocabulary words. It involves the following five steps.

1. List all the words that are potentially unknown, important, or difficult in a given passage.

2. Remove any words from the list that are not essential for comprehension.

3. Remove any words that can be understood through context or illustrations.

4. Mark all the academic words with an asterisk. Academic vocabulary refers to words that are not necessarily common or frequently encountered in informal conversations.

5. Circle the final words you will be teaching.

Isabel L. Beck and colleagues (2002) also propose a three-tiered system to help teachers select appropriate words to teach (see also table 8.1 for a summary of the three tiers of vocabulary instruction).

- **Tier 1:** This category includes basic words that most students would already know (such as *book, school, ball, food,* and *happy*). Teachers should not spend time to teach them unless they are dealing with English learners with very limited vocabulary or beginning first-grade students.

- **Tier 2:** This category includes words that occur frequently in language and are critical for passage comprehension (such as *evaluate, reluctant, avoid, generate, central, approach,* and *solution*).

- **Tier 3:** This category includes words that are relatively infrequent and specific to a particular content area or unit of study (like *peninsula, isomorph, isthmus, pumice,* and *protagonist*). Teachers should teach Tier 3 words only as they arise and if they are important for understanding that specific unit of study. Otherwise, use what is called "Show and Go" for Tier 3 words. Show what the word is briefly and move on.

**Table 8.1 The Three Tiers of Vocabulary Instruction**

| | Tier 1 | Tier 2 | Tier 3 |
|---|---|---|---|
| **Description** | Basic, high-frequency words typically acquired in early childhood | Words that are more complex and are encountered across multiple contexts | Specialized words, usually domain-specific and less commonly used in everyday language |
| **Examples** | *dog, happy, house, eat, sleep, blue* | *analyze, establish, abundant, ponder* | *ubiquitous, vicinity, cacophony, ephemeral* |
| **Teaching** | Rarely require instruction | Teach on a daily basis | Teach when a specific need arises |

Beck and colleagues (2002) recommend we teach Tier 2 words for the reasons outlined in the previous list. During instruction, do not hesitate to teach a word when you are uncertain whether it is a Tier 2 word or not. Likewise, just because we said earlier that teaching two words a day is likely sufficient, if a given passage includes four or five Tier 2 words that might be critical for passage understanding, you should teach all of them.

### Why We Should Keep Word Lists

Some researchers have created lists of words per grade level and subject area (Coxhead, 2000; Dang, Coxhead, & Webb, 2017; Gardner & Davies, 2014). Edward Fry (1999) also published a book called *The Vocabulary Teacher's Book of Lists* containing useful vocabulary per subject. Finally, in the appendix of their influential book *Bringing Words to Life*, Beck and colleagues (2002) recommend Tier 2 words that teachers can preteach for several popular students' books from kindergarten to eighth grade.

It is important to note here that these lists offer some recommendations to help teachers select words. It does not mean that these are the only words students should know per grade level to be fluent speakers and comprehenders. In fact, if you were to compare the words of a given grade level across two different word lists, you would realize that there is not a great overlap between them. Teaching vocabulary is not a matter of choosing words from a list (or out of context) and providing definitions for students to memorize.

Once, while visiting a school in Alberta, we noticed a teacher with one of these lists in her hand. When we asked her to tell us about it, she confessed that her principal—from her zeal to enhance the vocabulary skills of all her students—had given every teacher in her school a list of words she downloaded from the internet to teach five to six words daily. The principal had evenly split the job between the language arts, mathematics, and social studies teachers. Can you imagine a mathematics teacher beginning their class by teaching words from a list and out of context? We mention this to show you that having a list is not a solution; it is way better if every teacher knows how to apply the general guidelines mentioned earlier to identify and teach words that are critical for passage understanding or for a unit of study.

## How to Assess Vocabulary

The following sections present both informal and formal assessments for vocabulary. Similar to assessments available for other pillars of literacy, vocabulary assessments are plenty, widely varied, and often customizable.

### Informal Assessments

The vocabulary knowledge scale by Edgar Dale (1965) is probably the most widely used informal way of assessing how well students know the meaning of a given word. In this task, students are asked to rate their word knowledge on a scale from 1 to 4 (see figure 8.1).

| Words | 1 (Never heard this word before) | 2 (Heard this word but don't know what it means) | 3 (I know a little about what this word means) | 4 (I know very well what this word means) |
|---|---|---|---|---|
| Virulent | | | | |
| Formation | | | | |
| Suppress | | | | |
| Duly | | | | |

Figure 8.1: Vocabulary knowledge scale.

In a simpler form of Dale's (1965) scale, before teaching a word to students, you can show them the word and ask them to rank it on a scale of 1 to 5 by how well they know it. This will give students an opportunity to activate any prior knowledge of the word. See the scale in figure 8.2 for reference.

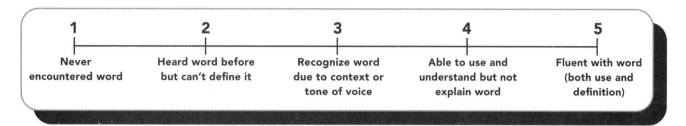

Figure 8.2: Word recognition scale.

One of the assessments within the Abecedarian battery is vocabulary (Wren & Watts, 2002). According to Sebastian Wren and Jennifer Watts (2002), by the end of the first grade, students should pass three vocabulary subtasks: production, antonyms, and synonyms. In the production task, students are given a word, and they are asked to tell what the word means (for example, "What does the word *soup* mean?"). In the antonyms task, students are given a word (like *thin*) and then three choices (like *weak*, *fat*, and *tall*) from which they must choose the one that means the opposite of the target word. Finally, in the synonyms task, students are given a word (like *chilly*) and then three choices (like *snow*, *winter*, and *cold*) from which they must choose the one that means the same thing as the target word. In each task, there are two alternate forms, and each task contains ten items. To pass a test, students should get at least eight out of ten items correct.

### Formal Assessments

Several formal assessments of vocabulary are available in different psychometric batteries. In the following sections, we describe the most popular ones according to the type of vocabulary measured.

### Receptive Vocabulary

Receptive vocabulary, which refers to the words an individual can understand when they hear or read them in text, is a frequently evaluated category. A measure of *receptive vocabulary* is the PPVT-5 (Dunn, 2018), a norm-referenced and individually administered test of receptive vocabulary. Individuals are given a word by the tester, and they are asked to point to a picture in a quadrant that depicts the word they were given. The task is appropriate for students ages two to ninety and takes about fifteen minutes to administer. It consists of 240 items, and it is discontinued after six consecutive errors. From our own experience administering this task, we noticed that even younger students go quite far in the task before you discontinue, and this results in longer administration times.

Similarly to the previous, the Listening Comprehension subtest of the WIAT-III (Wechsler, 2009) is also used to assess students' receptive vocabulary knowledge. It is constructed with the same philosophy as the PPVT-5. Students are told a word by the tester and then asked to preview a set of four pictures and point to the one that correctly represents the word. For example, the tester would say, "*Empty*. Point to the picture that shows *empty*." The items are ordered in terms of increasing difficulty. The task is discontinued after four consecutive errors, and a participant's score is the total number of correctly identified words (max = 19). The raw score can be converted into a standard score following the instructions in the manual. Because the task contains only nineteen items, it is much faster to administer than the PPVT-5.

### Expressive Vocabulary

Expressive vocabulary refers to the words an individual can actively use in speech or in writing; assessments measure how well students can express themselves through language. The vocabulary task from the Wechsler Intelligence Scale for Children, Fifth Edition (WISC-V; Wechsler, 2014), battery is a popular measure of *expressive vocabulary*. Students are asked to define words of increasing difficulty, and each item or answer is scored with 0 (incorrect), 1 (partly correct), or 2 (fully correct). A participant's score is the sum of scores aggregated across all responded items. The raw score can subsequently be converted into a standard score following the instructions in the manual. It takes about ten to fifteen minutes to administer this task. Even though the administration instructions come with a scoring guide, it is often very difficult to evaluate a student's answer on the spot. A solution is to record an individual's answers and then listen to the recordings to determine if an answer qualifies for two points or one point.

The Expressive One-Word Picture Vocabulary Test, Fourth Edition (EOWPVT-4), is an individually administered, norm-referenced assessment of how well persons age two years to over eighty years can name the objects, actions, or concepts presented in full-color pictures (Martin & Brownell, 2011). The task consists of 100 pictures arranged in terms of increasing difficulty. The task is discontinued after eight consecutive errors, and a participant's score is the total number of correct responses. It takes about fifteen to twenty minutes to administer. The authors have also developed a parallel task for receptive vocabulary (the Receptive One-Word Picture Vocabulary Test, Fourth Edition, or ROWPVT-4), in which a word is provided to the students and they have to point to one of four pictures in a quadrant that shows the word provided.

The TELL (Phillips & Hayward, 2016) includes both a receptive and an expressive vocabulary task and provides educators with norms for Canadian students three to eight years of age. More specifically, the Oral Vocabulary section of TELL comprises four tasks. The first two tasks ask students to label and provide definitions for a series of pictured nouns or verbs. The remaining two tasks ask students to provide definitions for a series of nonpictured nouns or verbs. The tasks administered are age dependent. Tasks involving labeling and providing definitions for pictured nouns or verbs are discontinued after five consecutive errors. All items are administered for the tasks involving definitions of nonpictured nouns or verbs. The total scores equal the number of correct items in each task. Standard scores and percentile ranks can be viewed relative to the student's age group and, if completed as part of the oral language test battery, will form part of the student's Oral Language composite score. Although testing time for the vocabulary tasks varies based on the number of tasks administered and the tester's familiarity with the tasks, it usually takes about twenty to twenty-five minutes to administer these tasks per child.

### Reading Vocabulary

Reading vocabulary assessments measure how well a student can recognize and understand words when reading a text. In Word Meaning from the Group Reading Assessment and Diagnostic Evaluation (GRADE), students are given a booklet that has twenty-seven rows of four pictures in each row (Williams, 2001). At the beginning of each row there is a printed word, and the students read it silently and then circle the picture that matches the meaning of the word in each row. The students are given about ten minutes to complete the task.

The Nelson-Denny Reading Test has two equivalent forms (I and J) and is appropriate for students ages fourteen all the way to year two and four at the university level (Fishco, 2019). Individuals are given fifteen minutes to answer eighty to a hundred multiple-choice vocabulary questions (for example, "*Indispensable* means [a] uncomfortable; [b] costly; [c] durable; [d] essential; or [e] timely"), and a participant's score is the total number of correct answers.

## How to Teach Vocabulary

Students learn new vocabulary in two ways: incidentally and through direct instruction. According to Michael F. Graves (2006; see also Graves, Schneider, & Ringstaff, 2018), a prominent figure in vocabulary instruction, to optimize vocabulary learning, we should (1) provide rich and varied language experiences, (2) teach specific words directly, (3) teach word-learning strategies, and (4) foster word consciousness. In this section of the chapter, we elaborate on each of these components.

### Provide Rich and Varied Language Experiences

Often, we hear students use some words as they speak, and we are fascinated by the breadth of their vocabulary. Some of these words they pick up from listening to their teacher, and others from listening to their parents or siblings. Given that learning of vocabulary may also happen incidentally, it is our responsibility as teachers to create those conditions that allow our students to be exposed to different words in oral conversations. We can provide rich and varied language experiences in three ways.

1. **By providing students the opportunity to engage daily in oral language activities:** Have rich vocabulary conversations with your students on a daily basis. When a word is repeated multiple times in your discussions, this will stimulate students' interest, and they may then look it up in their dictionary.

2. **By providing students the opportunity to listen to adults read to them:** As we mentioned earlier, when parents read to their children, it has a direct impact on their children's vocabulary. While reading a story, parents often pause and discuss the meaning of specific words (that is, they provide a definition). This helps build students' vocabulary.

3. **By providing students the opportunity to read extensively on their own:** The more students read on their own, the more words they will come across and learn their meaning. Independent reading has been found to be a significant predictor of vocabulary and reading comprehension (Cunningham & Stanovich, 1998; Torppa et al., 2020).

### Teach Specific Words Directly

Because of the importance of vocabulary in reading comprehension and because we want to close up the vocabulary gap, we need to directly teach certain words (like Tier 2 words). The following list includes an example of the steps involved in teaching a word. You should repeat these steps for every word you have decided to teach. Remember that students have a better chance to learn the meaning of a given word if they get multiple exposures to it (some say students need as many as twelve exposures to a word for it to become part of their vocabulary) and in different contexts. On page 240, sample lesson plan 1, "Building Vocabulary", provides a template for teaching a given word. An explicit vocabulary instruction routine includes four steps (Archer & Hughes, 2011).

1. **Introduce the word (pronounce it, write it, read it):** Call students' attention to the word's pronunciation and spelling. Have students pronounce and write the word, too. Check for students' pronunciation. Point to any relevant regular and irregular spelling patterns and syllable types in the word. You may even want to say what part of speech the word is (such as a noun, an adjective, or a verb).

2. **Present a student-friendly definition:** Give a definition of the word using known words that are easy for students to understand (not the dictionary's definition) and have the students read the definition with you. Explain the word's connection to other words. For example, let's pretend the word you will be teaching is *relieved*. You may say that when something difficult is over or never happened at all, you feel relieved.

3. **Illustrate the word with examples:** Use the word in sentences. Explain any multiple meanings. Use concrete examples, pictures, videos, and

gestures. Give examples as well as nonexamples. For example, you may say, "When I finished singing the national anthem in front of 10,000 fans, I felt relieved. Tell me about a time you felt relieved."

4. **Check for students' understanding:** Ask students deep processing questions or ask them to generate their own example. You may also provide a sentence starter that students complete using the right word. For example, you may say, "When John was told that the mathematics test was canceled, he said, 'I am relieved.' Why was John relieved?"

### Teach Word-Learning Strategies

Obviously, it is impossible for teachers to provide direct instruction for all the words students do not know. How then can we help students figure out the meaning of words they do not know and teachers won't directly teach in class? The answer is by teaching students some word-learning strategies like the following.

1. How to use dictionaries or glossaries

2. How to pay attention to meaningful parts within a word (known as morphology)

3. How to use contextual clues (such as illustrations or hints about the meaning of an unknown word provided in the words or phrases that surround the word)

We intentionally chose to elaborate here on the second word-learning strategy, paying attention to meaningful parts of a word—that is, morphology. This is for two reasons: first, because English is described as a *morphophonemic language*. In other words, the letters used in print correspond to sounds (phonemes). As we said in chapter 6 (page 105), teaching the letter-sound correspondences allows students to accurately read regular words. However, spelling in English has not evolved to represent only the sounds, but most importantly the meaning of words. Think for a second about the word *two*. Why is there a *w* in *two*? To signal its meaning connection to words like *twice*, *twin*, or even *twenty*. Thus, teaching morphology is akin to the characteristics of the English language. Second, several studies measuring in-service teachers' knowledge of language and literacy skills have shown that teachers have a very limited knowledge of morphology. For example, Erin K. Washburn and colleagues (2016) show that pre-service teachers in the United States have only a 20 percent average mean score in the questions related to morphology compared to 46 percent in Canada, 49 percent in the United Kingdom, and 33 percent in New Zealand. Thus, we are taking this opportunity to specifically talk about morphology.

### Morphology Terms Educators Should Know

Before we delve into the teaching of morphology, it is important to provide you with the definitions of the key terminology.

> **Spelling in English has not evolved to represent only the sounds, but most importantly the meaning of words.**

- **Morphology** is the part of the language system that is concerned with the internal structure of words, analyzing words into meaningful units called morphemes. It is a property of both oral and written language.

- **Morphemes** are the smallest units of meaning. Some words have only one morpheme (*cook, help, joy*) while many others are made up of two or more morphemes (*cook + ing, help + ful, joy + ous*). The words that have two or more morphemes are called multimorphemic words.

- **Affixes** are word parts that are "fixed to" either the beginning of words (these are called prefixes) or the ending of words (these are called suffixes). The word *unhelpful,* for example, has two affixes, a prefix (*un-*) and a suffix (*-ful*). Some words may have more than one prefix (*re + con + struct + ion*) or more than one suffix (help + *less + ness*). Suffixes can be further divided into two categories: inflectional suffixes (*-ing, -ed,* and *-s/es*) and derivational suffixes (*-ion, -ous, -ite,* and *-or*). Inflections change the grammatical nature of a base, such as number (in English, adding *-s* for plural), tense (adding *-ed* for the past tense), or gender (in French, *grand* [*tall*] is an adjective for masculine nouns, while *grande* is for feminine nouns). Derivations change the meaning of the word, for instance from *act* to *action,* sometimes changing the grammatical category (from verb to noun in this case, though *act* may also be a noun). Another distinction that is important to mention is that between free and bound morphemes. Free morphemes can stand alone as words, for instance *joy* or *look*. Bound morphemes cannot. Prefixes and suffixes are not words by themselves, so they are bound morphemes by definition.

- **Base words** are words that are not derived from other words. They are the words from which many other words are formed. For example, from the base word *help* we can get *helper, helping, helpless, helplessness, unhelpful,* and so on.

- **Root words** are the words from other languages that are the origin of many English words. About 60 percent of all English words have a Latin or Greek origin. For example, the word *instructor* is derived from the Latin root *struct,* which means to build (*in + struct + or* → *instructor*). From this root we can build words like *construction, destruction, instruction, constructive, constructivism,* and so on.

These are important terms for all members of your professional learning community to know. We highly recommend spending time learning about morphology as a team, using these terms as a starting point. The next section makes it clear that teaching morphology is an important part of vocabulary instruction.

Why We Should Teach Morphology

Teaching morphology is important for five reasons.

1. It helps students disambiguate the pronunciation of some words—for example, pronouncing *rethink* as *re + think*, not *reth + ink*, or *reached* as *reach + ed*, not *re + ached*.

2. It helps build students' vocabulary and comprehension. When a student comes across an unfamiliar word in a text, they can break it apart and use their knowledge of the root, prefixes, and suffixes to infer the meaning of the whole word. For example, knowing that the prefix *dys-* means "difficulty with" and *calculus* means "arithmetic," a student can infer that *dyscalculia* means difficulty with numbers and arithmetic.

3. It helps improve students' spelling. For example, students will notice that when you add a vowel suffix to a base word ending in *y*, the *y* changes to *i*.

   *try + es* → *tries*          *dry + es* → *dries*

   *cry + es* → *cries*          *fly + es* → *flies*

4. Similar to phonological awareness, morphological awareness is one of the linguistic skills that transfers from a student's first language (L1) to the student's second language (L2). For example, Gloria Ramirez, Xi Chen, Esther Geva, and Heider Kiefer (2010) show that morphological awareness in Spanish (L1) is predictive of students' word reading in English (L2), even after controlling for the effects of general cognitive ability, phonological awareness, and morphological awareness in English.

5. According to John R. Kirby and Peter N. Bowers (2017), morphology serves as a binding agent connecting phonology, orthography, and semantics. Morphemes are clearly units of meaning, so they are intimately related to semantics. In most languages, morphemes also have a very consistent spelling, so they are related to orthography. Finally, morphemes also relate to how sequences of letters are pronounced (like *rethink* as *re + think* and not *reth + ink*), so they are related to phonology. Together, this allows this strengthening of the mental representations of words.

> **Morphology serves as a binding agent connecting phonology, orthography, and semantics.**

### Scope and Sequence in Teaching Morphology

Because teaching morphology has been included in several English language arts curricula in the United States, Canada, and Australia, teachers might be wondering if there is a published scope and sequence they can use to teach morphology. The short answer is no. The scope and sequences that you can find on the internet are not based on any solid research but reflect personal choices. As pointed out by Peter N. Bowers (2009), the developer of Structured Word Inquiry (explained later in this section), the key point is not the teaching of certain morphemes in a specific order, but the teaching of certain orthographic concepts. The following are just a few of these key orthographic concepts.

- Every word is a base or a base with something else added to it. This could be another base (as in the case of compound words like *tooth + brush* → *toothbrush*) or an affix (prefix or suffix)

- We can break down multimorphemic words into their constituent morphemes with the use of word sums (identifying morphemes in words and examining how they combine together to make different words), and we can also show how they are all interrelated through a word matrix.

- There are three suffixing conventions (as in doubling the final consonant in a monosyllabic word when adding a vowel suffix; *stop + ed* → *stopped*), and they operate reliably.

- The primary goal of studying and understanding the suffixing conventions is not to improve students' spelling accuracy but to allow students to test hypotheses about connections between words.

- The structure and meaning test is used to determine that two words share a base. To do this, we need evidence from both structure (word sum) and meaning (etymology).

An instructional approach that teaches the connection between orthography and meaning (hence, tapping into morphology) is Structured Word Inquiry (SWI; Bowers, 2009; Bowers & Kirby, 2010). SWI is appropriate for all grade levels and can be done even with kindergarten students using hand gestures (for example, hold up your left fist and say, "This is play." Then put your right fist beside your left first and say, "This is *-er*. What happens if I put *-er* beside *play*?"). In SWI, students learn to generate and test hypotheses (hence the word *inquiry* in SWI) about the spelling-meaning connection of words. The inquiries include doing word sums, building word matrices, and learning about the etymology of words (by accessing online etymological dictionaries; www.etymonline.com). Four inquiry questions will provide a framework to guide the spelling-meaning-pronunciation investigations in SWI.

1. **What does it mean?** What is the definition of the word?

2. **How is it built?** Is it a base or a base with something else attached to it?

3. **What are the word's relatives?** What are the morphological relatives that share a base, or etymological relatives that share a historical root?

4. **What is the pronunciation?** What is the representation of phonemes across morphological boundaries and influence of word origin on grapheme choice?

An integral component of SWI is the process of "writing-out-loud word sums" and the creation of a word matrix. For example, the teacher will guide students to spell out the base *knight* ("kn: igh: t") and explicitly associate the *kn* digraph with the phoneme /n/, the trigraph *igh* with the phoneme /aɪ/, and the single-letter grapheme *t* with the phoneme /t/. Within the framework of word sums, students will be guided to announce prefixes (*de-*, *re-*) and suffixes (*-ed*, *-ment*, *-ure*, *-ing*).

Once the word sums are sufficiently practiced, students will be guided to build a word matrix (see figure 8.3). A matrix has a central base that can be combined with the other morphological elements (bases and affixes) to form complex words. Word sums show the morphological structure of individual words in a matrix. The vertical lines in the matrix correspond to the plus sign in the word sum. Horizontal lines cannot be crossed to form words. The matrix shows the full form of written morphemes in the cells, but the word sum can show suffixing changes (*make + ing → making*; *hop(p) + ing → hopping*; *try/i + es → tries*). The matrix and word sums provide concrete representations of the underlying morphological structure of words and the surface realizations that we see in print.

The word "sums" for *sign* are as follows.

- *sign + al → signal*
- *as + sign + ment → assignment*
- *re + de + sign → redesign*
- *sign + ate/ + ure → signature*

Note that the backslash in *signature* shows that the single, silent *e* is replaced by the vowel suffix *-ure*.

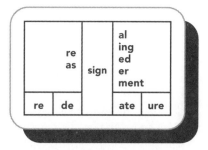

**Figure 8.3:** Word matrix for *sign* with associated word sums.

### Word Consciousness

The last component of Michael Graves' (2006) four-part vocabulary program introduced earlier in this chapter is fostering students' word consciousness. The term *word consciousness* refers to an awareness of and interest in words and their meanings (Graves & Watts-Taffe, 2002). According to Graves (2000), "if we can get students interested in playing with words and language, then we are at least halfway to the goal of creating the sort of word-conscious students who will make words a lifetime interest." Here are three types of word consciousness activities.

1. **Create a word-rich environment:** This can be achieved by filling up your classroom with books and other materials on many topics and by making sure that the provided books contain some new words for all students.

2. **Promote adept diction:** Make it a priority to use some sophisticated vocabulary and sometimes comment on your word choices. In addition, compliment students on their word choices in their discussions and writing.

3. **Promote word play:** Use word games (play well-known games like Word Bingo or Pictionary) for students to develop interest in words.

### Sample Lesson Plans

In appendix D (page 239), we include three sample lesson plans on how to teach vocabulary and morphological awareness. This is not meant to be a comprehensive program of teaching vocabulary but rather is a collection of ideas on how to teach each of the vocabulary subskills.

- Four-Step Model: Building Vocabulary (see page 240)
- Word Bags: Name the Word Family (see page 242)
- Morphological Analysis: Understanding Morphemes (see page 244)

## Conclusion

One of the best predictors of reading comprehension is vocabulary knowledge. In fact, the effects of vocabulary knowledge on reading comprehension increase over time because the texts become longer and include new vocabulary. Given the importance of vocabulary in later comprehension and the documented vocabulary gap in kindergarten, building students' vocabulary knowledge should start early in students' lives and be intentional and explicit. Obviously, parents can play an important role in fostering their students' vocabulary, but teachers should also incorporate vocabulary in their everyday teaching. In this chapter, we also highlighted the importance of morphological awareness, and we presented an example of an instructional approach that is used to teach it (SWI). Studying and understanding morphology allows students to discover the interconnections between different layers of our writing system and to apply that knowledge not only when they try to understand new words but also in spelling these words. Vocabulary and morphological awareness have been found to have a reciprocal relationship (Dulay et al., 2021; Grande, Diamanti, Protopapas, Melby-Lervåg, & Lervåg, 2024), and they both exert unique effects on reading comprehension, which is the focus of our next chapter.

# Key Readings and Resources

- Beck, I., McKeown, M., & Kucan, L. (2013). *Bringing words to life: Robust vocabulary instruction* (2nd ed.). New York: Guilford Press.

- Biemiller, A. (2009). *Words worth teaching: Closing the vocabulary gap.* New York: McGraw-Hill.

- Foorman, B. (2022). Improving comprehension through vocab: Effective instructional strategies in grades 4-8. *Literacy Today*, pp. 39-42. Accessed at https://fcrr.org/sites/g/files/upcbnu2836/files/media/PDFs/Foorman_ILA.pdf on November 10, 2024.

- Kirby, J., & Bowers, P. (2017). Morphological instruction and literacy. In K. Cain, D. Compton, & R. Parrila (Eds.), *Theories of reading development* (pp. 437-461). Amsterdam, Netherlands: Benjamins.

- Levesque, K. C., Breadmore, H. L., & Deacon, S. D. (2021). How morphology impacts reading and spelling: Advancing the role of morphology in models of literacy development. *Journal of Research in Reading*, 44(1), 10-26. https://doi.org/10.1111/1467-9817.12313

- Pearson, P. D., Hiebert, E. H., & Kamil, M. L. (2012). Vocabulary assessment: Making do with what we have while we create the tools we need. In J. Baumann & E. Kame'enui (Eds.), *Vocabulary instruction: Research to practice* (2nd ed.). New York: Guilford Press. Accessed at https://textproject.org/wp-content/uploads/papers/Pearson-Hiebert-Kamil-2012-Vocabulary-Assessment.pdf on November 10, 2024.

- Scott, J. A., & Nagy, W. E. (2004). Developing word consciousness. In J. F. Baumann & E. J. Kame'enui (Eds.), *Vocabulary instruction: Research to practice* (pp. 201-217). New York: Guilford Press.

- Wagner, R. K., Muse, A. E., & Tannenbaum, K. R. (Eds.) (2007). *Vocabulary instruction: Implications for reading comprehension*. New York: Guilford Press.

- Wright, T. S., & Cervetti, G. N. (2017). A systematic review of the research on vocabulary instruction that impacts text comprehension. *Reading Research Quarterly*, 52(2), 203-226. https://doi.org/10.1002/rrq.163

- Zucker, T. A., Cabell, S. Q., & Pico, D. L. (2021). Going nuts for words: Recommendations for teaching young students' academic vocabulary. *The Reading Teacher*, 74(5), 581-594.

continued ▶

Here are a few websites that include useful information and material for teaching vocabulary:

- **Florida Center for Reading Research (fcrr. org/student-center-activities):** This resource offers teachers vocabulary activities for students in kindergarten to grade 5. Each activity is accompanied by a lesson plan outlining the lesson's objectives, required materials, and step-by-step implementation instructions. All necessary materials are included within the resource, eliminating the need for teachers to develop additional materials.

- **Structured Word Inquiry (SWI) (wordworkskingston.com/WordWorks/ Home.html):** This website was developed by Peter N. Bowers, and it includes useful information on how to apply SWI in your classroom as well as links to videos. In this site you will also find links to useful tools such as how to build a word matrix, a word searcher, and word sums for different words.

- **Online Etymology (www.etymonline.com):** This site offers teachers and students access to the origin of thousands of words. It allows students to check if certain words belong to the same morphological family as their target word.

- **Jason Wade Education: The Root Repository (jwed.co.uk/2021/04/13/rootrepository):** On this site, Jason Wade provides weekly examples of root words along with their meaning, information on their origin (etymology), and examples of words that share this root.

- **Scholastic: Most Common Prefixes and Suffixes (teacher.scholastic.com/reading/ bestpractices/vocabulary/pdf/prefixes_ suffixes.pdf):** This resource provides a comprehensive list of the most common prefixes and suffixes that teachers can use to inform their instruction.

CHAPTER 9

# Reading Comprehension

If there is one thing researchers agree on, it is that the ultimate goal of reading is comprehension. Whether we lie down on a beach and read a book for pleasure or we read a newly posted message on a bulletin board at our school, we interact with the text, and we try to extract meaning from it. Despite the prominent place of reading comprehension in the pyramid of reading skills, evidence from different studies suggests that it is the skill that our students struggle with the most. For example, the results of the PISA international study have shown that fifteen-year-old Canadian students' performance in reading comprehension has been steadily declining over the years. In 2000 they obtained a score of 534, in 2012 they scored 523, and in 2022 they scored 507 (the lowest ever). Thus, in the last chapter of *Better Together* we will focus on reading comprehension. The National Reading Panel (2000) identified three themes that are important to remember as we discuss reading comprehension and how to best teach it.

1. Reading comprehension is a cognitive process that integrates complex skills and cannot be understood without paying attention to the critical role of vocabulary and its development.

2. Active strategic processes are critically necessary to the development of reading comprehension.

3. The preparation of teachers to best equip them to facilitate these complex processes is critical and intimately tied to the development of comprehension. This theme in particular is what motivated us to write this book.

In this chapter, we define reading comprehension, and we describe the most popular assessments of it. We also briefly present two popular instructional approaches that can easily be adapted to different grade levels and topics. Note that we do not present a scope and sequence for teaching reading comprehension, as reading comprehension goals may look different in different parts of North America and because teachers are allowed to use different texts to meet the goals of their curriculum.

## The Meaning of Reading Comprehension

Simply put, reading comprehension is the ability to understand what we read either in printed material or on electronic devices. This differentiates it from listening comprehension, which refers to understanding what is said orally. Reading comprehension is a complex, multicomponential construct that involves interactions between the reader (their decoding skills and inferential skills), what they bring to the task (such as previous knowledge about the topic), and variables related to the text they are asked to comprehend (the text type). This is partly the reason why pinning down the sources of a reading comprehension breakdown is quite challenging for teachers and also why the effects of intervention on comprehension tend to be lower than those targeting phonological awareness or decoding (Galuschka et al., 2014).

## Why We Should Teach Reading Comprehension

We should teach reading comprehension for three main reasons.

1.  Comprehension is the ultimate goal of reading. Assuming students struggle with reading comprehension, they will likely experience difficulties in many other subject areas (like mathematics or social studies) that require reading and comprehending text.

2.  Reading comprehension forms reciprocal relations with other cognitive-linguistic skills such as vocabulary, morphological awareness, and decoding (Manolitsis, Georgiou, Inoue, & Parrila, 2019; Sparapani et al., 2018). Therefore, if comprehension is impaired, the development of other skills will also be impacted.

3.  Reading comprehension allows students to develop reading enjoyment (van Bergen et al., 2023). Students with comprehension difficulties show significantly less interest in reading compared to students with strong reading comprehension skills and may develop task avoidance (Päivinen, Eklund, Hirvonen, Ahonen, & Kiuru, 2019).

## How to Assess Reading Comprehension

The assessment of reading comprehension is an interesting one because there is no perfect measure of it. Studies that have administered multiple measures of reading comprehension have revealed low correlations among individual measures (Cutting & Scarborough, 2006; Keenan, Betjemann, & Olson, 2008). In practice, this means that we cannot use these measures interchangeably and assume they all measure the same construct. To bypass this problem, Janice M. Keenan and colleagues (2008) recommend administering multiple reading comprehension tasks in order to get a finer picture of students' performance. Keenan and Chelsea E. Meenan (2014) also show that the average overlap between different comprehension tasks in diagnosing comprehension difficulties was only 43 percent. The consistency was greater for younger students (mean age = 9.32 years), when comprehension deficits are the result of weaker decoding skills, than for older students (mean age = 13.78 years). Interestingly, inconsistencies between comprehension tests were just as evident when identifying the top performers in comprehension.

Another important point worth noting is that reading comprehension measures differ in both their format and task demands. For example, some require oral reading of sentences or passages (YARC, GORT), while others require silent reading (TOSREC, GRADE). Some measures may follow a cloze format (they require individuals to either provide a word that completes the meaning of the sentence or select a word among choices to accurately complete the meaning of a sentence), use a multiple-choice format, or include open-ended questions. Some measures require students to read sentences or short passages (Woodcock-Johnson IV Passage Comprehension), while some involve reading whole passages (Nelson-Denny Reading Test).

Finally, it is important to remember that most reading comprehension tasks are time consuming (twenty to thirty minutes per student). We mention this because we often receive questions from teachers asking us to recommend quick and, at the same time, comprehensive measures of reading comprehension that will inform them about the comprehension strategies that their students may be lacking (summarization, making predictions, cause and effect). Even though some of the assessments we present in the following list (YARC, Nelson-Denny Reading Test) were developed to include questions that tap into these different comprehension strategies, the score that teachers will ultimately get from these tasks is not further broken down into the different comprehension strategies. Thus, assuming teachers want to know whether a given student has mastered certain comprehension skills, they must do a finer analysis of the student's scores in these assessments on their own. The following sections provide a review of formal and informal assessments, as well as assessments meant for individuals and those meant for groups.

> **The assessment of reading comprehension is an interesting one because there is no perfect measure of it.**

### Informal Assessments

The following is a list of informal assessments for measuring reading comprehension. Like the assessments for the other four pillars of literacy, these tests are variable and often customizable.

### CBM-Maze

The CBM-Maze requires students to read passages that include incomplete sentences (Deno, 1985; see also Fuchs & Fuchs, 1992). From these passages, the first sentence is always intact, and after the first sentence, every seventh word in the passage is replaced with the correct word and two distracters. Students must choose the word from among the three choices that best restores the meaning of that segment of the passage. The reader continues until time expires or until they complete the task. The CBM-Maze can be administered to a whole class at one time. Passages used for CBM-Maze should be at least 300 words in length. Fuchs and Fuchs (1992) also provide some norms for second through sixth grade (see table 9.1).

They did not provide norms for grade 1 as they argued CBM-Maze should not be used for progress monitoring in grade 1. Students scoring below the 25th percentile on CBM-Maze can be considered at risk for reading difficulties. The following is an example of a CBM-Maze task for sixth-grade students titled *No More TV* (Fuchs, 2017).

> Toby and his little brother, Brad, were quietly watching T.V. that Tuesday night their lives changed so much. Their mom, Mrs. Green, had gone [as/ to/ if] a P.T.A. meeting at their school. [Rug/ Buy/ The] school rarely had nighttime P.T.A. meetings, [he/ so/ I] Mrs. Green had made a special [great/ their/ effort] to attend this one since she couldn't [attend/ dreamy/ shrill] the afternoon meetings because of her [mad/ job/ the]. Toby and Brad weren't what you [puffy/ would/ dough] call hooked on T.V., but it [tar/ card/ was] definitely part of their routine. They [watched/ notion/ kettle] cartoons in the morning as they [land/ what/ ate] their breakfast and cartoons again in [the/ milk/ nut] afternoon after school and then comedy [like/ shows/ relax] and police shows after supper.

As you can see, the first sentence is intact, and then every seventh word is replaced with three choices. Students must circle the choice that completes the meaning of the passage accurately.

- **Example A:** Peter is a fifth-grade student and is assessed using CBM-Maze in the fall term. His score is 7. To check if Peter has comprehension difficulties, do the following.

    - Find his grade level in table 9.1.

    - Find the relevant scores under the term he was tested.

    - Compare his score to the cutoff scores provided. Since 7 is lower than the cutoff score associated with the 25th percentile for the fall term of grade 5 (12), we can conclude that Peter has reading comprehension difficulties.

- **Example B:** Mandy is in grade 2, and she is assessed using CBM-Maze in the spring term. Her score is 13. To check if Mandy has comprehension difficulties, do the following.

    - Find her grade level in table 9.1.

    - Find the relevant scores under the term she was tested.

- Compare her score to the cutoff scores provided. Since 13 is higher than the cutoff score associated with the 25th percentile for the spring term of grade 2 (8), we can conclude that Mandy does not have reading comprehension difficulties. In fact, her score would put her above the 50th percentile.

### Diagnostic Placement Test (Scholastic)

In this task, there are ten phonics questions, fifteen vocabulary questions, and twenty-five comprehension questions. In the comprehension section of the test, students are asked to read four passages and then answer multiple-choice questions that are associated with each passage. The total score out of 50 can be used to identify those students who are reading below grade level, at grade level, or above grade level. A total score of less than 60 percent correct indicates that the student is reading below grade level, between 60 and 89 percent that the student is reading at grade level, and 90 percent or higher that the student is reading above grade level. It is important to note that the comprehension questions in this task were designed to tap into the different comprehension strategies (making predictions, compare and contrast, context clues, main idea, summarization, and more). Unfortunately, as with all comprehension tasks, when you get the student's total score, there is no breakdown of the strategies in which the student is doing poorly so you can target through instruction.

**Table 9.1: Recommended Norms for CBM-Maze, Grades 2–6**

| Grade Level | Assessment Term | | |
|---|---|---|---|
| **Grade 2** | **Fall** | **Winter** | **Spring** |
| 25th | 3 | 5 | 8 |
| 50th | 4 | 9 | 12 |
| 75th | 7 | 13 | 16 |
| **Grade 3** | **Fall** | **Winter** | **Spring** |
| 25th | 8 | 11 | 13 |
| 50th | 11 | 14 | 16 |
| 75th | 14 | 17 | 20 |
| **Grade 4** | **Fall** | **Winter** | **Spring** |
| 25th | 9 | 13 | 16 |
| 50th | 11 | 17 | 19 |
| 75th | 15 | 21 | 23 |
| **Grade 5** | **Fall** | **Winter** | **Spring** |
| 25th | 12 | 15 | 16 |
| 50th | 17 | 20 | 22 |
| 75th | 22 | 26 | 28 |
| **Grade 6** | **Fall** | **Winter** | **Spring** |
| 25th | 12 | 16 | 17 |
| 50th | 18 | 23 | 22 |
| 75th | 24 | 30 | 30 |

## Formal Assessments

There are several commercially available and norm-referenced measures of reading comprehension. Most of them are part of psychometric batteries of achievement along with other measures. In the following list we divide assessments into those that are administered individually and those that can be administered in a group setting.

### Administer Individually

The following assessments help teachers understand an individual's reading comprehension level.

- **Sentence Comprehension (Wide Range Achievement Test, Fifth Edition [WRAT-5]; Wilkinson & Robertson, 2017):** Individuals are asked to silently read fifty sentences of increasing difficulty and provide the missing word in each sentence that accurately completes the meaning of the sentence. The task is discontinued after seven consecutive errors, and a participant's score is the total number of correct answers. It usually takes about fifteen minutes to administer this task.

- **Woodcock-Johnson IV Tests of Achievement (Schrank et al., 2014):** In this task, students are asked to silently read a short passage and then provide the missing word to correctly complete the sentence in a sensible manner ("The man ran over and began to _____. He dug and dug."). A student's score is the total number of correct answers. It usually takes about fifteen to twenty minutes to administer this task, and it may be even longer when working with struggling readers.

- **Test of Reading Comprehension, Fourth Edition (TORC-4; Brown, Hammill, & Wiederholt, 2009):** The test has five subtests, and scores from each subtest are combined to form a composite score, or "reading comprehension index." This is the same as a standard score with a mean of 100 and a standard deviation of 15. This index represents students' ability to understand contextual printed material. Here is a short description of each subtest.

    - *Relational vocabulary*—From the student question booklet, the student reads a set of three words that are in some way related to each other. The student is then to read silently another four words and choose two words that are related to the first set of three words.

    - *Sentence completion*—From the student question booklet, the student silently reads a sentence that is missing two words. The student then silently reads a list of word pairs and chooses the word pair that best completes the sentence.

    - *Paragraph construction*—The student is asked to rearrange a list of sentences that are not in logical order to form a coherent paragraph.

    - *Text comprehension*—Students silently read a short passage and then answer five multiple-choice questions relative to the passage.

    - *Contextual fluency*—This subtest measures how many individual words students can recognize, in three minutes, in a series of passages taken from the text comprehension subtest. Each passage, printed in uppercase letters without punctuation or spaces between words, becomes progressively more difficult in content, vocabulary, and grammar. As students read the segments, they draw a line between as many words as they can in the time allotted.

    TORC-4 can be given to individuals from seven to seventeen years of age and takes about thirty to thirty-five minutes to complete.

- **York Assessment of Reading for Comprehension (YARC; Snowling et al., 2012):** The YARC is a standardized assessment used to measure text comprehension skills (reading comprehension concerning literal and inferential meaning). The passages included in the YARC tap into a range of skills: word-level decoding, reading fluency, vocabulary knowledge, grammar, ability to make inferences, knowledge of the world, knowledge of story structure and text format, and comprehension monitoring and error-correction strategies. YARC has two versions: for primary-age students (ages five to eleven) and secondary-age students (ages twelve to sixteen). In the primary version of YARC, students are required to read two passages out loud, and each passage consists of two parts: a text passage (to measure accuracy and rate) and eight comprehension questions. In the secondary version of YARC, the passages are read silently.

### Administer in a Group

The following assessments help teachers understand a group's current level on their respective comprehension topics.

- **Sentence Comprehension and Passage Comprehension (GRADE; Williams, 2001):** In this test, there are two subtasks that jointly give you a comprehension score: Sentence Comprehension and Passage Comprehension. In Sentence Comprehension, students are asked to read short sentences and then select among four choices the word that accurately completes the meaning of the sentence—for example, "Cars and buses drive on the (A) told, (B) road, (C) goat, (D) roar." Sentence Comprehension has nineteen items. In Passage Comprehension, students are asked to silently read eight short passages and answer three multiple-choice questions that follow each passage (for a total score of 24).

- **Test of Silent Reading Efficiency and Comprehension (TOSREC; Wagner et al., 2010):** We included this task here as well as in chapter 7 (page 125) because it captures both reading efficiency and comprehension. In our own work in schools, the scores from TOSREC correlate strongly with those of other measures of reading comprehension (Woodcock-Johnson IV Passage Comprehension). Other researchers have also provided evidence that scores from the TOSREC load on the same factor as other measures of comprehension (Lonigan & Burgess, 2017), and therefore we feel confident enough to include it here even though on the surface it does not look like it requires higher-level comprehension skills.

  In the TOSREC, students are asked to silently read simple sentences (for example, *Ice is hot*) and circle *Y* (Yes) if the meaning of the sentence is true or *N* (No) if the meaning of the sentence is false. The *Y* and *N* are printed at the end of each sentence. Students are given three minutes to read as many of the sixty sentences as possible, and their score is calculated by subtracting the number of incorrect responses from the number of correct (this is done to correct for guessing). There is a different kit for each grade level (grades 1–12), and there are four parallel forms within each grade level kit.

- **Gates MacGinitie Reading Test, Fourth Edition (GMRT-4; MacGinitie, MacGinitie, Maria, & Dreyer, 2000):** The GMRT-4 is a timed, standardized, and norm-referenced reading comprehension task for students in grades K–12 that is administered either individually or in a group setting. The GMRT-4 includes eleven passages and forty-eight multiple-choice questions related to these passages. The expository and narrative passages, each containing three to fifteen sentences, are read silently. The questions that follow each passage require constructing an understanding based on information that is either explicitly or implicitly stated in the passage. Students independently read the passages and questions and then record their answers on a separate answer sheet. Administration of the test takes approximately forty-five minutes (ten minutes for the pretest, then thirty-five minutes for the actual test administration). A student's score is the total number of questions answered correctly.

- **Nelson-Denny Reading Test (Fishco, 2019):** This task has two equivalent forms (I and J) and is appropriate for students from fourteen years old all the way to second and fourth year at the university level. In the comprehension task, individuals are given a maximum of twenty minutes to answer as many multiple-choice questions as possible that follow each of the seven passages. A student's score is the total number of correct answers.

> **Decoding and language comprehension (or, broadly speaking, oral language skills) are the two most important skills in fostering reading comprehension.**

## How to Teach Reading Comprehension

There are usually two approaches to improve reading comprehension. The first one concerns the teaching of foundational skills. We already know from the "simple view of reading" (Gough & Tunmer, 1986) that decoding and language comprehension (or, broadly speaking, oral language skills) are the two most important skills in fostering reading comprehension. Therefore, instruction that focuses on decoding (accuracy and fluency), vocabulary, and language comprehension is critical for improving reading comprehension (see chapters 6–8, pages 105–150, on how to teach these skills). This has been documented in several empirical studies, including intervention studies with students with reading disabilities (Edmonds et al., 2009; Stevens et al., 2017).

Another approach to improving reading comprehension is through explicit teaching of reading comprehension strategies. According to Timothy Shanahan (2023), professor emeritus at the University of Illinois Chicago (UIC) and founding director of the UIC Center for Literacy, comprehension strategies serve two purposes: First, they get readers to think about a text more than they would if they were to just read it. If readers think more about the ideas in a text, they are more likely to remember them when they are asked questions later. Second, strategies may guide students' attention to key information in the text. For example, when reading something that is hard to understand, you may write down the most important idea from each paragraph, which then allows you to pay attention to all the key ideas, without having any unnecessary details distracting you.

Despite the attention that comprehension strategies have received since the early 2000s (see Filderman, Austin, Boucher, O'Donnell, & Swanson, 2022; see also Peng, Wang, Filderman, Zhang, & Lin, 2024, for a meta-analytic study on reading comprehension strategies), there are still some unknowns around their nature and contribution. First, it remains unclear if comprehension strategies make an independent contribution to reading comprehension over and beyond the contribution of decoding and language comprehension. Christopher J. Lonigan, Stephen R. Burgess, and Christopher Schatschneider (2018), for example, show that decoding and language comprehension jointly explain almost all of the variance in students' reading comprehension performance. If this is true, then what is left for comprehension strategies to explain? Second, it remains unclear how long strategy teaching should last in order to be effective. According to Shanahan (2023), teachers can teach a strategy well in three to four weeks, if they have their students practicing with lots of different texts. Peng Peng and colleagues' (2024) meta-analysis shows, however, that intervention length does not really matter and that short-strategy interventions have similar effects to longer ones. Finally, even though teaching multiple comprehension strategies together seems to produce better results than teaching one strategy at a time, it remains unclear what set of comprehension strategies produces the best outcomes. Oddly enough, most English language arts curricula in the United States and Canada treat comprehension strategies as individual mastery goals, and teachers are encouraged to move to teaching the next strategy only when their students have demonstrated a good mastery of the previous one. Unfortunately, we also frequently witness in different classes that the choice of simple texts does not really allow students to deploy any comprehension strategies. In table 9.2 we summarize some of the most commonly used comprehension strategies that have been found to improve reading comprehension.

> **It remains unclear if comprehension strategies make an independent contribution to reading comprehension over and beyond the contribution of decoding and language comprehension.**

**Table 9.2: Comprehension Strategy Summaries**

| Strategy | Description of Strategy |
|---|---|
| **Comprehension monitoring** | Being actively aware of whether one is understanding the text or not through ways such as self-questioning (including asking questions such as "Does this makes sense?" and "Am I missing something here?") and coherence checking. |
| **Activating prior knowledge and predicting** | Using what is already known from the text and background knowledge to hypothesize the content of the text and evaluate this hypothesis against the actual content. |
| **Text structure** | Recognizing the underlying structure of texts to help focus attention on key concepts and relationships, anticipate what is to come, and monitor their comprehension as they read. |
| **Asking questions** | Asking questions about the text being read. This can serve as a form of self-assessment. |
| **Answering questions** | Answering questions posed by the teacher and receiving feedback on the correctness of one's answers. |
| **Inference generation** | Integrating information within text and between the text and one's general knowledge of the topic to understand ideas not explicitly stated in the text. |
| **Retell and summarization** | Attempting to identify and write the main important ideas that integrate the other meanings of the text into a coherent whole. |
| **Graphic organizers** | Using teacher-made graphic representations of the material to assist comprehension. |

### Prerequisite Skills for Reading Comprehension

Researchers have explored the role of both cognitive and noncognitive (environmental and motivational) skills that may underlie reading comprehension. The list would have been quite long, and for this reason we focus on the most important ones.

- Decoding
- Oral language skills
- Working memory
- Background knowledge
- Comprehension monitoring

The following section elaborates on each of these items.

#### Decoding and Oral Language Skills

One of the most influential theories of reading, called the "simple view of reading" by Phillip B. Gough and William E. Tunmer (1986), argues that reading comprehension (RC) is the product of language comprehension (LC) and decoding (D); thus, $RC = LC \times D$. *Decoding* is the ability to associate print with sounds accurately and fluently. In turn, *language comprehension* is the ability to understand spoken language (usually measured by vocabulary or listening comprehension). Even though the theory is rather simplistic, it helps us in two important ways.

1. The "simple view of reading" theory signals that while language comprehension and decoding are necessary components, they are not sufficient on their own for reading comprehension to occur. This is why Gough and Tunmer (1986) view reading comprehension as a product rather than the sum of the two skills. If one of the two components is poor, adequate comprehension cannot be achieved. If you cannot decode the words in a text correctly, you cannot comprehend what the text is about. Likewise, if you can read accurately but lack the knowledge of the meaning of the words, you cannot comprehend the text either. For example, because Finnish is a transparent orthography (this means every letter corresponds to one sound), after learning the sound associated with each letter, we can decode accurately almost all words in a text, but we cannot comprehend what the text is about because we do not know the meaning of the words we decoded accurately.

2. The theory has helped researchers and practitioners classify students into different types of reading disabilities. Students with relatively good language comprehension but poor decoding (standard scores below 85 in word reading) have dyslexia (a specific word reading difficulty). Students with relatively poor language comprehension (standard scores below 85 in listening comprehension) and at least average decoding have a specific poor comprehension deficit (they read text accurately and fluently, but they do not understand what they read). Finally, students with relatively poor performance in both are known as "garden variety poor readers" (Gough & Tunmer, 1986), and students with good performance in both are considered good readers.

The importance of these two skills in reading comprehension changes over time. During the early years, decoding plays a more important role than language comprehension. As students master decoding, the contribution of decoding to reading comprehension decreases, and the contribution of language comprehension increases.

### Working Memory

Working memory is the capacity to store and process information simultaneously (Baddeley, 2012). It is important for reading comprehension because while we are reading a given text, we need to temporarily store some important information about the text (such as who the main character is or where the story takes place) and then integrate all the pieces together to make a coherent representation of the text. Many students with specific poor comprehension have a deficit in working memory (Georgiou & Das, 2015; Nation, Adams, Bowyer-Crane, & Snowling, 1999). Unfortunately, deficits in working memory are difficult to remediate. Meta-analytic studies have reported small effects of working memory training and that these effects do not transfer to other skills such as reading comprehension (Melby-Lervåg & Hulme, 2013; Melby-Lervåg, Redick, & Hulme, 2016). Monica Melby-Lervåg and Charles Hulme (2013), for example, conclude that "memory training programs appear to produce short-term, specific training effects that do not generalize" (p. 270).

### Background Knowledge

When individuals read a given passage, they try to integrate the information they get from the passage to what they already know about the topic. Obviously, if they have limited knowledge of the topic, this will not support their comprehension. To demonstrate the importance of background knowledge, consider the following example. Most people would think that if you can accurately read a list of words like the one following this text and you also know their meaning, you should not have any problems understanding a short passage that is made up of these words. Let's give it a try. We assume you can read this list of words correctly and you also know what they mean.

| | | | |
|---|---|---|---|
| are | draws | making | relation |
| curve | known | points | corresponding |
| isolated | one | variables | if |
| with | values | continuously | often |
| table | consists | graph | set |
| between | variation | only | |

Now, please read the following text that contains these words from the book *Basic College Math* by M. Michael Michaelson (1945). After you finish reading this short passage, can you tell us what it means in your own words?

> If the known relation between the variables consists of a table of corresponding values, the graph consists only of the corresponding set of isolated points. If the variables are known to vary continuously, one often draws a curve to show the variation.

If you are like most adults who do not have a background in mathematics, the preceding text will be difficult to understand—not because you do not know the meaning of these words in isolation, but because you do not have the necessary background knowledge to support your understanding of this text.

### Comprehension Monitoring

Students who are good at monitoring their own comprehension are aware of whether they understand what they are reading and when their comprehension is compromised. When they realize that they did not understand a certain word or a section in the text, they deploy "fix-up" strategies to resolve problems or confusion. Jane Oakhill, Joanne Hartt, and Deborah Samols (2005) have repeatedly shown that students with a specific reading comprehension deficit perform worse than their chronological-age controls on measures of comprehension monitoring. They measured comprehension monitoring by asking students to read stories and to indicate any problems in these stories (such as blatantly contradictory pieces of information in the text). Students who were not effectively monitoring their understanding found it more difficult to detect inconsistencies between pieces of information in text, particularly when the items of information that need to be integrated were not in adjacent sentences.

A special category of reading disabilities is called specific reading comprehension deficit. It is a condition whereby an individual can read accurately, fluently, and at age-appropriate levels, but fails to understand much of what they read. Because of the nature of this reading disability, many students fall off the radar of teachers and remain undiagnosed. Because teachers often ask students to read out loud in their class, it is easier to identify a student who is not reading accurately. It is more challenging for teachers to detect comprehension deficits because it would require them asking questions to all students even if they are silent and do not raise their hand. Charles Hulme and Margaret J. Snowling (2011) report that about 10 percent of school-age students have a specific reading comprehension deficit.

## What to Teach Before, During, and After Reading

In the following section we elaborate on two instructional approaches that have been used to boost students' reading comprehension by training multiple comprehension strategies before, during, and after reading a given text.

### Self-Regulated Strategy Development

An approach that is well researched and has produced significant effects on reading comprehension is self-regulated strategy development (SRSD; Graham & Harris,

1993; Harris & Graham, 2017; Mason, 2013; Sanders, 2020). SRSD is an explicit and scaffolded instructional approach with a GRR that occurs over six recursive stages (develop background knowledge, discuss it, model it, memorize it, support it, and encourage independent performance). The approach also integrates self-regulation techniques such as self-monitoring and goal setting to ultimately facilitate students' independent application of the strategy. It is intended to be a criterion-based instructional method, allowing students to progress through the stages at their own pace and only move to the next stage when they have met at least the minimum requirements of the preceding stage (Harris & Graham, 2017). Here, we describe each of the six stages of SRSD.

### Stage 1: Develop Background Knowledge

During this stage, the teacher may discuss what skilled readers do, emphasizing the importance of effective reading practices. Students may be prompted to identify situations where remembering what they have read is particularly important, and to reflect on their current comprehension abilities.

### Stage 2: Discuss It

In the second stage, students learn about the benefits of using a strategy to increase reading comprehension. The selected strategy is introduced and explained in a step-by-step manner, with the teacher explicitly discussing the purpose of each step. A mnemonic may also be introduced to help students remember the strategy. Self-regulation techniques, such as self-monitoring and goal setting, are integrated into this stage.

### Stage 3: Model It

The third stage often incorporates a think-aloud, with the teacher articulating their thought process while employing the strategy. Using instructions in each step and explicitly integrating the self-regulation strategies discussed in the previous stage, the teacher demonstrates the strategy by reading a specific passage and verbalizing the steps taken to comprehend the text.

### Stage 4: Memorize It

The fourth stage focuses on the memorization of the chosen strategy. As mentioned earlier, a mnemonic can be helpful in aiding students' memorization of the steps. However, it is important to ensure that students not only memorize each step but can also describe the purpose of each step and its components. Students should advance to the next stage only when they can accurately recite the strategy's steps and provide an adequate explanation of the requirements and purpose of each step.

### Stage 5: Support It

In the fifth stage, the teacher supports students in applying the strategy and gradually reduces the level of guidance provided. This stage may involve the teacher working with groups of students or individual students, with the teacher assisting students in self-monitoring the use of the strategy. The aim of this stage is for the use of the strategy, along with the self-regulatory processes, to become less teacher directed as students take on more responsibility.

### Stage 6: Encourage Independent Performance

In the final stage, students independently implement the strategy. When presented with a passage, students are expected to apply the strategy without prompts or guidance. The teacher oversees students' performance, gradually removing all guidance as students consistently and accurately employ the strategy. To help facilitate generalization, teachers should provide opportunities for students to apply the strategy across various texts and subjects.

## Collaborative Strategic Reading

Collaborative strategic reading (CSR) consists of four strategies (preview, click and clunk, get the gist, and wrap up) designed to help students in upper elementary and middle school to understand narrative or informational text (Boardman et al., 2016; Klingner et al., 2004; Klingner, Vaughn, Boardman, & Swanson 2012; Vaughn et al., 2011). It actually forces students to think of their own comprehension before, during, and after reading the text. A CSR learning log, titled "Making the 'Clunk' Click" appears in appendix E (page 250). Students will use this learning log to take important notes as they go through the four CSR strategies that we describe in the following steps. A sample lesson on CSR can also be seen in appendix E (page 247).

### Step 1: Preview

The first CSR strategy, conducted before reading a passage, helps students activate their prior knowledge about the topic they will be reading and make predictions about what the text might be about. For example, if the book is about rainforests, the teacher may ask students to say what they already know about rainforests, where we can find rainforests, and the like.

### Step 2: Click and Clunk

The second CSR strategy, conducted during reading a passage, helps students monitor their understanding while reading. "Clicks" are those words or concepts that students already know. Materials that are difficult to understand are called "clunks." For every clunk, there are four strategies that students can use to turn it into a click. First, they can reread the sentence or section of text, omitting the clunk, and consider what information is in the rest of the sentence that would make the clunk make sense. Second, they can reread the sentences before and after the sentence with the clunk and determine if there are any clues to help them make sense of the clunk. Third, they can look for prefixes or suffixes in the clunk because, as mentioned in chapter 8 (page 133), morphemes carry meaning and may clarify the clunk. Finally, they can break the clunk into smaller, more familiar words.

### Step 3: Get the Gist

The third CSR strategy, conducted during reading a passage, helps students determine the main idea of a paragraph or section of text. It consists of two stages: First, students must determine what person, place, or thing is the most important in the paragraph. Second, they must use their own words to describe the main idea related to this person, place, or thing.

### Step 4: Wrap Up

The fourth CSR strategy, conducted after reading of the passage is completed, helps students generate questions and review important information in the text. It consists of two stages: First, students ask and answer their own questions pertaining to the most important information in the text: who, what, where, why, when, and how. Second, they review the key points and the most important information in the text.

### *Sample Lesson Plans*

In appendix E (page 247), we include two sample lesson plans on how to teach comprehension using the SRSD and CSR instructional approaches. This is not meant to be a comprehensive program of teaching reading comprehension, but rather is a collection of ideas on how to teach each of the comprehension subskills.

- Summarizing Text (see page 248)
- Making the "Clunk" Click (see page 250)

## Conclusion

The ultimate goal of reading is comprehension. We read text in order to extract meaning from the words included in that text. Despite the fact that many students are able to comprehend without any difficulty, a significant number of students (estimated to be about 10 percent of the general population) do not comprehend what they read despite the fact that their decoding is adequate. This category of students is known to have a specific comprehension deficit. Several hypotheses have been proposed regarding the underlying causes of poor comprehension. Current evidence indicates that most students with poor comprehension present a wealth of deficits such as poor vocabulary, poor working memory, limited background knowledge, and poor comprehension monitoring. Because comprehension is the product of several underlying skills, a breakdown in comprehension could be due to a breakdown in any of these skills or a combination of them. Obviously, this makes it difficult to pin down the exact cause and may explain (at least partly) why the effect sizes of comprehension interventions have been lower than the effect sizes for decoding or reading fluency.

# Key Readings and Resources

- Duke, N. K., Ward, A. E., & Pearson, P. D. (2021). The science of reading comprehension instruction. *The Reading Teacher*, 74(6), 663-672. https://doi.org/10.1002/trtr.1993

- Elleman, A. M., & Oslund, E. L. (2019). Reading comprehension research: Implications for practice and policy. *Policy Insights From the Behavioral and Brain Sciences*, 6(1), 3-11. https://doi.org/10.1177/2372732218816339

- Filderman, M. J., Austin, C. R., Boucher, A. N., O'Donnell, K., & Swanson, E. A. (2021). A meta-analysis of the effects of reading comprehension interventions on the reading comprehension outcomes of struggling readers in third through 12th grades. *Exceptional Students*, 88(2), 163-184. https://doi.org/10.1177/00144029211050860

- Foorman, B. (2022, October/November/December). Improving comprehension through vocabulary: Effective instructional strategies in grades 4-8. *Literacy Today*, pp. 39-42. Accessed at https://fcrr.org/sites/g/files/upcbnu2836/files/media/PDFs/Foorman_ILA.pdf on November 16, 2024.

- Hulme, C., & Snowling, M. J. (2011). Students' reading comprehension difficulties: Nature, causes, and treatments. *Current Directions in Psychological Science*, 3, 139-142.

- Klingner, J. K., Vaughn, S., & Boardman, A. (2007). Teaching reading comprehension to students with learning disabilities. New York: Guilford Press.

- Landi, N., & Ryherd, K. (2017). Understanding specific reading comprehension deficit: A review. *Language and Linguistics Compass*, 11(2), 1-24. https://doi.org/10.1111/lnc3.12234

- Nation, K. (2005). Students' reading comprehension difficulties. In M. J. Snowling and C. Hulme (Eds.), *The science of reading: A handbook* (pp. 248-265). Malden, MA: Blackwell.

- Shanahan, T., Callison, K., Carriere, C., Duke, N. K., Pearson, P. D., Schatschneider, C., & Torgesen, J. (2010). *Improving reading comprehension in kindergarten through 3rd grade: A practice guide* (NCEE 2010-4038).

- National Center for Education Evaluation and Regional Assistance, Institute of Education Sciences, U.S. Department of Education. Accessed at whatworks.ed.gov/publications/practiceguides on November 16, 2024.

- Wagner, R. K., Muse, A. E., & Tannenbaum, K. R. (Eds.) (2007). *Vocabulary instruction: Implications for reading comprehension*. New York: Guilford Press.

Here are a few websites that include useful information and material for reading comprehension.

- **Florida Center for Reading Research (fcrr. org/student-center-activities):** This resource offers teachers comprehension activities for students from kindergarten to grade 5. Each activity is accompanied by a lesson plan outlining the lesson's objectives, required materials, and step-by-step implementation instructions. All necessary materials are included within the resource, eliminating the need for teachers to develop additional materials.

- **Reading Universe: Graphic Organizers (https://readinguniverse.org/pdf/explore-teaching-topics/reading-comprehension/strategies-and-activities/graphic-organizers-for-reading-comprehension):** This resource includes six different graphic organizers for various types of text. Teachers can use this resource to help students organize, break down, and summarize important information within a text.

- **Self-Regulated Strategy Development (https://srsdonline.org):** This site contains resources and additional information about SRSD.

- **ReadWorks (www.readworks.org):** On this site, teachers can find different passages per grade level and subject along with the Tier 2 vocabulary that goes with the specific passage and comprehension questions. An important feature of this site is that you can choose the difficulty level of the passage (number of words, Lexile), which means that you can find texts that are appropriate for students of different reading ability level.

# EPILOGUE

Reading is undoubtedly one of the most important skills students should master in their early school career. Failure to do so is linked to higher dropout rates, an increased risk of mental health problems, lower salaries, poorer health, and even incarceration (Mulcahy, Bernardes, & Baars, 2016). Given that reading is not natural and must be taught explicitly, teachers have an enormous responsibility to provide high-quality classroom instruction so that 95 percent of all students become competent readers.

Although hundreds of studies on literacy acquisition have revealed how students learn to read and what skills need to be taught to support literacy acquisition, current evidence draws a rather gloomy picture (Hall et al., 2023; National Reading Panel, 2000). The reading scores of fourth-grade students on nationwide reading assessments in the United States haven't changed since 2003, with only 30 to 35 percent of these students reading at or above the expected level of reading proficiency. Across the border, the PISA results for Canadian students reached a historic low in 2024, and for the first time in Canadian history we have a Human Rights Commission report for the right to read, calling upon governments and postsecondary institutions to take action to boost students' reading performance. In the midst of this, teachers' knowledge of "what" needs to be taught and "how" to best teach it remains limited, despite the fact that the first studies to identify a significant gap in teachers' knowledge of spoken and written language structure were published in the 1990s (Moats, 1994; Moats & Lyon, 1996; Parrila et al., 2024; Piasta, Ramirez, Farley, Justice, & Park, 2020).

Can we then turn the tide and create schools where 95 percent of students reach proficiency levels in reading? This question provided the impetus of *Better Together*. In writing this book, we sought to bridge the gap between the science of reading and educational practice, as what we have learned as scientists since 1990 has unfortunately had little impact on what happens in the classroom (Seidenberg et al., 2020). We learned through our own experience working in schools (and admittedly through our own mistakes) that providing one-off professional development to teachers and giving them access to a plethora of materials and resources they can use at their own discretion does not lead to better student reading performance. Moving the needle on literacy cannot be achieved when teachers work in silos, and it doesn't work when the administrators (principals and superintendents) are not part of the solution process. When schools operate as PLCs, the schools learn to embrace teacher learning, implement effective instruction, and improve student outcomes. Hence, *Better Together* provides a road map of the "whats" and "hows" of changing your school culture to a PLC, one that embraces adult learning, draws on data to inform decisions, and fosters reciprocal accountability.

As described in chapter 3 (page 39), within the structure of the PLC process, there is a set of five action steps for principals to successfully transition their school to evidence-based reading instruction.

1. Form a guiding coalition.
2. Facilitate job-embedded professional development.
3. Collect schoolwide reliable and valid data.
4. Create time for intervention.
5. Create a system of reciprocal accountability.

All of these steps need to be implemented as part of a systemic approach to improving reading performance. Simply put, neither administrators nor teachers can pick or choose what is easy, familiar, or comfortable to implement.

The second part of this book has aimed to help teachers in implementing evidence-based reading instruction that focuses on the five pillars of literacy instruction. We realized over the years that many teachers do not know what skills to teach, in what order to teach them, and what materials to use to teach these skills more effectively. The proliferation of social media and literacy websites has worsened the problem as teachers can download almost everything from the internet without asking if this is an evidence-based program or not. In addition, teachers and researchers may have a totally different view on what is considered "evidence." For example, presenting data collected from a single school somewhere in the United States doesn't make a given program "evidence-based."

In writing this section of *Better Together*, we first explained what these concepts are and why they are important for reading. We also provided several recommendations on how to assess the five pillars of literacy and how to teach them. We encourage teachers to explore these recommendations and, in collaboration with the guiding coalition within their school, set a plan on how to use these resources and how to measure their effectiveness.

We acknowledge that changing the culture of a school into one that focuses on continuous adult learning and data-informed decisions is easier said than done. However, we need to start from somewhere, and this starting point has to be the example of schools that were successful in moving the needle on literacy. *Better Together* brings forward these examples and allows both principals and teachers to benefit from it and ultimately achieve the goal of developing proficient readers.

APPENDIX A
# PHONOLOGICAL AWARENESS LESSON PLANS

In this appendix, we include reproducible activities to increase phonological awareness as whole-group and individual exercises. The activities, such as syllable awareness, onset and rime, phoneme isolation, phoneme blending, and phoneme deletion, are meant to be conducted in the classroom so the teacher can oversee progress and provide guidance. These activities are designed for kindergarten, grade 1, and grade 2.

## PHONOLOGICAL AWARENESS
*Syllable Awareness*

# Syllable Clap

### Learning Objective

Students will identify syllables in spoken words they **hear.**

### Materials

- Pictures of objects or animals (optional)

### Activity

Review with students that words we **hear** can be separated into **syllables**, the "beats of a word." Model how to orally segment words into syllables.

1. Say the word *baby*.
2. Segment the word into syllables, clapping once for each part of the word, /bā/ (clap) /bē/ (clap).
3. Have students say and clap the syllables in the word on their own.
4. Continue modeling, giving students different words.

### Example Words
- One-syllable words: *hop, wet, car, rain, fast, small, drink, green, park, knight*
- Two-syllable words: *basket, robot, paper, spider, table, circle, bubble, tiny*
- Three-syllable words: *basketball, strawberry, lemonade, potato, September*

### Modifications and Extensions

- Students may tap or jump instead of clapping each syllable.
- Show a picture of an object or animal. Have students name the picture and then clap its syllables.
- Say a word and then ask the students to tell you how many syllables the word has (For example, say *number*. The word *number* has two syllables /nŭm/ /ber/).

# PHONOLOGICAL AWARENESS
*Onset and Rime*

## Onset and Rime Time

 **Learning Objective**

Students will segment and match onsets and rimes in words they **hear**. The onset is the initial phonological unit of a word (/h/ in *hat*), and the rime is the string of letters that follow (/ăt/ in *hat*).

## Materials

- Picture cards (Line Masters [LM] 1–3)
- Blank tiles or cubes (optional)

## Activity

1. Show the picture card of a cat.
2. Say the word *cat*.
3. Segment *cat* into its onset and rime, briefly pausing between /k/ and /ăt/.
4. Repeat with the picture cards for *hat* and *bat*. **Emphasize that all the words end in the same rime /ăt/.**
5. Present other picture cards and have students name each picture and then segment the word into its onset and rime.

## Modifications and Extensions

- Mix up the picture cards. Have students identify and then match the picture cards that share the same rime (/ăn/ in *pan, van, can, fan*).
- Use blank tiles or cubes to concretely represent the onset and rime under each picture.

# PHONOLOGICAL AWARENESS
*Onset and Rime*

**LM 1: Rime /ăt/**

# PHONOLOGICAL AWARENESS
*Onset and Rime*

**LM 2: Rime /ăn/**

# PHONOLOGICAL AWARENESS
*Onset and Rime*

**LM 3: Rime /ŏg/**

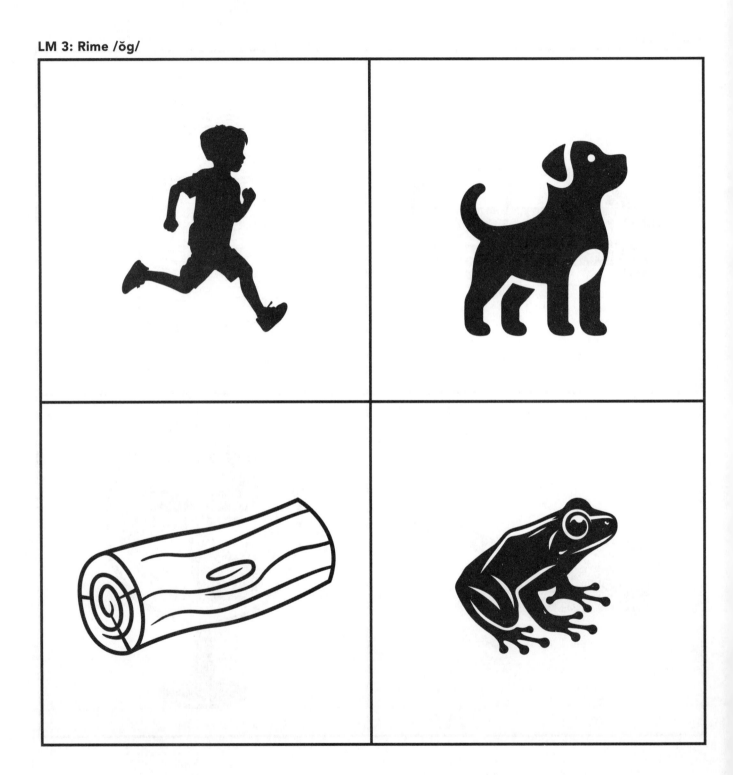

## PHONOLOGICAL AWARENESS
Phoneme Isolation

# Where's the Sound? ☐☐☐

 ## Learning Objective

Students will identify the beginning, end, and medial phonemes in words they **hear.**

## Materials

- Picture cards (Line Masters [LM] 1–4)
- Pencil (optional)

## Activity

1. Show the picture card *cat*.
2. Say the name of the picture card /k/ /ă/ /t/.
3. Direct students to tell you where they hear the /k/ sound in the word *cat*.
   Say: "Where's the /k/ sound? Is it at the beginning, middle, or end?"
4. Under the picture, ask students to place a mark in the box that indicates the /k/ sound in *cat*.
5. Continue this activity with new pictures targeting other phonemes
   (for *cat*, say: "Where is the /t/ sound?"). Encourage students to say each sound in the word.

## Modifications and Extensions

- Start with beginning sounds before introducing end sounds. Identify middle sounds last.
- Begin with consonants before isolating short and long vowels.
- Distribute picture cards to students to complete the activity independently.
- Create additional picture cards to explore a variety of phonemes.

## PHONOLOGICAL AWARENESS
*Phoneme Isolation*

**LM 1: Phoneme /k/**

# PHONOLOGICAL AWARENESS
*Phoneme Isolation*

**LM 2: Phoneme /p/**

# PHONOLOGICAL AWARENESS
*Phoneme Isolation*

**LM 3: Phoneme /ă/**

# PHONOLOGICAL AWARENESS
*Phoneme Isolation*

## Say the Sound

block /b/

 ### Learning Objective

Students will recognize and pronounce the individual sounds in words they **hear**. They will isolate beginning, medial, and end phonemes in words.

## Materials

- Isolating sounds word lists (Learning Masters [LM] 1–3)
- Blank tiles or cubes (optional)

## Activity

1. Explain to students that you will say a word and they will say the sound they hear at the beginning of that word.
2. Select some words to model from the Isolating Beginning Sounds word list (LM 1). Say the first word, *bus*.
3. Direct students to say the sound they hear at the beginning of *bus*.
4. Say: "Listen to the word *bus*. What is the beginning sound in *bus*?" (/b/)
5. Continue the activity, dictating other words from the word list.
6. In later lessons, have students isolate and pronounce the end sounds, then the middle sounds, in words.

*Here's a tip: start with one-syllable words containing short vowels before moving onto words that have long vowels or vowel combinations.*

## Modifications and Extensions

- Use blank tiles or cubes to show the sounds in each word concretely.
- Practice isolating phonemes in nonwords (ip, bik, rup, siplet, getfom).
- Encourage students to think of other words that contain similar beginning, middle, or end sounds they learn.

# PHONOLOGICAL AWARENESS
*Phoneme Isolation*

## LM 1: Isolating Beginning Sounds

| One-syllable | One-syllable | Two-syllable | Three-syllable |
|---|---|---|---|
| bus /b/ | block /b/ | inside /ĭ/ | basketball /b/ |
| car /k/ | soft /s/ | under /ŭ/ | strawberry /s/ |
| rug /r/ | knight /n/ | flying /f/ | family /f/ |
| hat /h/ | hide /h/ | sleepy /s/ | dinosaur /d/ |
| jet /j/ | junk /j/ | glasses /g/ | library /l/ |
| fit /f/ | fly /f/ | little /l/ | octopus /ŏ/ |
| dig /d/ | stop /s/ | zipper /z/ | telephone /t/ |
| get /g/ | quilt /kw/ | yellow /y/ | broccoli /b/ |
| bed /b/ | tell /t/ | money /m/ | rectangle /r/ |
| lap /l/ | mine /m/ | rabbit /r/ | camera /k/ |
| wet /w/ | nest /n/ | tiger /t/ | violin /v/ |
| sun /s/ | rink /r/ | bunny /b/ | banana /b/ |
| zip /z/ | vase /v/ | necklace /n/ | computer /k/ |
| yet /y/ | kite /k/ | letter /l/ | pineapple /p/ |
| van /v/ | waste /w/ | doorbell /d/ | umbrella /ŭ/ |
| up /ŭ/ | snake /s/ | basket /b/ | animal /ă/ |
| in /ĭ/ | lamp /l/ | forest /f/ | volcano /v/ |
| ask /ă/ | horse /h/ | garbage /g/ | wonderful /w/ |
| egg /ĕ/ | desk /d/ | flower /f/ | elephant /ĕ/ |
| on /ŏ/ | rain /r/ | thinking /th/ | hamburger /h/ |
| ship /sh/ | joke /j/ | weather /w/ | microscope /m/ |
| chop /ch/ | slide /s/ | showtime /sh/ | carpenter /k/ |
| felt /f/ | flag /f/ | chatter /ch/ | afternoon /ă/ |
| gift /g/ | must /m/ | trimming /t/ | underneath /ŭ/ |
| act /ă/ | zoo /z/ | crumble /k/ | energy /ĕ/ |
| cake /k/ | wish /w/ | pizza /p/ | quietly /kw/ |
| shine /sh/ | ant /ă/ | very /v/ | remember /r/ |
| think /th/ | end /ĕ/ | robin /r/ | forgetful /f/ |

# REPRODUCIBLE

# PHONOLOGICAL AWARENESS
*Phoneme Isolation*

## LM 2: Isolating End Sounds

| One-syllable | One-syllable | Two-syllable | Three-syllable |
|---|---|---|---|
| left /t/ | scrub /b/ | outside /d/ | ladybug /g/ |
| nap /p/ | hiss /s/ | blackbird /d/ | daffodil /l/ |
| mug /g/ | ten /n/ | cabin /n/ | hibernate /t/ |
| ham /m/ | night /t/ | cabbage /j/ | character /er/ |
| crab /b/ | shop /p/ | washcloth /th/ | Saturday /ā/ |
| bed /d/ | sock /k/ | water /er/ | radio /ō/ |
| line /n/ | wax /ks/ | bedtime /m/ | lemonade /d/ |
| car /ar/ | moth /th/ | music /k/ | pajamas /s/ |
| bell /l/ | zap /p/ | pizza /ă/ | photograph /f/ |
| more /or/ | paint /t/ | beachball /l/ | fantastic /k/ |
| frog /g/ | some /m/ | season /n/ | underneath /th/ |
| hush /sh/ | said /d/ | pilot /t/ | banana /ă/ |
| touch /ch/ | need /d/ | zebra /â/ | instrument /t/ |
| ice /s/ | rope /p/ | popcorn /n/ | jellyfish /sh/ |
| plate /t/ | star /ar/ | jacket /t/ | butterfly /ī/ |
| tooth /th/ | raft /t/ | bathtub /b/ | fingernail /l/ |
| bridge /j/ | cats /s/ | pencil /l/ | happiness /s/ |
| drink /k/ | dogs /z/ | fifteen /n/ | potato /ō/ |
| kind /d/ | teeth /th/ | about /t/ | microwave /v/ |
| twirl /l/ | mush /sh/ | happy /ē/ | hamburger /er/ |
| split /t/ | page /j/ | water /er/ | bakery /ē/ |
| tenth /th/ | knife /f/ | hero /ō/ | apartment /t/ |
| crush /sh/ | thumb /m/ | olive /v/ | rattlesnake /k/ |
| quack /k/ | peach /ch/ | subway /ā/ | toboggan /n/ |
| saw /aw/ | buzz /z/ | magnet /t/ | mosquito /ō/ |
| fuzz /z/ | fetch /ch/ | garden /n/ | porcupine /n/ |
| edge /j/ | north /th/ | student /t/ | remember /er/ |
| think /k/ | burn /n/ | monkey /ē/ | iguana /ă/ |

**Better Together** © 2025 Solution Tree Press • SolutionTree.com
Visit **go.SolutionTree.com/literacy** to download this page.

# PHONOLOGICAL AWARENESS
*Phoneme Isolation*

## LM 3: Isolating Middle Sounds

| One-syllable | One-syllable |
|---|---|
| let /ĕ/ | rob /ŏ/ |
| map /ă/ | miss /ĭ/ |
| hug /ŭ/ | slow /l/ |
| not /ŏ/ | cry /r/ |
| cub /ŭ/ | foam /ō/ |
| win /ĭ/ | cane /ā/ |
| pen /ĕ/ | sly /l/ |
| fuss /ŭ/ | bath /ă/ |
| mop /ŏ/ | cute /ū/ |
| math /ă/ | that /ă/ |
| neck /ĕ/ | chip /ĭ/ |
| hush /ŭ/ | comb /ō/ |
| touch /ŭ/ | park /ar/ |
| mitt /ĭ/ | fort /or/ |
| gate /ā/ | phone /ō/ |
| moss /ŏ/ | meet /ē/ |
| hive /ī/ | mule /ū/ |
| beat /ē/ | shape /ā/ |
| fish /ĭ/ | teeth /ē/ |
| team /ē/ | short /or/ |
| luck /ŭ/ | wide /ī/ |
| teeth /ē/ | toad /ō/ |
| cart /ar/ | shirt /er/ |
| quack /ă/ | free /r/ |
| toss /ŏ/ | chill /ĭ/ |
| fuzz /ŭ/ | glue /l/ |
| fry /r/ | crow /r/ |
| loan /ō/ | yes /ĕ/ |

# PHONOLOGICAL AWARENESS
Phoneme Blending

## Blend It!

### Learning Objective

Students will **isolate** and **blend phonemes** they **hear** to make words. They will successively **blend** the sounds together, **saying** the first sound followed by the second and then immediately the third, to pronounce a whole word.

### Materials

- Blend It! word cards (Learning Masters [LM] 1–4)

### Activity

1. Show the picture card *bat*.
2. Direct students how to *blend* the sounds together to say the word.
3. Say: "Look at the picture. Let's blend the sounds together to say the word /băt/. Under the picture, tap each square as you say each sound, /b/ /ă/ /t/.
   Then, place your finger on the arrow and slide it. Start at the beginning sound and move through to the middle, then to the end, as you blend the sounds quickly together to say the word /băt/.
4. Continue this activity, showing other pictures targeting new phonemes (/f/ /ĭ/ /sh/, *fish*). Encourage students to say each sound in the word, then successively blend them together to say the whole word.

### Modifications and Extensions

- Complete the activity without pictures. Dictate two-phoneme words (*it, an, on, it*) followed by three-phoneme words (*tan, hop, pet*), having students tap the sounds before blending them together.
- Create pictures for blending more three-phoneme words with LM 4.

#### Examples of other *three-phoneme* words:

| tell | ship | chat |
|---|---|---|
| /t/ /ĕ/ /l/ | /sh/ /ĭ/ /p/ | /ch/ /ă/ /t/ |
| pick | shop | bath |
| /p/ /ĭ/ /k/ | /sh/ /ŏ/ /p/ | /b/ /ă/ /th/ |

# PHONOLOGICAL AWARENESS
*Phoneme Blending*

**LM 1: Blend It!**

REPRODUCIBLE

# PHONOLOGICAL AWARENESS
*Phoneme Blending*

**LM 2: Blend It!**

Better Together © 2025 Solution Tree Press • SolutionTree.com
Visit **go.SolutionTree.com/literacy** to download this page.

# PHONOLOGICAL AWARENESS
*Phoneme Blending*

**LM 3: Blend It!**

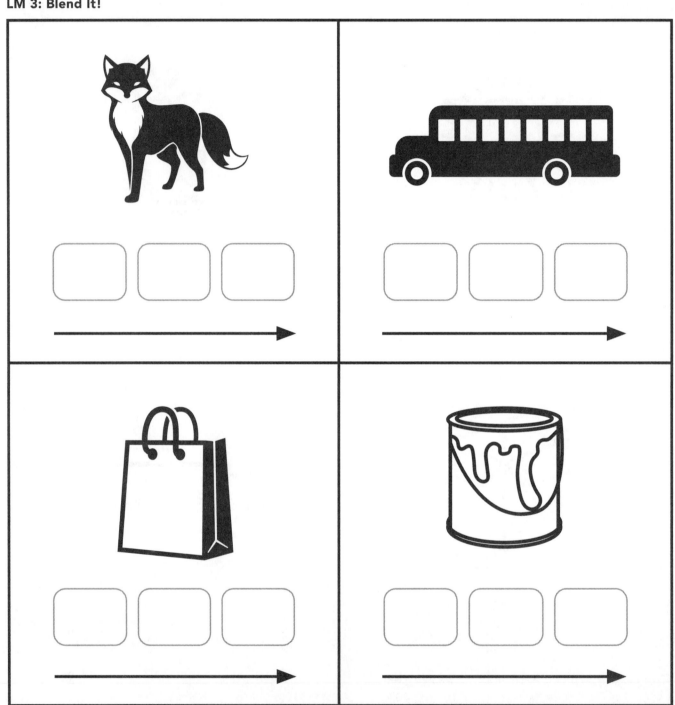

# PHONOLOGICAL AWARENESS
*Phoneme Blending*

**LM 4: Blend It!**

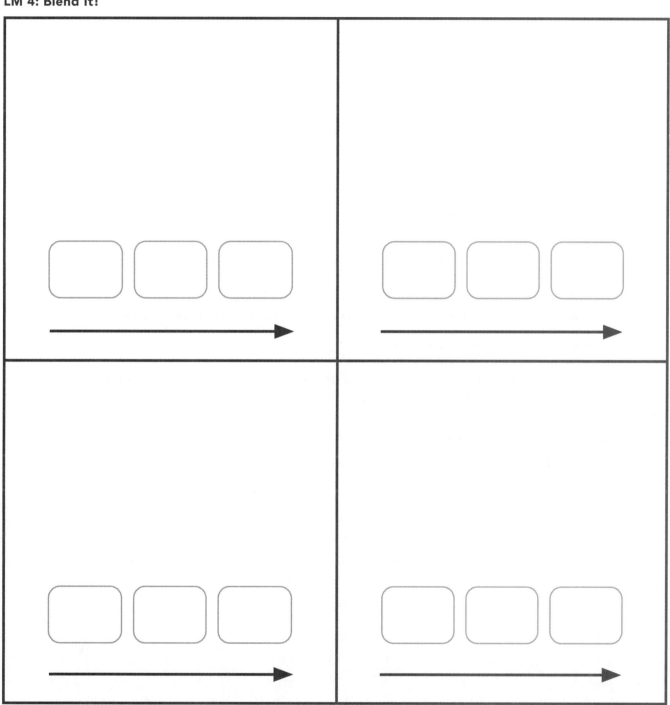

# PHONOLOGICAL AWARENESS
*Phoneme Deletion*

## Take Away  /măt/ − /m/ = /ăt/

### Learning Objective

Students will **take away** (delete) a **phoneme** from a word they **say**, then pronounce the new word made.

### Materials

- Dictation card (Learning Masters [LM] 1): Beginning Sound Deletion
- Dictation card (LM 2): End Sound Deletion (optional)
- Dictation card (LM 3): Medial Sound Deletion (optional)
- Blank tiles or cubes (optional)

### Activity

Modeling:

1. Direct students to listen carefully to your instructions. Explain that you will say a word, take away the beginning sound in that word, and then say the new word it makes.
2. Read aloud the first dictation card: Beginning Sound Deletion (LM 1).
3. "Say *mat*. Now say *mat* without saying /m/. What's left [*at*]?" Provide additional explanation if needed.
   Say: "What was the first word I said [*mat*]?
   What was the beginning sound I took away [/m/]?
   What new word did I make [*at*]?"
4. Continue this activity by dictating exercises from LM 1. Encourage students to tap the sounds they hear in the word dictated and in the new word they make.

### Modifications and Extensions

- Begin with the deletion of beginning phonemes and then continue to end phonemes.
- Use blank tiles or cubes to represent phonemes concretely. When a phoneme is deleted, remove the tile/cube that is associated with that sound. Draw attention to the position of the phoneme removed.

REPRODUCIBLE

# PHONOLOGICAL AWARENESS
*Phoneme Deletion*

## What's Left?

**LM 1: Beginning Sound Deletion**

| | |
|---|---|
| **DICTATION 1**<br><br>Say *mat*.<br><br>Now say *mat* without saying /m/.<br><br>What's left?<br><br>*at* | **DICTATION 2**<br><br>Say *sit*.<br><br>Now say *sit* without saying /s/.<br><br>What's left?<br><br>*it* |
| **DICTATION 3**<br><br>Say *cup*.<br><br>Now say *cup* without saying /k/.<br><br>What's left?<br><br>*up* | **DICTATION 4**<br><br>Say *nap*.<br><br>Now say *nap* without saying /n/.<br><br>What's left?<br><br>*app* |
| **DICTATION 5**<br><br>Say *bad*.<br><br>Now say *bad* without saying /b/.<br><br>What's left?<br><br>*add* | **DICTATION 6**<br><br>Say *leg*.<br><br>Now say *leg* without saying /l/.<br><br>What's left?<br><br>*egg* |
| **DICTATION 7**<br><br>Say *spot*.<br><br>Now say *spot* without saying /s/.<br><br>What's left?<br><br>*pot* | **DICTATION 8**<br><br>Say *clap*.<br><br>Now say *clap* without saying /k/.<br><br>What's left?<br><br>*lap* |

**Better Together** © 2025 Solution Tree Press • SolutionTree.com
Visit **go.SolutionTree.com/literacy** to download this page.

## PHONOLOGICAL AWARENESS
*Phoneme Deletion*

### What's Left?

**LM2: End Sound Deletion**

| | |
|---|---|
| **DICTATION 1**<br><br>Say *meet.*<br><br>Now say *meet* without saying /t/.<br><br>What's left?<br><br>*me* | **DICTATION 2**<br><br>Say *tent.*<br><br>Now say *tent* without saying /t/ at the end.<br><br>What's left?<br><br>*ten* |
| **DICTATION 3**<br><br>Say *beach.*<br><br>Now say *beach* without saying /ch/.<br><br>What's left?<br><br>*bee* | **DICTATION 4**<br><br>Say *seed.*<br><br>Now say *seed* without saying /d/.<br><br>What's left?<br><br>*see* |
| **DICTATION 5**<br><br>Say *ants.*<br><br>Now say *ants* without saying /s/.<br><br>What's left?<br><br>*ant* | **DICTATION 6**<br><br>Say *team.*<br><br>Now say *team* without saying /m/.<br><br>What's left?<br><br>*tea* |
| **DICTATION 7**<br><br>Say *short.*<br><br>Now say *short* without saying /t/.<br><br>What's left?<br><br>*shore* | **DICTATION 8**<br><br>Say *stopped.*<br><br>Now say *stopped* without saying /d/.<br><br>What's left?<br><br>*stop* |

**Better Together** © 2025 Solution Tree Press • SolutionTree.com
Visit **go.SolutionTree.com/literacy** to download this page.

REPRODUCIBLE

# PHONOLOGICAL AWARENESS
*Phoneme Deletion*

### What's Left?
**LM 3: Medial Sound Deletion**

| | |
|---|---|
| **DICTATION 1**<br><br>Say *frog.*<br><br>Now say *frog* without saying /r/.<br><br>What's left?<br><br>*fog* | **DICTATION 2**<br><br>Say *lamp.*<br><br>Now say *lamp* without saying /m/.<br><br>What's left?<br><br>*lap* |
| **DICTATION 3**<br><br>Say *smell.*<br><br>Now say *smell* without saying /m/.<br><br>What's left?<br><br>*sell* | **DICTATION 4**<br><br>Say *stick.*<br><br>Now say *stick* without saying /t/.<br><br>What's left?<br><br>*sick* |
| **DICTATION 5**<br><br>Say *past.*<br><br>Now say *past* without saying /s/.<br><br>What's left?<br><br>*pat* | **DICTATION 6**<br><br>Say *great.*<br><br>Now say *great* without saying /r/.<br><br>What's left?<br><br>*gate* |
| **DICTATION 7**<br><br>Say *string.*<br><br>Now say *string* without saying /r/.<br><br>What's left?<br><br>*sting* | **DICTATION 8**<br><br>Say *black.*<br><br>Now say *black* without saying /l/.<br><br>What's left?<br><br>*back* |

**Better Together** © 2025 Solution Tree Press • SolutionTree.com
Visit **go.SolutionTree.com/literacy** to download this page.

# PHONOLOGICAL AWARENESS
*Phoneme Segmentation*

## Sound Count

/d/ /ŏ/ /g/

### Learning Objective

Students will **segment** and then **count** the number of **phonemes** they **hear** in words.

### Materials

- Sound Count word cards (Learning Masters [LM] 1–4)
- Sound Count answers card (LM 5)

### Activity

**Modeling:**

1. Show the picture card for the word *dog*.
2. Direct students how to *segment* (pull apart) the word to say its sounds and then *count* how many sounds are in the word. Model counting each sound on your fingers.
3. Say: "Look at the picture. What is it? *dog*. Let's sound out the word *dog* one sound at a time, /d/ [pause] /ŏ/ [pause] /g/ [pause]. How many sounds do you hear in the word *dog*? Count each sound with your fingers. Hold up one finger for each sound you hear [three sounds, /d/ /ŏ/ /g/]."
4. Continue this activity by showing other pictures targeting different phonemes (*sheep*, three phonemes, /sh/ /ē/ /p/). Encourage students to say the whole word, segment each sound in the word (one sound at a time), then say the whole word again. Have them count the number of phonemes they hear with their fingers.

### Modifications and Extensions

- Start with words that begin with continuous sounds (f, v, m, s) then progress to stop sounds (t, p, k).
- Create pictures for segmenting additional words with two or more phonemes.

**Examples of other words with three or more phonemes:**

| shell | stop | trim |
|---|---|---|
| /sh/ /ĕ/ /l/ | /s/ /t/ /ŏ/ /p/ | /t/ /r/ /ĭ/ /m/ |
| bite | flame | black |
| /b/ /ī/ /t/ | /f/ /l/ /ā/ /m/ | /b/ /l/ /ă/ /k/ |

# PHONOLOGICAL AWARENESS
*Phoneme Segmentation*

**LM 1: Sound Count**

# PHONOLOGICAL AWARENESS
*Phoneme Segmentation*

**LM 2: Sound Count**

# PHONOLOGICAL AWARENESS
*Phoneme Segmentation*

**LM 3: Sound Count**

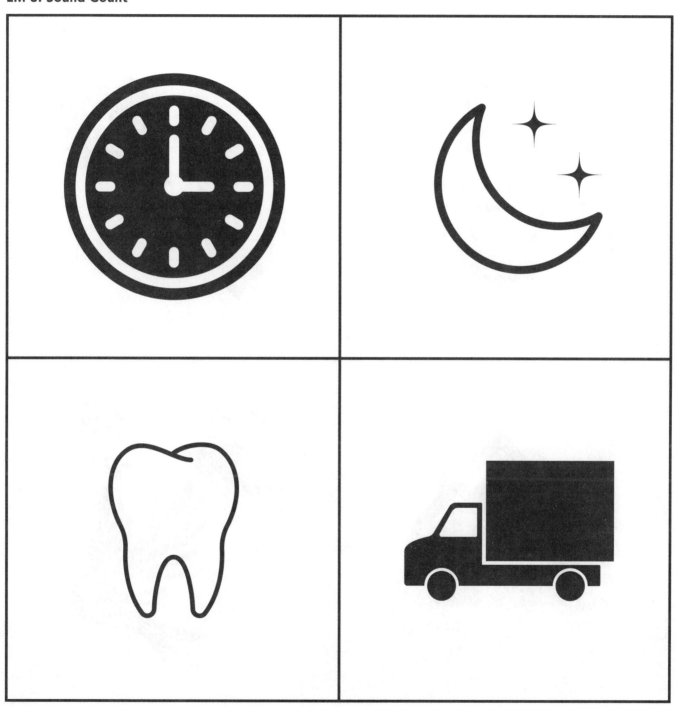

# PHONOLOGICAL AWARENESS
*Phoneme Segmentation*

**LM 4: Sound Count**

REPRODUCIBLE

# PHONOLOGICAL AWARENESS
*Phoneme Segmentation*

## LM 5: Sound Count
**Sound Count Answers**

| Card | Words | Number of Phonemes |
|---|---|---|
| 1 | dog | /d/ /ŏ/ /g/ (3) |
| | ant, bug, insect | /ă/ /n/ /t/ (3) /b/ /ŭ/ /g/ (3) /ĭ/ /n/ /s/ /ĕ/ /k/ /t/ (6) |
| | duck | /d/ /ŭ/ /k/ (3) |
| | sheep | /sh/ /ē/ /p/ (3) |
| 2 | sun | /s/ /ŭ/ /n/ (3) |
| | bone | /b/ /ō/ /n/ (3) |
| | cheese | /ch/ /ē/ /z/ (3) |
| | bed | /b/ /ĕ/ /d/ (3) |
| 3 | clock, time | /k/ /l/ /ŏ/ /k/ (4) /t/ /ī/ /m/ (3) |
| | moon | /m/ /oo/ /n/ (3) |
| | tooth | /t/ /oo/ /th/ (3) |
| | truck | /t/ /r/ /ŭ/ /k/ (4) |
| 4 | plant | /p/ /l/ /ă/ /n/ /t/ (5) |
| | kite | /k/ /ī/ /t/ (3) |
| | house, home | /h/ /ow/ /s/ (3) /h/ /ō/ /m/ (3) |
| | birds, fly | /b/ /er/ /d/ /s/ (4) /f/ /l/ /ī/ (3) |

**Better Together** © 2025 Solution Tree Press • SolutionTree.com

Visit **go.SolutionTree.com/literacy** to download this page.

# PHONOLOGICAL AWARENESS
*Phoneme Substitution*

## Sound Switch  /măt/ /b/ = /băt/

### Learning Objective

Students will **substitute** (switch) a **phoneme** from a word they **say**, then pronounce the new word they make.

### Materials

- Dictation card (Learning Masters [LM] 1): Beginning Sound Substitution
- Dictation card (LM 2): End Sound Substitution (optional)
- Dictation card (LM 3): Medial Sound Substitution (optional)
- Blank tiles or cubes (optional)

### Activity

1. Direct students to listen carefully to your instructions. Explain that you will say a word, change the beginning sound in that word, and then say the new word it makes.
2. Read aloud the first dictation card: Beginning Sound Substitution (LM 1).
3. "Say *mat*. Now switch the beginning sound to /b/. What word do you hear [*bat*]?" Provide additional explanation if needed.
   Say: "What was the first word I said [*mat*]? What beginning sound did I switch [/m/ changed to /b/]? What new word did I make [*bat*]?"
4. Continue this activity by dictating exercises from LM 1. Encourage students to tap the sounds they hear in the word dictated and in the new word they make.

### Modifications and Extensions

- Begin with the substitution of beginning phonemes and then continue to end phonemes.
- Use blank tiles or cubes to represent phonemes concretely. When a phoneme is switched, draw attention to its position and the sound that replaced it.

REPRODUCIBLE

# PHONOLOGICAL AWARENESS
*Phoneme Substitution*

**Sound Switch**

**LM 1: Beginning Sound Substitution**

| | |
|---|---|
| **DICTATION 1**<br><br>Say *mat*.<br><br>Switch /m/ to /b/.<br><br>What's the new word?<br><br>*bat* | **DICTATION 2**<br><br>Say *sit*.<br><br>Switch /s/ to /l/.<br><br>What's the new word?<br><br>*lit* |
| **DICTATION 3**<br><br>Say *cup*.<br><br>Switch /k/ to /p/.<br><br>What's the new word?<br><br>*pup* | **DICTATION 4**<br><br>Say *nap*.<br><br>Switch /n/ to /t/.<br><br>What's the new word?<br><br>*tap* |
| **DICTATION 5**<br><br>Say *rug*.<br><br>Switch /r/ to /h/.<br><br>What's the new word?<br><br>*hug* | **DICTATION 6**<br><br>Say *far*.<br><br>Switch /f/ to /k/.<br><br>What's the new word?<br><br>*car* |
| **DICTATION 7**<br><br>Say *nail*.<br><br>Switch /n/ to /m/.<br><br>What's the new word?<br><br>*mail* | **DICTATION 8**<br><br>Say *flip*.<br><br>Switch /f/ to /s/.<br><br>What's the new word?<br><br>*slip* |

**Better Together** © 2025 Solution Tree Press • SolutionTree.com

Visit **go.SolutionTree.com/literacy** to download this page.

# PHONOLOGICAL AWARENESS
*Phoneme Substitution*

### Sound Switch
**LM 2: End Sound Substitution**

| | |
|---|---|
| **DICTATION 1**<br><br>Say *bug.*<br><br>Switch /g/ to /s/.<br><br>What's the new word?<br><br>*bus* | **DICTATION 2**<br><br>Say *lip.*<br><br>Switch /p/ to /d/.<br><br>What's the new word?<br><br>*lid* |
| **DICTATION 3**<br><br>Say *cut.*<br><br>Switch /t/ to /b/.<br><br>What's the new word?<br><br>*cub* | **DICTATION 4**<br><br>Say *web.*<br><br>Switch /b/ to /t/.<br><br>What's the new word?<br><br>*wet* |
| **DICTATION 5**<br><br>Say *him.*<br><br>Switch /m/ to /s/.<br><br>What's the new word?<br><br>*hiss* | **DICTATION 6**<br><br>Say *bun.*<br><br>Switch /n/ to /z/.<br><br>What's the new word?<br><br>*buzz* |
| **DICTATION 7**<br><br>Say *bat.*<br><br>Switch /t/ to /th/.<br><br>What's the new word?<br><br>*bath* | **DICTATION 8**<br><br>Say *den.*<br><br>Switch /n/ to /k/.<br><br>What's the new word?<br><br>*deck* |

**Better Together** © 2025 Solution Tree Press • SolutionTree.com
Visit **go.SolutionTree.com/literacy** to download this page.

# PHONOLOGICAL AWARENESS
*Phoneme Substitution*

### Sound Switch
**LM 3: Medial Sound Substitution**

| | |
|---|---|
| **DICTATION 1**<br><br>Say *big.*<br><br>Switch /ĭ/ to /ŭ/.<br><br>What's the new word?<br><br>*bug* | **DICTATION 2**<br><br>Say *pat.*<br><br>Switch /ă/ to /ĕ/.<br><br>What's the new word?<br><br>*pet* |
| **DICTATION 3**<br><br>Say *pen.*<br><br>Switch /ĕ/ to /ă/.<br><br>What's the new word?<br><br>*pan* | **DICTATION 4**<br><br>Say *tap.*<br><br>Switch /ă/ to /ĭ/.<br><br>What's the new word?<br><br>*tip* |
| **DICTATION 5**<br><br>Say *stick.*<br><br>Switch /ĭ/ to /ŭ/.<br><br>What's the new word?<br><br>*stuck* | **DICTATION 6**<br><br>Say *flop.*<br><br>Switch /ŏ/ to /ĭ/.<br><br>What's the new word?<br><br>*flip* |
| **DICTATION 7**<br><br>Say *chip.*<br><br>Switch /ĭ/ to /ŏ/.<br><br>What's the new word?<br><br>*chop* | **DICTATION 8**<br><br>Say *block.*<br><br>Switch /ŏ/ to /ă/.<br><br>What's the new word?<br><br>*black* |

APPENDIX B
# PHONICS LESSON PLANS

In this appendix, we present phonics activities for the whole classroom and individual use. Word cards are meant to be used daily and filled out by the student.

# Sorting Words

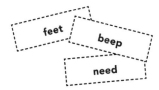

## Learning Objective

Students will recognize that vowel sounds can be represented by more than one letter combination. They will blend sounds together to decode words.

## Materials

- Sorting Chart (Learning Masters [LM] 1)
- Long *e* Word Cards (LM 2–4)
- Sorting Chart Template (LM 5)
- Word Cards Template (LM 6)

## Activity

1. Write the letter combination *ea* on the whiteboard. Say: "The letter combination *ea* makes the vowel sound long *e*." Ask students to practice saying the vowel sound long *e* with you. Then, say: "Can you think of any words that contain the letter combination *ea* that says the sound long *e*?"

2. Have students share examples of words and write them on a whiteboard or chart paper (for example, *seat, meal*). Repeat the same procedure with the letter combination *ee*, emphasizing that both letter combinations represent the vowel sound long *e*.

3. Next, explain to students that they will read words that say the sound long *e*. The letter combination *ea* can make the long *e* sound as in the word *team*. The letter combination *ee* also makes the long *e* sound as in the word *feet*.

4. Distribute a Sorting Chart (LM 1) and Long *e* Word Cards (LM 2–4) to each student. Alternatively, this activity can be done in pairs of two students.

5. Model for students how to decode and sort a few long *e* words under the correct column on the Sorting Chart. For example, select the word cards *treat* and *feed*. Guide students on how to blend the sounds to pronounce each word. Then, have them identify the letter sound correspondence in each word that makes the sound long *e*.

6. Direct students to place the word card *treat* on the Sorting Chart under the *ea* column. The word card *feed* is placed under the *ee* column.

7. Ask students to read each word aloud before continuing.

8. Continue the activity, inviting students to decode the words and sort them under the associated columns.

## Modifications and Extensions

- Instead of providing word cards, give students a word list. They can sort and then write the long *e* words under each column of the Sorting Chart.
- For a challenge, dictate long *e* words to students. Have them spell the words and then write them words on the Sorting Chart.
- Encourage students to think of other words that contain the sound long *e* made with the letter combinations *ea* and *ee*. Then, have them add the new words to their Sorting Charts.

## Shared Book Reading

Select a short decodable text passage to practice reading. The text should contain high frequency words covered in the Sorting Words activity. Begin by reading the text to students, inviting them to follow along with you. Gradually release the responsibility of reading, inviting the students (one at a time) to read words that contain the long **e** sound (that is, words with **ea** and **ee** such as **read** and **tree**).

Replicate this activity with other letter-sound correspondences that make the same sound. Use the Sorting Chart and Word Cards Templates (LM 5 and LM 6) to create other words to sort.

**LM 1: Sorting Chart**
Sorting Long e

| ea | ee |
|---|---|
|  |  |
|  |  |
|  |  |
|  |  |
|  |  |
|  |  |
|  |  |
|  |  |
|  |  |
|  |  |
|  |  |
|  |  |
|  |  |

**LM 2: Long *e* Word Cards**
Long *e* Word Cards

| feet | read |
|------|------|
| beam | need |
| team | lean |
| been | feel |
| leap | meal |
| seed | neat |
| deep | beep |

# PHONICS
*Word Sorting*

210  REPRODUCIBLE

## LM 3: Long *e* Word Cards

**Long *e* Word Cards**

| | |
|---|---|
| clean | cheek |
| treat | steam |
| green | sleep |
| street | three |
| sheet | cheat |
| least | dream |
| sweet | peach |

**Better Together** © 2025 Solution Tree Press • SolutionTree.com
Visit **go.SolutionTree.com/literacy** to download this page.

page 5 of 8

**PHONICS** — *Word Sorting*

**LM 4: Long *e* Word Cards**
Long *e* Word Cards

| feast | cleats |
|---|---|
| screen | heater |
| steamed | wheels |
| wreath | speaking |
| leaky | creamy |
| leaves | sleeves |
| peaked | freezer |

# PHONICS
*Word Sorting*

## LM 5: Sorting Chart Template

Sorting: _____

# REPRODUCIBLE

**PHONICS**
*Word Sorting*

### LM 6: Word Cards Template

_____ **Word Cards**

**Better Together** © 2025 Solution Tree Press • SolutionTree.com
Visit **go.SolutionTree.com/literacy** to download this page.

REPRODUCIBLE

# Tap, Map, Blend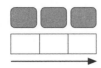

## Learning Objective

Students will segment phonemes in consonant-vowel-consonant (CVC) words they hear. They will then map (write) the letter or letter combination that represents each phoneme and blend the phonemes together to decode words.

## Materials

- Tap, Map, Blend picture cards (Learning Masters [LM] 1–3)
- Tap, Map, Blend template (LM 4)

## Activity

1. Show the picture card (for example, *bat*).

2. Model for students how to *blend* the sounds they hear together to say the word.
   Say: "Look at the picture. Let's blend the sounds together to say the word /băt/. Under the picture, tap each square as you say each sound, /b/ /ă/ /t/. How many sounds do you hear in the word *bat*?"

3. Invite students to map (write) the corresponding letter or letter combination for each sound in the boxes provided.
   Say: "What letter says /b/ [letter *b*]? Write the letter *b* in the first box. What letter says the short vowel /ă/ [letter *a*]? Write the letter *a* in the second box. What letter says /t/ [letter *t*]? Write the letter *t* in the final box."

4. Model how to blend the letter sounds together to decode the word.
   Say: "Place your finger on the arrow and slide it as you blend the letter sounds together. Start at the first box and move through to the middle box and then to the last box as you blend the sounds together to say the word *bat*."

5. Continue the activity with the other Tap, Map, Blend picture cards (LM 1–3). Encourage students to say and tap the sounds in each word and then map (write) the letter or letter combination that matches the sounds in the associated boxes. Invite students to decode each word aloud by blending the letter sounds together.

## Modifications and Extensions

- Complete the activity without pictures. Instead, dictate words to students, having them tap, map, and blend the letter sounds together.
- Replicate the activity by creating other CVC words using the Tap, Map, Blend Template (LM 4).
- Extend practice.

## Shared Book Reading

Select a short decodable text passage to practice reading. The text should contain high frequency words covered in the Tap, Map, Blend activity. Begin by reading the text to students, inviting them to follow along with you. Gradually release the responsibility of reading, inviting the students (one at a time) to read the words in the passage.

Replicate this activity using words that contain more complex letter patterns (for example, CCVC, CVCC, CVVC, CCVVC, and so on). If you choose to use sound boxes, adapt the number of boxes to match the number of sounds that will be mapped to the letters or letter combinations.

**LM 1: Tap, Map, Blend**

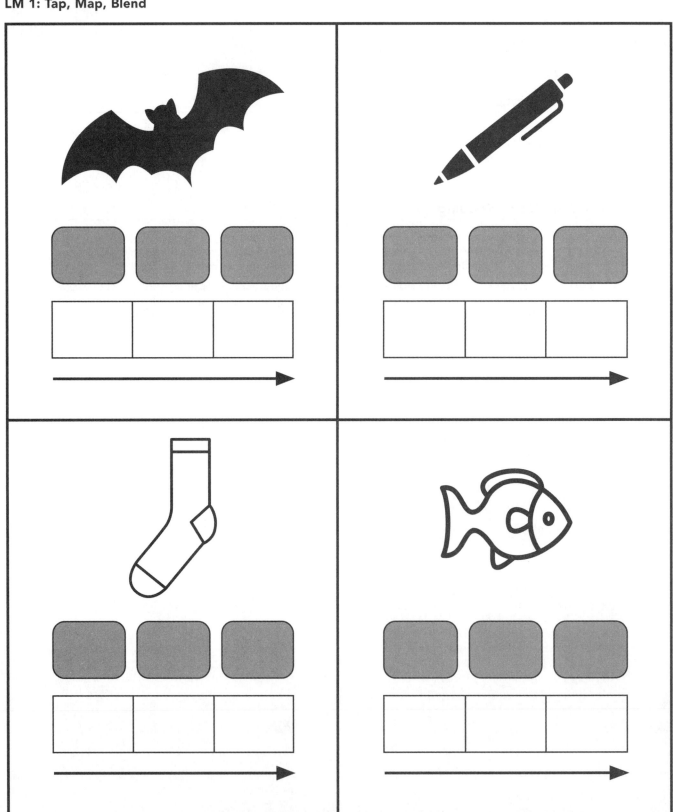

**LM 2: Tap, Map, Blend**

**PHONICS**
*Phoneme Blending*

**LM 3: Tap, Map, Blend**

**LM 4: Tap, Map, Blend Template**

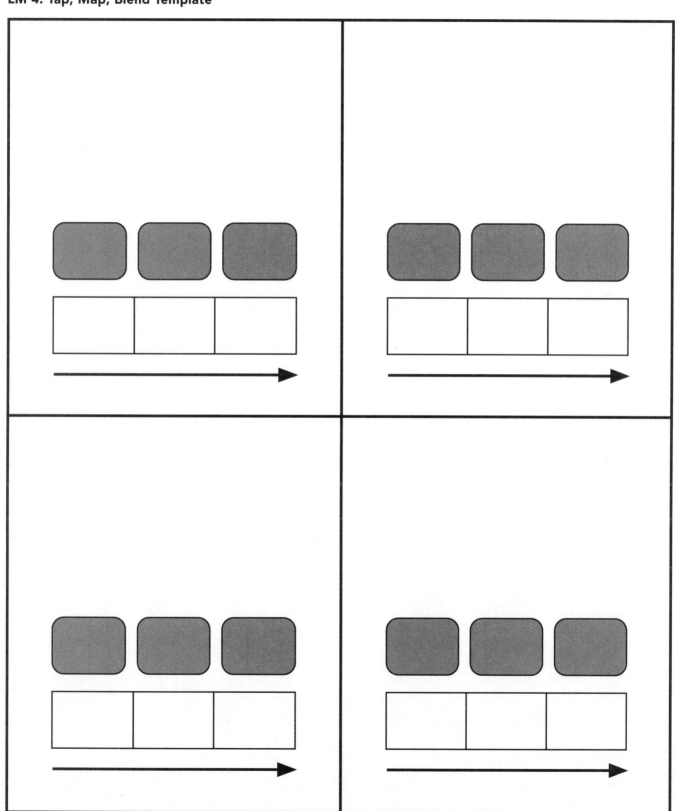

APPENDIX C
# FLUENCY LESSON PLANS

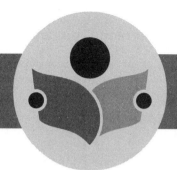

In this part of the book, we present some lesson plans for reading fluency instruction for the whole classroom. We have lesson plans for word- and sentence-reading fluency. We also present lessons on punctuation.

# READING FLUENCY
## Word Triangles

## Onset and Rime

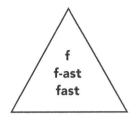

 **Learning Objective**

Students will **build** reading **fluency** using word triangles. They will **successively blend** the onset and rime of words together to **decode** whole words **smoothly**.

## Materials

- Onset and Rime Word Fluency Lists
  - Learning Masters [LM] 1: Short Vowel Consonant-Vowel-Consonant
  - LM 2: Beginning Blends and Digraphs
  - LM 3: Ending Blends and Digraphs
  - LM 4: Vowel Teams and R-Controlled Vowels
- Word Fluency Triangle Template (LM 5)

## Activity

1. Select an Onset and Rime Word Fluency List to practice with students.
2. Draw a large triangle on a piece of chart paper or on the whiteboard. Then, copy the word inside the triangle as shown on the word list.
3. Direct the students to read the triangle from top to bottom starting with the onset (/f/). Then, have them read the second line, the rime (/ăst/). The students then complete the triangle by reading the whole word (/făst/, *fast*).
4. Have the students practice reading the word multiple times and then work on other words from the Onset and Rime Word Fluency Lists provided (LM 1–4) or words you have preselected.

## Modifications and Extensions

- Provide Onset and Rime Word Fluency Triangle cards (LM 5) for students to practice independently or in small groups.
- Create more words to practice building fluency, including other high-frequency words, word families, and three- and four-syllable words.
- Eventually remove the support triangles and have students read the words on paper.

# READING FLUENCY
*Word Triangles*

## LM 1: Short Vowel Consonant-Vowel-Consonant

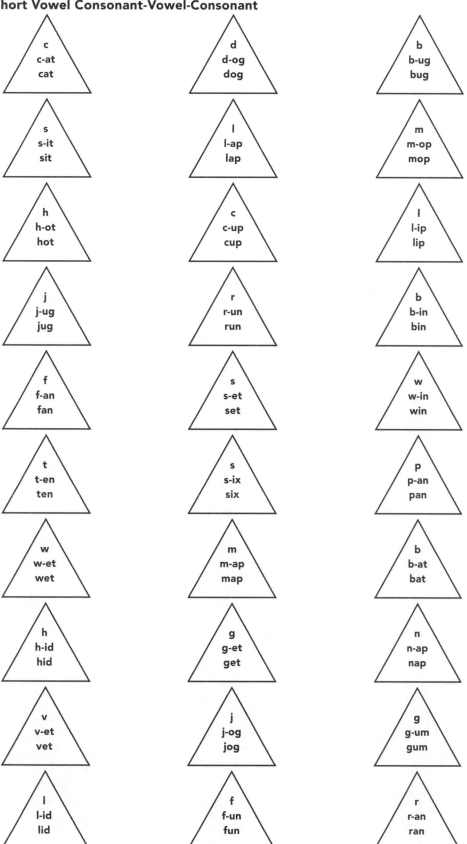

# READING FLUENCY
*Word Triangles*

## LM 2: Beginning Blends and Digraphs

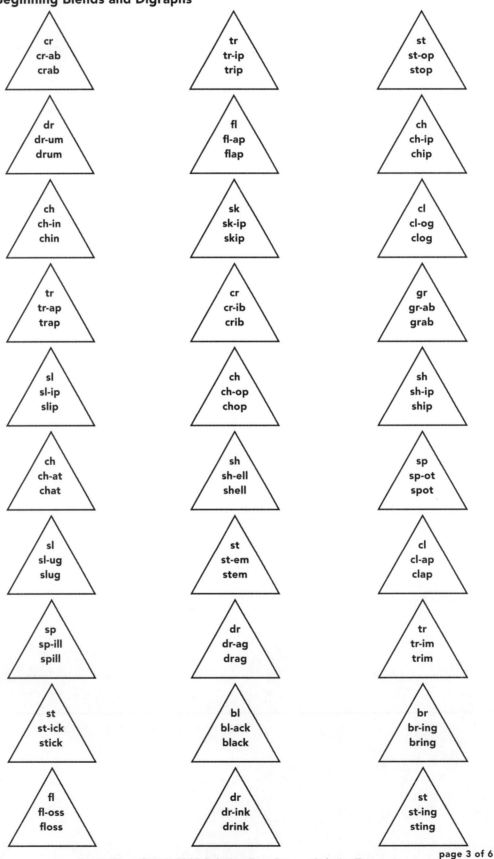

| | | |
|---|---|---|
| cr / cr-ab / crab | tr / tr-ip / trip | st / st-op / stop |
| dr / dr-um / drum | fl / fl-ap / flap | ch / ch-ip / chip |
| ch / ch-in / chin | sk / sk-ip / skip | cl / cl-og / clog |
| tr / tr-ap / trap | cr / cr-ib / crib | gr / gr-ab / grab |
| sl / sl-ip / slip | ch / ch-op / chop | sh / sh-ip / ship |
| ch / ch-at / chat | sh / sh-ell / shell | sp / sp-ot / spot |
| sl / sl-ug / slug | st / st-em / stem | cl / cl-ap / clap |
| sp / sp-ill / spill | dr / dr-ag / drag | tr / tr-im / trim |
| st / st-ick / stick | bl / bl-ack / black | br / br-ing / bring |
| fl / fl-oss / floss | dr / dr-ink / drink | st / st-ing / sting |

# READING FLUENCY
*Word Triangles*

## LM 3: Ending Blends and Digraphs

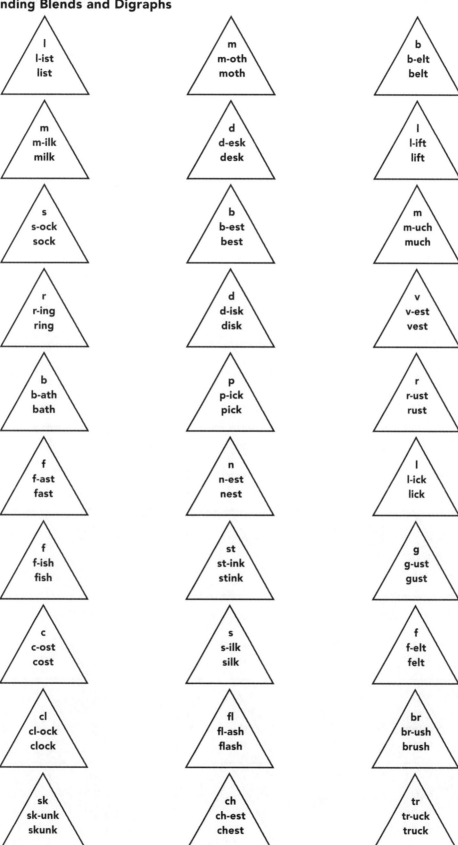

page 4 of 6

# READING FLUENCY
*Word Triangles*

## LM 4: Vowel Teams and *R*-Controlled Vowels

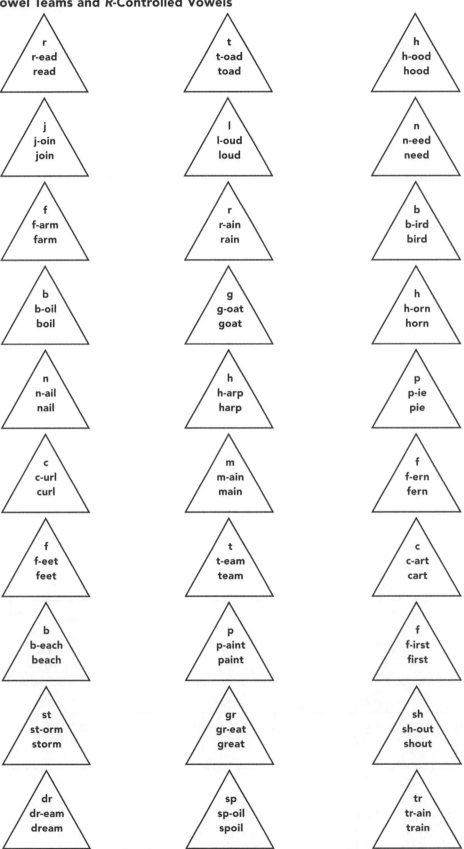

# READING FLUENCY
*Word Triangles*

**LM 5: Word Fluency Triangle Template**

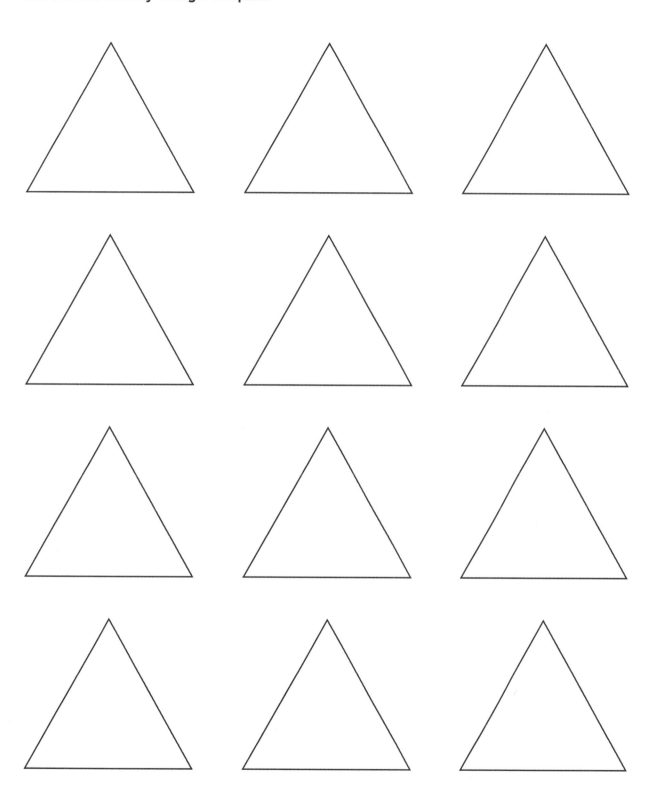

# READING FLUENCY
*Sentence Triangles*

## Sentence Fluency

### Learning Objective

Students will **build** expression, word automaticity, rhythm and phrasing, and smoothness using Sentence Fluency Triangles. They will **decode** words to read sentences **accurately** and **smoothly**.

### Materials

- Sentence Fluency Triangle Lists (Learning Masters [LM] 1–3)
- Sentence Fluency Triangle Template (LM 4)

### Activity

1. Select a Sentence Fluency Triangle List (LM 1–3) to practice with students.
2. Draw a large triangle on a piece of chart paper or on the whiteboard. Then, copy the words inside the triangle as they are shown on the word list.
3. Direct the students to read the triangle from top to bottom starting with the first word in the sentence (*I*). Then read the second line that contains the first two words in the sentence (*I like*), followed by the third line (*I like the*). Then, finish the triangle by reading the complete sentence (*I like the dog*).
4. Have the students practice reading the sentence multiple times. Then, work on other sentences from the lists provided or sentences you have preselected.

### Modifications and Extensions

- Provide Sentence Fluency Triangle cards (LM 4) for students to practice independently or in small groups with high-frequency words.
- Create more sentences to practice building fluency with longer sentences that contain high-frequency and multisyllabic words.
- Eventually remove the support triangles and have students read the sentences on paper.
- Practice using end punctuation to read with expression (for those triangles that end in an exclamation point or a question mark).

# READING FLUENCY
*Sentence Triangles*

## LM 1: Sentence Fluency

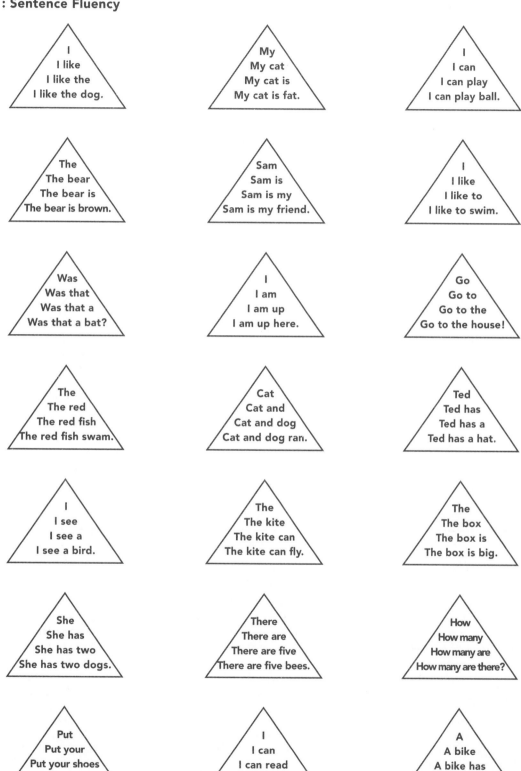

# READING FLUENCY
*Sentence Triangles*

**LM 2: Sentence Fluency**

page 3 of 5

**Better Together** © 2025 Solution Tree Press • SolutionTree.com
Visit **go.SolutionTree.com/literacy** to download this page.

# REPRODUCIBLE

231

## READING FLUENCY
*Sentence Triangles*

**LM 3: Sentence Fluency**

Draw
Draw a
Draw a picture
Draw a picture on
Draw a picture on the
Draw a picture on the paper.

We
We built
We built a
We built a brand
We built a brand new
We built a brand new house.

The
The storm
The storm clouds
The storm clouds covered
The storm clouds covered the
The storm clouds covered the sky.

We
We slept
We slept because
We slept because we
We slept because we were
We slept because we were tired.

The
The cars
The cars zoomed
The cars zoomed down
The cars zoomed down the
The cars zoomed down the street.

Rags
Rags wagged
Rags wagged his
Rags wagged his tail
Rags wagged his tail and
Rags wagged his tail and smiled.

Always
Always say
Always say please
Always say please and
Always say please and thank
Always say please and thank you.

Have
Have you
Have you seen
Have you seen my
Have you seen my cat
Have you seen my cat Fluffy?

Do
Do your
Do your homework
Do your homework before
Do your homework before you
Do your homework before you play!

After
After breakfast
After breakfast we
After breakfast we went
After breakfast we went to
After breakfast we went to school.

**Better Together** © 2025 Solution Tree Press • SolutionTree.com

page 4 of 5

Visit **go.SolutionTree.com/literacy** to download this page.

# READING FLUENCY
*Sentence Triangles*

**LM 5: Sentence Fluency Triangle Template**

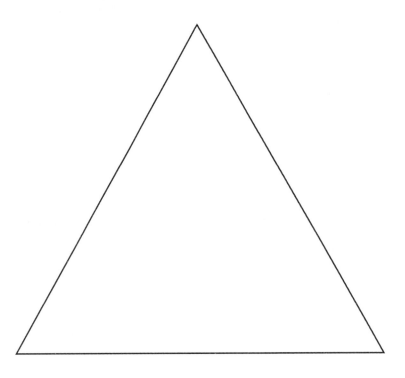

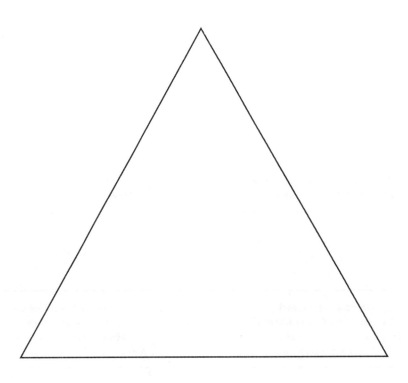

# READING FLUENCY
*Expressive Fluency*

## Emphasize It!

### Learning Objective

Students will **understand** how expression supports fluency in reading. They will read sentences, emphasizing boldfaced words with intonation. Emphasizing certain words in a sentence can impact their meaning.

### Materials

- Emphasize It! (Learning Masters [LM] 1–3)

### Activity

1. Select the Emphasize It! (LM 1: Banana Pancakes) text to model with students.
2. Copy the text on a large sheet of chart paper or project the text onto a digital whiteboard.
3. Have the students read through each sentence of LM 1: Banana Pancakes on their own.
4. Point to where the words in each sentence are boldfaced. Model how to intonate one's voice each time the boldfaced words are read. Explain how emphasizing each word can impact the sentence's meaning. For example, in the sentence *Sam didn't want banana pancakes for breakfast* the word *didn't* emphasizes that someone thought Sam liked banana pancakes when in fact she didn't. She likes different types of pancakes.
5. Finally, have the students read each sentence aloud, emphasizing the boldfaced word in each sentence, and explain how the meaning changes.

### Modifications and Extensions

- Copy and distribute another Emphasize It! page (LM 2 or LM 3). Have the students work in partners to read the sentences aloud, emphasize the boldfaced words, and debate the meaning of the sentences.
- Create other sentences with boldfaced words to be emphasized.

# READING FLUENCY
*Sentence Triangles*

### LM 1: Emphasize It!: Banana Pancakes
**Sam didn't want banana pancakes for breakfast.**

Sam **didn't** want banana pancakes for breakfast.

Sam didn't **want** banana pancakes for breakfast.

Sam didn't want **banana** pancakes for breakfast.

Sam didn't want banana **pancakes** for breakfast.

Sam didn't want banana pancakes for **breakfast**.

### LM 2: Emphasize It!: Hockey Game
**Ben watched the hockey game on Friday night.**

**Ben** watched the hockey game on Friday night.

Ben **watched** the hockey game on Friday night.

Ben watched the **hockey** game on Friday night.

Ben watched the hockey **game** on Friday night.

Ben watched the hockey game on **Friday** night.

Ben watched the hockey game on Friday **night**.

### LM 3: Emphasize It!: Roller Coasters
**I love riding fast roller coasters with my friends.**

**I** love riding fast roller coasters with my friends.

I **love** riding fast roller coasters with my friends.

I love **riding** fast roller coasters with my friends.

I love riding **fast** roller coasters with my friends.

I love riding fast **roller coasters** with my friends.

I love riding fast roller coasters with **my** friends.

I love riding fast roller coasters with my **friends**.

REPRODUCIBLE

235

# READING FLUENCY
*Punctuation Practice*

# Punctuation Practice  . ! ?

## Learning Objective

Students will **understand** how punctuation supports expression in reading. Punctuation markers will direct their intonation to emphasize the meaning of text.

## Materials

- Punctuation Practice Samples (Learning Masters [LM] 1–3)

## Activity

1. **Select a Punctuation Practice Sample to model with students.**

2. **Copy the text on a large sheet of chart paper or project the text onto a digital whiteboard. For example, write the alphabet letters shown on LM 1.**

3. **Before presenting the text to the students, premark punctuation beside selected letters. For example, place a question mark (?) to the right of the letter C, an exclamation mark (!) to the right of the letter S, and a period (.) to the right of the letter Z. Add as many or few punctuation marks beside each of the twenty-six letters on the page as you wish.**

4. **During reading, have the students read the letter chorally (together in unison). Read the text again, this time modeling points where punctuation has been added. If introducing punctuation for the first time, you will need to teach the marks of punctuation. Thus, a period (.) indicates a pause before starting to read the next letter, an exclamation point (!) means to raise your voice to show a strong feeling, and a question mark (?) means we pause for a second and our voice goes up at the end.**

5. **Have students practice reading the text again, attending to the punctuation to read with expression. Repeat, reading the passage multiple times.**

## Modifications and Extensions

- Copy and create other premarked passages with punctuation for students to practice reading chorally, individually, or with a partner.

**Better Together** © 2025 Solution Tree Press • SolutionTree.com
Visit **go.SolutionTree.com/literacy** to download this page.

**page 1 of 4**

# READING FLUENCY
*Punctuation Practice*

**LM 1: Punctuation Practice: The Alphabet**

| | | | |
|---|---|---|---|
| A | B | C | D |
| E | F | G | H |
| I | J | K | L |
| M | N | O | P |
| Q | R | S | T |
| U | V | W | X |
| Y | Z | | |

**Better Together** © 2025 Solution Tree Press • SolutionTree.com
Visit **go.SolutionTree.com/literacy** to download this page.

**page 2 of 4**

REPRODUCIBLE

# READING FLUENCY
*Punctuation Practice*

**LM 2: Punctuation Practice: Numbers**

| | | | |
|---|---|---|---|
| 1 | 2 | 3 | 4 |
| 5 | 6 | 7 | 8 |
| 9 | 10 | 11 | 12 |
| 13 | 14 | 15 | 16 |
| 17 | 18 | 19 | 20 |
| 21 | 22 | 23 | 24 |

**Better Together** © 2025 Solution Tree Press • SolutionTree.com
Visit **go.SolutionTree.com/literacy** to download this page.

page 3 of 4

# READING FLUENCY
*Punctuation Practice*

**LM 3: Punctuation Practice: Words**

| | | |
|---|---|---|
| No | No | No |
| No | No | No |
| No | No | No |
| No | No | No |
| No | No | No |
| No | No | No |

APPENDIX D
# VOCABULARY LESSON PLANS

In this appendix, we present some lesson plans for vocabulary instruction for the whole classroom. We present the four-step model for building vocabulary as well as two morphological analysis worksheets.

## VOCABULARY
*Four-Step Model*

# Building Vocabulary

## Learning Objective

Students will develop an understanding of Tier 2 vocabulary.

## Materials

- Selected or self-written text

## Activity: The Four-Step Vocabulary Instruction Model

Use the four-step vocabulary instruction model to preteach new vocabulary that is important to understanding a selected text. Select a text passage or write a sample text that contains Tier 2 words. The following lesson example is provided.

## Sample Text Passage

One of Canada's most impressive engineering wonders is the Confederation Bridge. It connects the province of Prince Edward Island to the mainland of Canada over the Northumberland Strait in the Gulf of Saint Lawrence. The Confederation Bridge is 12.9 kilometers long and 11 meters wide and took 4 years to construct. It is a concrete box girder toll bridge that rests on 62 piers. The Confederation Bridge is the longest bridge in the world that stands over ice-covered waters.

Tier 2 vocabulary to preteach from this passage may include *connects*, *longest*, and *wide*.

## Preteaching Vocabulary Words

The following lesson demonstrates how to apply the four-step model with the word *connects*. Apply the same four-step model to teaching the other Tier 2 vocabulary from the text passage.

### Step 1: Introduce the Word *Connects*
- Write the word *connects* on the board.
- Read the word *connects*. Have students repeat the word back to you.
- Say: "The word I read is *connects*. What word is it?" (Students reply *connects*.)

### Step 2: Present a Student-Friendly Definition
- Tell students an explanation of the word *connects* or have them read the following explanation to you.

  "When we put or bring two things together, we *connect* them. A bridge *connects* one part of land to another."
  So, if a bridge brings two parts of land together, it _____ them. (*connects*)

### Step 3: Illustrate the Word With Examples
- Use concrete, visual, or verbal examples that demonstrate the meaning of the word *connects*.
- For example, show a picture of the Confederation Bridge to students, explaining how the bridge *connects* Prince Edward Island to the mainland of Canada. Or provide a verbal example of the word *connects*. For example, "A cord connects my iPhone to an outlet to get electricity."
- Ask students to demonstrate their understanding of the word *connects*. They may provide a complete sentence that uses the word.

### Step 4: Check Students' Understanding
- Have students generate examples of things that connect.
  *Say:* "Tell your partner some examples of things that connect."
- Have students generate a complete sentence that contains the word *connects*. For example, "A highway . . ." or "A train track . . ."

## Modifications and Extensions

- Provide students with a variety of cloze sentences to help them write a complete sentence with the word *connects*.

  Examples: "The train track _____ cities."

  "The ferry _____ us to the island."

  "A cord _____ my computer to the internet."

  "A highway _____ cities and towns."

- Have students visually demonstrate their understanding of the word *connects*. For example, they may sketch a drawing of the Confederation Bridge connecting from Prince Edward Island to the mainland of Canada. Then, using the drawing, have them provide a short oral presentation that demonstrates their understanding of *connects*.

## MORPHOLOGY
*Word Bags*

# Name the Word Family

*replay* *player*
*played* — (*play*) — *playing*

## Learning Objective

Students will identify words that belong to the same **morphological word family**.

## Materials

- Selected or self-written text
- A small bag and index cards
- Hoop (optional)
- Chart paper and colored markers

The following lesson demonstrates how to play the game Name the Word Family using words that contain the base word *play*. Apply the game to teaching the other morphological families from text passages you select or create.

## Sample Text Passage

**"I've noticed that many of you like to play hockey at recess. How many of you are playing in the rink? It must be crowded with all of you playing there. Have you ever played kickball in the field? I prefer to play kickball because I get lots of chances to kick the ball and there is more space to run. You may want to try playing kickball at recess too."**

### Before Completing the Activity

Preselect the base word *play* to work with from the sample of text provided. The sample uses the base word *play* in context. Write the following words on index cards or strips of paper and place them in the word bag: **playing**, **played**, **replay**, **player**, **plate**, **plane**, and **run**. **Do not include the word play**! This is the base word of the morphological family that you want the students to figure out.

## Explaining the Game

**Explain to students that inside the word bag are words written on cards. The objective of the game is to read each word out loud, then figure out what the words have in common. Say: "To be part of the same morphological word family, words must share a common meaning and spelling. The part of a word that shares a common spelling and meaning is called the base."**

*Note:* If you choose to include words that do not belong to the same morphological family, tell students to watch for these words.

**Better Together** © 2025 Solution Tree Press • SolutionTree.com
Visit **go.SolutionTree.com/literacy** to download this page.

**page 1 of 2**

# MORPHOLOGY
*Word Bags*

## Playing the Game

1. Invite students one at a time to pull a word card from the bag. Ask them to read and spell the word out loud. Then, show the word and have the class or group read it out loud.

2. Lay the word card in the center of a circle after each one is read. The circle may be written on a whiteboard or chart paper, or a hoop may be placed on the floor.

3. Repeat turns with students, having each one pull and read the cards until the bag is empty. Encourage students to think about the meaning and spelling structure of the words to determine what the words have in common.

   Note: The words playing, played, replay, and player are part of the same morphological family because they share a common meaning and spelling structure. The words plate, plane, and run are not.

4. Once students have determined the common meaning and structure of the words drawn, they share the name of the morphological family. The name of the morphological family is play.

5. Represent the morphological family in a word web on chart paper or on the whiteboard.

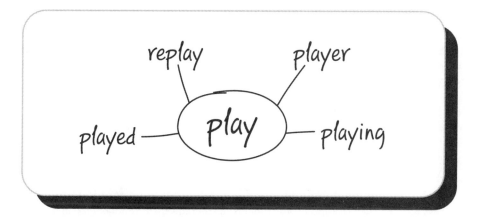

## Modifications and Extensions

- Include additional words that contain the base word play in the word bag for sorting (*playful*, *playfulness*, *playground*, *playmate*).
- Have students create their own word webs and circle the base word play in each word.

# Understanding Morphemes    ab + rupt → abrupt

## Learning Objective

Students will understand the meaning of morphemes in words.

## Materials

- Whiteboard or chart paper
- Copy of sample text passage for each student

The following lesson provides a seven-step model for examining words with the root *rupt*. Apply the model to the other multimorphemic words you choose to work with from text passages you select or create.

## Sample Text Passage

### How Disruptive!

"Don't be so abrupt! You interrupted me while I was playing my video game again. Why are you such a disrupter? Every time you disrupt me, I lose money in my gaming account. I'm about to go bankrupt! So, go away before you cause another disruption. I'm about ready to erupt!"

## Before Completing the Activity

Prepare and distribute the sample text to each student. You may display the text on chart paper or a whiteboard. Ask students to have a pencil ready.

## Activity

1. Read the text passage *How Disruptive!* to students. Encourage them to follow along as you read. Emphasize the words *disruptive, abrupt, interrupted, disrupter, disrupt, bankrupt, disruption,* and *erupt*.

2. **Present the word.** Write the word *disruptive* on the whiteboard. Read the word and then have students repeat the word back to you.

3. **Define the word.** Ask students to share what they think the word *disruptive* means. They may use the word in a sentence to demonstrate their understanding (for example, *The noisy crowd was being disruptive during the hockey game*).

4. Explain to students that the word *disruptive* is an adjective that means to disrupt or throw into disorder. When there is a loud noise, it can be disruptive to people and animals. The root *rupt* comes from Latin, meaning "break." When we break silence and make too much noise, we can be *disruptive*.

5. **How many morphemes are in the word?** Have students determine how many morphemes are in the word. Direct them to look for any affixes (prefixes and/or suffixes) in the word to help them figure out the root *rupt*.
Say: "How many morphemes are in the word *disruptive*?" (There are three morphemes, *dis-, rupt,* and *-ive*.)

6. **Present the word sum.** Write the word sum for *disruptive* on the whiteboard, *dis + rupt + ive* → *disruptive*. Ask students to identify the prefix (*dis-*), the root (*rupt*), and the suffix (*-ive*). If students can write the word sum for *disruptive* on their own, encourage them to do so on the back of their paper.

7. **Generate words.** Ask students to tell you other words that contain the root *rupt*. Encourage them to read through the text to find it. Students may also tell you words that are not in the text (*corrupt, eruption, interrupted*). Model writing words with the root *rupt* in a list or in a word web on the whiteboard or chart paper.

# MORPHOLOGY
*Morphological Analysis*

**Review: In subsequent days, students may reread the text *How Disruptive!*, identifying words that contain the root *rupt*. Have them define each word and identify/count the morphemes that they contain.**

## Modifications and Extensions

- Have students create their own word webs. They may circle the root rupt in the words they write.
- Students can write out word sums for other words that contain the root rupt (***abrupt***, ***interrupted***, ***disrupter***, ***bankrupt***).

ab + rupt → abrupt          dis + rupt + er → disrupter

inter + rupt + ed → interrupted          bank + rupt → bankrupt

APPENDIX E
# READING COMPREHENSION LESSON PLANS

The following activities are designed to evaluate your students' reading comprehension. Some are labeled as self-regulated development strategies and others are designated collaborative activities.

**TEXT COMPREHENSION**
*Self-Regulated Development Strategy*

# Summarizing Text

## Learning Objective

Students will develop an understanding of the text they read.

## Materials

- Selected text (The fairy tale *Little Red Riding Hood*)
- Chart paper or a whiteboard
- Summarize SWBST organizer (one per student, optional)

## Self-Regulated Strategy Development

Use the self-regulated strategy development (SRSD) model to support students in building a deeper understanding of a selected text. The following SRSD lesson teaches the summarizing strategy Somebody, Wanted, But, So, and Then (SWBST) with the fairy tale *Little Red Riding Hood*.

## Before Teaching

Create a chart that outlines the SWBST mnemonic for summarizing text. Use the chart to model how to summarize the story. You may distribute a SWBST organizer for students to fill out as you are teaching.

## Self-Regulated Strategy Development

### Stage 1: Develop and Activate Background Knowledge

1. Discuss with students what skilled readers do. Prompt them to share examples of what they do to better understand a topic.
   Say: "Skilled readers think about what they already know about a topic and connect their knowledge to help them better understand what they read."

2. Review the names of different types of literary structures (narrative text: fiction, fairy tales, poetry, folk tales; expository text: nonfiction, informational). Explain to students that they will be reading a narrative passage, specifically a fairy tale called *Little Red Riding Hood*. A fairy tale is a fictional short story that often has magic and fantastical creatures.

3. Prompt discussion to develop and activate background knowledge about fairy tales that students may know. Ask: "What do you know about fairy tales? What is the purpose of a fairy tale? What are some fairy tales you know? What types of characters do you find in fairy tales?"

### Stage 2: Discuss It

Explicitly teach the summarization mnemonic Somebody, Wanted, But, So, and Then (SWBST) to students after reading *Little Red Riding Hood*. Discuss each step beginning with *Somebody* and move down the list. Discuss the importance of summarizing, introduce each section of the mnemonic with the associated question, and encourage students to think about each question as it relates to the story.

**Somebody:** Who is the main character?

**Wanted:** What did the character want?

**But:** What was the problem?

**So:** How did the character try to solve the problem?

**Then:** What was the resolution of the story?

## TEXT COMPREHENSION
*Self-Regulated Development Strategy*

### Stage 3: Model It
As you are moving through the SWBST summary, model how to think through answering each question (If I don't know the answer, what can I do to find the answer?). Model thinking aloud, self-instruction, and self-reinforcement. For example, talk about how to confirm your answers to each question. Talk through how to write a sentence (or two) in each section as you demonstrate how to print it on the chart. Place a check mark beside each section after you have completed it. Explain to students that learning the SWBST mnemonic is a useful and easy way of summarizing the story. They can apply it to all different texts.

### Stage 4: Memorize It
After students have completed the summary with you, have them recite the steps of the SWBST mnemonic. Have them take turns describing what is required at each step. Assist students throughout the process as needed and encourage them to share their ideas independently.

### Stage 5: Support It
Work collaboratively with students, gradually releasing the role of responsibility. For example, move from writing the sentence for students to having them summarize and write each sentence on their own. Provide specific feedback and positive reinforcement for self-monitoring.

### Stage 6: Independent Performance
Read another fairy tale. Have students work independently using the SWBST mnemonic with their own chart. Provide guidance throughout the process, encouraging self-regulation and self-monitoring. Continue practicing the SWBST summary strategy with different literature in a variety of genres across tasks and subjects.

**TEXT COMPREHENSION**
*Self-Regulated Development Strategy*

# Making the "Clunk" Click

## Learning Objective

Students will develop an understanding of the text they read.

## Materials

- Selected or self-written text
- CSR learning log (optional)

## Collaborative Strategic Reading

Use the collaborative strategic reading (CSR) model to support students in building a deeper understanding of a text passage. Select a text passage or write a sample text. The following CSR lesson is provided based on the first section of a text passage titled *The Confederation Bridge*.

## Sample Text Passage: The Confederation Bridge

There are many famous bridges in North America. Those you might know are the Golden Gate Bridge in San Francisco and the Brooklyn Bridge in New York City. But did you know that Canada holds one of the most impressive engineering wonders in the world? The Confederation Bridge connects the province of Prince Edward Island to the mainland of Canada over the Northumberland Strait in the Gulf of Saint Lawrence. It took 4 years to construct and officially opened on May 31, 1997. The Confederation Bridge is 12.9 kilometers long and 11 meters wide. It is a concrete box girder toll bridge that rests on 62 piers. The bridge was built by over 2,500 workers who fabricated and connected 175 structural pieces from pier bases to main girders. The

Confederation Bridge is the longest bridge in the world that stands over ice-covered waters.

## Collaborative Strategic Reading

### Step 1: Preview
*Before reading the passage,* prompt discussion to activate background knowledge about the topic of bridges. For example, ask: "What do you know about bridges? What is the purpose of a bridge? What are bridges made of? Are there different types of bridges? What are the names of bridges that you know of in the world?"

### Step 2: Click and Clunk
*During reading,* support students in monitoring their understanding of the text passage. Begin with the first section of the passage. Have students read the section aloud. When they come to a "clunk" (a word or concept that is difficult to understand), pause and access one or more of the following strategies to make the "clunk" a "click," a word or concept they understand.

For example, stuck on a word? Direct students to use one or more of the following strategies:

- **Strategy 1:** Reread the sentence of text, omitting the unknown word (the clunk). Consider what information is in the rest of the sentence that can help the clunk make sense.
- **Strategy 2:** Reread the sentences before and after the sentence with the clunk and determine if there are any clues to help you make sense of the unknown word.

# REPRODUCIBLE

## TEXT COMPREHENSION
*Self-Regulated Development Strategy*

- Strategy 3: Look for prefixes or suffixes in the clunk to help you read and make sense of the word in the sentence.

### Step 3: Get the Gist
*During reading*, support students in determining the main idea of a section of text (one paragraph at a time).

1. Have students determine what person, place, or thing is the most important in the paragraph. (The Confederation Bridge)

2. Have students describe the main idea related to the person, place, or thing in their own words. (The Confederation Bridge is the longest bridge in Canada and connects Prince Edward Island to the mainland.)

Repeat this step with the next section followed by the next until finished.

### Step 4: Wrap Up
*After reading the passage*, support students in generating questions and reviewing important information from the text they read.

1. Ask students to ask and answer their own questions about the text (that is, *what, where, why, when,* and *how*). What: The Confederation Bridge. Where: Atlantic Canada. Why: Built to connect the mainland of Canada to the province of Prince Edward Island. When: Took 4 years to build. It officially opened on May 31, 1997. How: Built by over 2,500 workers who fabricated and connected 175 structural pieces from pier bases to main girders.

2. Have students review the important information in the text—for example, the location of the Confederation Bridge, its purpose, and how it was built.

**Better Together** © 2025 Solution Tree Press • SolutionTree.com

Visit **go.SolutionTree.com/literacy** to download this page.

page 2 of 3

# TEXT COMPREHENSION
*Self-Regulated Development Strategy*

| | | | | |
|---|---|---|---|---|
| **Before Reading** | **Preview** | What I already know about the topic:<br><br><br>What I think I will learn: | | |
| **During Reading** | **Clunks and Gists** | First section of the passage: | Second section of the passage: | Third section of the passage: |
| **After Reading** | **Wrap Up** | Questions about the important ideas of the passage:<br><br><br>What I learned: | | |

# GLOSSARY OF TERMS

**accountability meetings:** Meetings of the guiding coalition and the teacher teams designed to ensure both teams are working to accomplish shared goals. The meetings focus on instruction of essential standards, assessment, data analysis, intervention planning, and goal setting. They provide an opportunity for the leadership and teacher teams to hold each other accountable for shared commitments designed to improve student learning.

**active learning:** An instructional approach that involves engaging students as active participants in the learning process. Students are engaged through a variety of activities, which may include group discussions, hands-on experiences, or problem solving.

**adaptive instruction:** A flexible approach to classroom instruction that allows teachers to adjust their instruction and materials to account for the diverse learning needs and abilities of students within a classroom.

**alphabetic principle:** Understanding that the sounds heard in words correspond to letters in print.

**apprenticeship of observation:** A theory by Dan Lortie (2002) that surmises that teachers' beliefs and practices are influenced by their observations of teacher behavior while they were students. These observations lead to assumptions about classroom teaching and student learning that may not align with research-based practices.

**art and science of teaching:** The intuition, flexibility, and adaptability each teacher brings to the classroom to engage students in the learning process. The science of teaching refers to the research-supported best practices teachers need to participate in and learn about to maximize classroom instructional effectiveness.

**balanced literacy:** An instructional approach to teaching reading and writing that attempted to combine both whole language and phonics-based instruction.

**base word:** The part of a word that gives the word its basic meaning (for example, *help* is the base word in *helpful*); also known as a *root word*.

**cognitive dissonance:** A psychological state where an individual experiences discomfort due to their conflicting beliefs, attitudes, or behaviors, which often motivates a change to resolve the inconsistency.

**cognitive rigor:** The level of intellectual challenge and depth of thinking required by a task, often assessed using frameworks like Bloom's taxonomy or Webb's Depth of Knowledge (DOK) model.

**cognitive task analysis (CTA):** A process used by teams to break down essential standards into a scaffold of student-friendly learning targets. Targets include an assessment of the cognitive demand required to demonstrate proficiency. This process, commonly referred to as *unpacking*, is used to inform instructional design and assessment.

**collaborative team:** A group of educators who engage in frequent job-embedded professional development on research-supported practices designed to improve their instructional effectiveness. These educators embrace improved adult learning as the pathway to improved student learning.

**collective teacher efficacy:** The shared belief among educators in a school that they can positively impact student learning by combining their efforts and working together as members of an effective collaborative team.

**common formative assessments:** Assessments aligned with essential standards that are collaboratively created and used by teacher teams to measure student learning and inform instructional practices.

**comprehension:** Understanding of the meaning of a text.

**consonants:** Letters in the alphabet other than *a*, *e*, *i*, *o*, or *u*; the letter *y* is a consonant in some words and a vowel in others.

**continuous improvement:** An ongoing process undertaken by teams within a school where they continuously examine their instruction, assessment, and systems of support through the lens of improved student learning. Teams commit to the analysis of student learning data to enhance their effectiveness and positively impact student learning outcomes. It is the continuous improvement of teacher practice that leads to the improvement of student outcomes.

**data protocol:** A structured process used by teacher teams to guide their analysis of common assessment data. The protocol identifies student performance by learning target, provides an opportunity for reflection on the effectiveness of instructional practice, and facilitates intervention planning.

**decoding:** The ability to apply knowledge of the relationship between letters and sounds (grapheme-phoneme correspondence) to correctly pronounce written words.

**digraph:** Two letters that represent one phoneme, or sound (for example, in *church*, the digraph *ch* represents the single sound /ch/).

**distributed leadership:** A leadership approach in a school that shares responsibility and authority for decision making between school leaders and teachers. In a PLC, this group is the guiding coalition.

**enrichment:** Instruction or activities that extend learning beyond the core curriculum, challenging students who have mastered grade-level content.

**essential standard:** A grade-level standard that has been identified by teacher teams as containing essential knowledge and skills for continued success in school. Essential standards determine the learning required in the school's guaranteed and viable curriculum.

**evidence-based reading instruction:** Instructional practices used to teach reading whose effectiveness is supported by the research contained within the science of reading.

**explicit instruction:** An approach that provides clear, structured, and direct teaching of specific skills or concepts. Explicit instruction can be given using an instructional framework like gradual release of responsibility (GRR), which follows "I do" (focused teacher instruction), "We do" (guided practice), "You all do" (collaborative practice), and "You do alone" (independent practice) stages to scaffold and guide students from teacher-directed learning to independent mastery.

**fluency:** Reading text accurately, quickly, and with proper expression.

**forgetting curve:** A model that outlines the quick decline in memory retention over time when information is not actively reviewed and implemented.

**formative assessments:** Assessments that classroom teachers conduct to inform next steps in their practice. Formative assessments are used to determine student progress, instructional effectiveness, and areas for teacher growth. Data from formative assessments allow teachers to adapt instruction to the tailored needs of their students.

**four critical questions of a PLC:** The questions that collaborative teams of teachers are asked to answer as they work through the PLC process. The four critical questions are (1) What do we want all students to know and be able to do? (2) How will we know if they have learned it? (3) How will we respond when some students do not learn? and (4) How will we extend the learning for students who are already proficient?

**grade-level reading proficiency:** The level of reading skill expected for each student enrolled in a specific grade.

**gradual release of responsibility (GRR):** An explicit instructional framework where teachers progressively transfer responsibility for learning from themselves to students through stages: "I do" (teacher modeling), "We do" (guided practice), "You do together" (collaborative practice), and "You do alone" (independent practice).

**grapheme:** A letter or combination of letters that represents one phoneme, or sound (for example, *b* and *sh* are graphemes that each represent one phoneme).

**grapheme-phoneme correspondence (GPC):** The relationship between a written letter or combination of letters and its sound (for example, the relationship between the letter *m* and the sound this letter makes, /m/).

**guaranteed and viable curriculum:** A prioritized curriculum developed by teacher teams that describes the knowledge and skills all students will learn in a school. Teachers commit to ensuring that the curriculum is taught in every classroom (the guarantee) and that every student will learn it to grade level during the school year (viability).

**guiding coalition:** A diverse team of educational leaders who manage the implementation of the professional learning community process within a school. The team provides an opportunity for distributed leadership by including teacher leaders in the decision-making process.

**high-frequency words:** The words that appear most often in printed text.

**intensive intervention (Tier 3):** The most intensive tier of support in a multitiered system of supports (MTSS), which is reserved for students who don't respond to Tier 1 instruction or Tier 2 intervention.

**intrinsic motivation:** The internal drive to engage in a behavior or activity for personal satisfaction and interest, rather than external rewards or pressures.

**irregular word:** A word that does not follow one or more of the letter-sound correspondence rules (for example, *said* is irregular because the letter combination *ai* makes the sound /ĕ/ and not /ā/, which is the typical sound corresponding to the letter combination *ai*, as in *wait*).

**job-embedded learning:** Frequent professional learning that occurs at the school level and focuses on improved teacher knowledge and classroom practice. It is a framework for teacher learning that supports the immediate and successful application of new skills or information.

**learning targets:** Often written as *I can* statements, targets that define what students should know, understand, and be able to do as a result of their participation in a lesson.

**lesson study:** A professional development process where teachers collaborate to create, implement, observe, and reflect on classroom lessons. The goal of this collaborative practice is to continuously improve lessons' effectiveness so they positively impact student learning.

**letter combination:** Two or more letters in a word that are pronounced as one sound (for example, *ch* and *sh*). Some letter combinations can represent more than one sound (for example, the letter combination *oo* represents different sounds in *moon* and *book*).

**Leveled Literacy Instruction:** A system of reading intervention, based on whole language instruction, that uses leveled books to gradually increase reading complexity and comprehension skills.

**morpheme:** The smallest unit of meaning (for example, *unhelpful* is composed of three morphemes—the prefix *un-*, meaning "opposite"; the suffix *-ful*, meaning "full of"; and the base word *help*—and the meaning of each morpheme contributes to the meaning of *unhelpful*). *See also* base word, prefix, *and* suffix.

**morphological awareness:** The ability to use understanding of morphemes to support the reading and writing of words. *See also* morpheme *and* morphology.

**morphology:** The study of words and how they are formed.

**motivational framework:** A framework that encourages the development of intrinsic motivation in teachers. The framework includes addressing a teacher's need for relevance, purpose, mastery, and autonomy.

**multimodal instruction:** Teaching that incorporates various modalities (visual, auditory, and kinesthetic) to enhance learning using a variety of instructional methods.

**multitiered system of supports (MTSS):** A framework that provides targeted support to students based on their needs. It is typically organized into three tiers of support ranging from supports for all students to more targeted and specific supports for students with complex learning needs.

**National Reading Panel (NRP):** A panel of experts established in 1997 by the U.S. Congress to review research on reading instruction. The NRP's 2000 report identified five key components of effective reading instruction: (1) phonemic awareness, (2) phonics, (3) fluency, (4) vocabulary, and (5) comprehension.

**norm-referenced assessment:** An often standardized assessment that compares an individual student's performance to the performance of a predetermined developmentally appropriate group of students.

**one-size-fits-all instruction:** An instructional approach that does not differentiate or adapt the methodology, regardless of the needs and abilities of students in the class. This approach often leads to disengagement and poor performance for many students.

**onset:** The sound or sounds that come before a vowel in a syllable (for example, in *farm*, /f/ is the onset).

**orthographic mapping:** The process of linking the phonemes (sounds) in a word to the graphemes (written letters) that represent them.

**orthography:** The spelling conventions in a given language.

**Peter Effect:** A concept referring to the fact that teachers who lack knowledge or motivation in an area of study may be unable to effectively impart those qualities to their students. For example, teachers who lack foundational knowledge of evidence-based reading instruction will be unable to use these strategies to teach their students how to read.

**phoneme:** The smallest unit of sound (for example, there are three phonemes in *cat*—/k/ /ă/ /t/— as well as in *fish*—/f/ /ĭ/ /sh/).

**phoneme blending:** Blending together sounds to say a word (for example, blending the phonemes /k/ /ă/ /t/ to say *cat*).

**phoneme elision:** Deleting a sound in a word and saying what is left (for example, deleting /f/ from *fat* makes *at*).

**phoneme segmentation:** Separating the different phonemes in a word (for example, recognizing that *fish* is composed of the phonemes /f/ /ĭ/ /sh/).

**phoneme substitution:** Replacing one sound with a different sound (for example, replacing /b/ in *bat* with /f/ to produce *fat*).

**phonemic awareness:** The ability to recognize and manipulate the individual sounds (phonemes) in spoken words.

**phonics:** An approach to reading and spelling instruction that focuses on the relationship between letters and sounds. Direct and systematic instruction in phonics is required to help students decode words.

**phonograms:** Letter groups within words that share a pattern across words (for example, *-ice* as in *nice*, *mice*, and *dice*).

**phonological awareness:** The ability to identify and work with sounds in a spoken language.

**phonological encoding:** Following phonetic rules to spell spoken words.

**phonological recoding:** Using graphemes (letters and letter combinations) in a written word to pronounce the word.

**prefix:** One or more letters added at the beginning of a word to make a new word with a different meaning (for example, when the prefix *re-*, meaning "again," is added to the word *write*, the new word *rewrite* is formed).

**professional learning community (PLC):** A school or district committed to improving student outcomes by ensuring teachers work in teams and engage in meaningful, continuous, job-embedded professional development weekly. This work develops a culture focused on student learning, collaboration, and results. PLCs seek to improve teachers' understanding of curriculum, assessment, intervention, and enrichment so all students experience a high-quality education, regardless of their teacher.

**proficiency scale:** A scale teacher teams develop for each essential standard that describes levels of student performance (typically four). It ensures a common understanding of the skills and knowledge each student must learn to demonstrate grade-level performance on the standard. The levels represent a continuum of learning that includes descriptions of below-grade-level, close-to-grade-level, grade-level, and above-grade-level learning.

**prosody:** Reading with expression.

**reading wars:** The phrase used to describe the often-volatile relationship between proponents of whole language instruction and those who believe in the direct instruction of phonics to teach reading.

**reading year plan:** A long-term plan outlining the scope, sequence, and pacing of reading skills across a school year. The plan ensures comprehensive coverage of essential reading skills for all students.

**R.E.A.L. criteria:** Criteria developed to aid teacher teams in the selection of essential standards. An essential standard must satisfy one or more of the criteria of readiness (prerequisite), endurance (representative of a lifelong skill), assessment (connected to a standardized test), and leverage (used across subjects).

**reciprocal accountability:** A concept where teachers and school leaders share responsibility for increasing student learning by holding each other accountable for fulfilling their respective roles in achieving shared goals.

**regular word:** A word that can be pronounced correctly by applying letter-sound correspondences (for example, *pan*). *See also* irregular word.

**rime:** The part of a syllable that includes the vowel and any consonant sounds that come after.

**root word:** *See* base word.

**Rose report:** A 2006 report out of the United Kingdom, authored by Jim Rose, which emphasizes the importance of systematic phonics in early reading instruction. This report was instrumental in leading reading reform in the United Kingdom.

**science of reading:** The large body of scientific research related to the skill of reading. This research outlines how humans learn to read, the breadth of skills required to become a proficient reader, and the most effective instructional strategies for teaching reading. Its scope extends past the field of education to include research from cognitive psychology, communication sciences, developmental psychology, special education, implementation science, linguistics, neuroscience, and school psychology.

**scope and sequence:** A detailed outline of the content (scope) and the order in which it is taught (sequence). It provides a structured progression for knowledge and skills contained within the curriculum over the course of the year.

**scripted instruction:** An instructional approach where teachers follow a prescribed script or lesson plan, often word for word, to ensure consistency and fidelity in delivering content.

**segment:** *See* phoneme segmentation.

**self-regulated strategy development (SRSD):** An evidence-based instructional approach to explicitly writing strategies while also helping students develop self-regulation skills such as goal setting, self-monitoring, and self-reinforcement.

**short vowel:** The sound a vowel usually makes when it appears between two consonants (for example, the vowels in *tap*, *set*, *did*, *log*, and *cup* all make their short vowel sounds). A scoop called a *breve* is placed over a vowel to indicate a short vowel sound (for example, /ĕ/).

**simultaneous loose-tight culture:** The culture developed within a professional learning community that clearly outlines the non-negotiable actions (tight) undertaken by teacher teams as well as the scope of autonomous decision making (loose) afforded to each team. For example, a school will be tight about the creation of a guaranteed and viable curriculum but loose about the decisions a team makes regarding the inclusion and exclusion of standards.

**SMART goals:** Goals written by teacher teams that are specific, measurable, attainable, relevant, and time bound. These goals are collective achievement targets that outline a team's short-term objectives for a unit of study or their long-term objectives over the course of the school year. To achieve a SMART goal, teams must work interdependently, take collective responsibility, and hold each other mutually accountable.

**SMART goal writing process:** A process used by collaborative teams to develop meaningful SMART goals. The process requires teams to determine an area for improvement, accumulate benchmark performance data, closely examine the skill deficits of underperforming students, determine a focus group of students, develop a plan to accelerate learning for the focus group, monitor the group's progress, adapt instruction based on progress monitoring, and reflect on the effectiveness of their plan.

**standard score:** A statistical measure used to compare a student's performance against a predetermined group of students. A standard score is calculated based on the mean (average) and the standard deviation of the dataset (norm). It shows how far an individual's score is from the mean and whether it is above or below the average.

**structured literacy:** An approach to literacy instruction that emphasizes the teaching of foundational skills in a logical and organized way from simple to more complex. The key areas of focus are phonology, sound-symbol association, syllable instruction, morphology, syntax, and semantics.

**suffix:** One or more letters added to the end of a word (sometimes with spelling changes to the word) to make a new word, usually with a different meaning (for example, adding the suffix *-ed* to the verb *look* shifts the meaning from present tense to past tense; when adding *-ed* to *stop*, a second *p* is added—*stopped*).

**supplemental intervention (Tier 2):** Additional time and support offered to students who require more time or a different approach to learn essential grade-level standards.

**syllable:** A speech unit that contains one vowel sound, with or without surrounding consonants (for example, *open* has two syllables—*o/pen*).

**target words:** A set of words, provided in each lesson, that each contain the letter-sound correspondence taught in the lesson.

**teacher isolation:** When teachers work by themselves, making all classroom decisions individually rather than in coordination with other teachers in the school.

**Tier 2 intervention:** The additional time and support provided on grade-level core standards to a select group of students.

**Tier 3 intervention:** Specific and targeted instruction for students with gaps in foundational skills.

**top-down approach:** A leadership approach that emphasizes and promotes classroom decisions made by high-level leaders in the school or district with minimal or no input by teachers.

**trigraph:** Three letters that together represent one phoneme, or sound (for example, in *edge*, the trigraph *dge* represents the single sound /j/).

**vertical alignment:** The process of aligning standards and learning targets with grades above and below to ensure that the essential knowledge and skills learned will build a foundation of success in the next grade level.

**vocabulary:** The number of words someone knows and how well they know them.

**vowels:** The letters *a*, *e*, *i*, *o*, and *u*; the letter *y* is a vowel in some words and a consonant in others.

**whole language approach:** A philosophy of teaching reading that emphasizes meaning by using strategies focused on context clues, background knowledge, and the structure of language. This philosophy excludes direct and systematic phonics and phonemic awareness instruction as a component of learning to read.

**word recognition:** The ability to recognize written words without having to sound them out.

# REFERENCES AND RESOURCES

Accountability. (n.d.). In *Merriam-Webster's online dictionary*. Accessed at https://www.merriam-webster.com/dictionary/accountability on January 7, 2024.

Adams, M. J. (1990). *Beginning to read: Thinking and learning about print*. Cambridge, MA: MIT Press.

Affandi, L. H., Ermiana, I., & Makki, M. (2019). Effective Professional Learning Community model for improving elementary school teachers' performance. In *Proceedings of the 3rd International Conference on Current Issues in Education (ICCIE 2018)* (Vol. 54). Advances in Social Science, Education and Humanities Research. https://doi.org/10.2991/iccie-18.2019.54

Ainsworth, L. (2015a). *Common formative assessments 2.0: How teacher teams intentionally align standards, instruction, and assessment*. Thousand Oaks, CA: Corwin Press.

Ainsworth, L. (2015b, February 24). *Priority standards: The power of focus*. Accessed at https://www.edweek.org/teaching-learning/opinion-priority-standards-the-power-of-focus/2015/02 on June 19, 2024.

Al Otaiba, S., Allor, J., Werfel, K. L., & Clemens, N. (2016). Critical components of phonemic awareness instruction and intervention: Recommendations for teacher training and for future research. In R. Schiff & R. M. Joshi (Eds.), *Interventions in learning disabilities: A handbook on systematic training programs for individuals with learning disabilities* (pp. 9–27). Cham, Switzerland: Springer.

Al Otaiba, S., Kosanovich, M. L., & Torgeson, J. K. (2012). Assessment and instruction for phonemic awareness and word recognition skills. In A. G. Kamhi & H. W. Catts (Eds.), *Language and reading disabilities* (3rd ed., pp. 112–145). London: Pearson.

Anderson, L. W., Krathwohl, D. R., Airasian, P. W., Cruikshank, K. A., Mayer, R. E., Pintrich, P. R., et al. (2001). *A taxonomy for learning, teaching, and assessing: A revision of Bloom's taxonomy of educational objectives (Abridged ed.)*. London: Pearson.

Anderson, R. C., Hiebert, E. H., Scott, J. A., & Wilkinson, I. A. G. (1985). *Becoming a nation of readers: The report of the Commission on Reading*. Washington, DC: National Academy of Education. Accessed at https://naeducation.org/wp-content/uploads/2021/08/Anderson-Hiebert-Scott-Wilkinson-Becoming-a-Nation-of-Readers.pdf on June 19, 2024.

Ankrum, J., Morewood, A., Parsons, S., Vaughn, M., Parsons, A., & Hawkins, P. (2020). Documenting adaptive literacy instruction: The adaptive teaching observation protocol (ATOP). *Reading Psychology, 41*, 71–86. https://doi.org/10.1080/02702711.2020.1726845

Anrig, G. (2013). *Beyond the education wars: Evidence that collaboration builds effective schools.* New York: Century Foundation Press. Accessed at https://production-tcf.imgix.net/app/uplo ads/2013/04/04180908/20130404-beyond-the-education-wars-intro-8.pdf on June 19, 2024.

Anthony, J. L., & Francis, D. J. (2005). Development of phonological awareness. *Current Directions in Psychological Science, 14*(5), 255–259. https://doi.org/10.1111/j.0963 -7214.2005.00376.x

Archer, A., & Hughes, C. (2011). *Explicit instruction: Effective and efficient teaching.* New York: Guilford Press.

Athanases, S. Z., Bennett, L. H., & Wahleithner, J. M. (2015). Adaptive teaching for English language arts: Following the pathway of classroom data in preservice teacher inquiry. *Journal of Literacy Research, 47*(1), 83–114. https://doi.org/10.1177/1086296X15590915

August, D., & Shanahan, T. (2006). *Developing literacy in second language learners: Report of the national literacy panel on language-minority children and youth.* Mahwah, NJ: Lawrence Erlbaum Associates.

Baddeley, A. (2012). Working memory: Theories, models, and controversies. *Annual Review of Psychology, 63,* 1–29. https://doi.org/10.1146/annurev-psych-120710-100422

Barth, R. S. (2001). *Learning by heart.* San Francisco: Jossey-Bass.

Beck, I., & McKeown, M. (1991). Conditions of vocabulary acquisition. In R. Barr, M. L. Kamil, P. B. Mosenthal, & P. D. Pearson (Eds.), *Handbook of reading research* (Vol. 2, pp. 789–814). Mahwah, NJ: Lawrence Erlbaum Associates.

Beck, I. L., McKeown, M. G., & Kucan, L. (2002). *Bringing words to life: Robust vocabulary instruction.* New York: Guilford Press.

Beckman, M. E. (1996). The parsing of prosody. *Language and Cognitive Processes, 11*(1–2), 17–68. https://doi.org/10.1080/016909696387213

Berwick, R. C., Friederici, A. D., Chomsky, N., & Bolhuis, J. J. (2013). Evolution, brain, and the nature of language. *Trends in Cognitive Sciences, 17*(2), 89–98. https://doi.org/10.1016/j .tics.2012.12.002

Biemiller, A. (2003). Vocabulary: Needed if more children are to read well. *Reading Psychology, 24*(3–4), 323–335.

Biemiller, A. (2005). Vocabulary development and instruction: A prerequisite for school learning. In D. K. Dickinson & S. B. Neuman (Eds.) *Handbook of early literacy research* (Vol. 2, pp. 41–51). New York: Guilford Press.

Bigozzi, L., Tarchi, C., Vagnoli, L., Valente, E., & Pinto, G. (2017). Reading fluency as a predictor of school outcomes across grades 4–9. *Frontiers in Psychology, 8,* 200. https://doi .org/10.3389/fpsyg.2017.00200

Binder, K. S., Cote, N. G., Lee, C., Bessette, E., & Vu, H. (2017). Beyond breadth: The contributions of vocabulary depth to reading comprehension among skilled readers. *Journal of Research in Reading, 40*(3), 333–343. https://doi.org/10.1111/1467-9817.12069

Binks-Cantrell, E., Washburn, E. K., Joshi, R. M., & Hougen, M. (2012). Peter effect in the preparation of reading teachers. *Scientific Studies of Reading, 16*(6), 526–536. https://doi.org/10 .1080/10888438.2011.601434

Blachman, B. A., Tangel, D. M., Ball, E. W., Black, R., & McGraw, C. K. (1999). Developing phonological awareness and word recognition skills: A two-year intervention with low-income, inner-city children. *Reading and Writing, 11*(3), 239–273.

Bleses, D., Moos, M., Purpura, D. J., & Dale, P. S. (2023). General and math vocabulary contributions to early numeracy skills in a large population-representative sample. *Frontiers in Developmental Psychology, 1*, Article 1279691. https://doi.org/10.3389/fdpys.2023.1279691

Boardman, A. G., Vaughn, S., Buckley, P., Reutebuch, C., Roberts, G., & Klingner, J. (2016). Collaborative strategic reading for students with learning disabilities in upper elementary classrooms. *Exceptional Children, 82*(4), 409–427.

Bowers, J. S., & Bowers, P. N. (2017). Beyond phonics: The case for teaching children the logic of the English spelling system. *Educational Psychologist, 52*, 124–141. https://doi.org/10.1080/004 61520.2017.1288571

Bowers, J. S., & Bowers, P. N. (2018). The importance of correctly characterising the English spelling system when devising and evaluating methods of reading instruction: Comment on Taylor, Davis, and Rastle (2017). *Quarterly Journal of Experimental Psychology, 71*(7), 1497–1500. https://doi.org/10.1177/1747021818759477

Bowers, P. G., & Wolf, M. (1993). Theoretical links among naming speed, precise timing mechanisms and orthographic skill in dyslexia. *Reading and Writing, 5*(1), 69–85.

Bowers, P. N. (2009). *Teaching how the written word works*. Wolfe Island, Ontario, Canada: WordWorks Literacy Centre. Accessed at www.wordworksinternational.com on June 19, 2024.

Bowers, P. N., & Kirby, J. R. (2010). Effects of morphological instruction on vocabulary acquisition. *Reading and Writing, 23*(5), 515–537. https://doi.org/10.1007/s11145-009-9172-z

Brady, S. A. (2011). Efficacy of phonics teaching for reading outcomes: Indications from post-NRP research. In S. A. Brady, D. Braze, & C. A. Fowler (Eds.), *Explaining individual differences in reading: Theory and evidence* (pp. 69–96). London: Psychology Press.

Brady, S. A. (2020). A 2020 perspective on research findings on alphabetics (phoneme awareness and phonics): Implications for instruction. *The Reading League Journal, 1*(3), 20–28.

Breznitz, Z. (2006). *Fluency in reading: Synchronization of processes*. Mahwah, NJ: Lawrence Erlbaum Associates.

Brown, V. L., Hammill, D. D., & Wiederholt, J. L. (2009). *Test of Reading Comprehension* (TORC-4; 4th ed.) [Measurement instrument]. Austin, TX: Pro-Ed.

Buffum, A., Mattos, M., & Malone, J. (2018). *Taking action: A handbook for RTI at Work*. Bloomington, IN: Solution Tree Press.

Cain, K. (2010). *Reading development and difficulties*. Chichester, West Sussex, England: BPS Blackwell.

Caravolas, M., Lervåg, A., Defior, S., Seidlová Málková, G., & Hulme, C. (2013). Different patterns, but equivalent predictors, of growth in reading in consistent and inconsistent orthographies. *Psychological Science, 24*(8), 1398–1407. http://dx.doi.org/10.1177/0956 797612473122

Cárdenas-Hagan, E. (2020). *Literacy foundations for English learners: A comprehensive guide to evidence-based instruction*. Baltimore: Brookes.

Castles, A., Rastle, K., & Nation, K. (2018). Ending the reading wars: Reading acquisition from novice to expert. *Psychological Science in the Public Interest, 19*(1), 5–51. https://doi.org/10.11 77/1529100618772271

Catts, H. W., Wilcox, K. A., Wood-Jackson, C., Larrivee, L. S., & Scott, V. G. (1997). Toward an understanding of phonological awareness. In C. K. Leong & R. M. Joshi (Eds.), *Cross-language studies of learning to read and spell: Phonologic and orthographic processing* (pp. 31–52). Dordrecht, Netherlands: Kluwer Academic.

Chall, J. S. (1967). *Learning to read: The great debate*. New York: McGraw-Hill.

Chall, J. S. (1996). *Learning to read: The great debate* (3rd ed.). San Diego, CA: Harcourt Brace College.

Chapman, J. W., & Tunmer, W. E. (2015, July). *The literacy performance of ex-Reading Recovery students between two and four years following participation on the program: Is this intervention effective for students with early reading difficulties?* Paper presented at the 39th Annual Conference of the International Academy for Research in Learning Disabilities (IARLD), Vancouver, Canada.

Chard, D. J., Vaughn, S., & Tyler, B.-J. (2002). A synthesis of research on effective interventions for building reading fluency with elementary students with learning disabilities. *Journal of Learning Disabilities, 35*(5), 386–406.

Cheung, W. M., & Wong, W. Y. (2014). Does Lesson Study work? A systematic review on the effects of Lesson Study and Learning Study on teachers and students. *International Journal for Lesson and Learning Studies, 3*(2), 137–149. https://doi.org/10.1108/ijlls-05-2013-0024

Chung, K. K. H. (2015). Socioeconomic status and academic achievement. In J. D. Wright (Ed.), *International encyclopedia of the social & behavioral sciences* (2nd ed., pp. 924–930). Amsterdam, Netherlands: Elsevier. https://doi.org/10.1016/B978-0-08-097086-8.92141-X

Cialdini, R. B. (2007). *Influence: The psychology of persuasion*. New York: Collins Business Essentials.

Colenbrander, D., Wang, H.-C., Arrow, T., & Castles, A. (2020). Teaching irregular words: What we know, what we don't know, and where we can go from here. *Educational and Developmental Psychologist, 37*(2), 97–104. https://doi.org/10.1017/edp.2020.11

Colker, L. J. (2014). The word gap: The early years make the difference. *Teaching Young Children, 7*(3), 26–28.

Collins, J. (2001). *Good to great: Why some companies make the leap . . . and others don't*. New York: Harper Business.

Conzemius, A., & O'Neill, J. (2014). *Handbook for SMART school teams: Revitalizing best practices for collaboration* (2nd ed.). Bloomington, IN: Solution Tree Press.

Coulmas, F. (2003). *Writing systems: An introduction to their linguistic analysis*. Cambridge, England: Cambridge University Press.

Coulter, G. A., & Lambert, M. C. (2015). Access to general education curriculum: The effect of preteaching key words upon fluency and accuracy in expository text. *Learning Disability Quarterly, 38*(4), 248–256. https://doi.org/10.1177/0731948715580438

Coxhead, A. (2000). A new academic word list. *TESOL Quarterly, 34*(2), 213–238.

Cunningham, A. E., & Stanovich, K. E. (1998). What reading does for the mind. *American Educator, 22*(1–2), 8–15.

Cutting, L. E., & Scarborough, H. S. (2006). Prediction of reading comprehension: Relative contributions of word recognition, language proficiency, and other cognitive skills can depend on how comprehension is measured. *Scientific Studies of Reading, 10*(3), 277–299. https://doi.org/10.1207/s1532799xssr1003_5

Dale, E. (1965). Vocabulary measurement: Techniques and major findings. *Elementary English, 42*, 82–88.

Dale, P. S., Paul, A., Rosholm, M., & Bleses, D. (2023). Prediction from early childhood vocabulary to academic achievement at the end of compulsory schooling in Denmark. *International Journal of Behavioral Development, 47*(2), 123–134. https://doi.org/10.1177/01650254221116878

Dang, T. N. Y., Coxhead, A., & Webb, S. (2017). The academic spoken word list. *Language Learning, 67*(4), 959–997.

Darling-Hammond, L., Hyler, M. E., & Gardner, M. (2017, June). *Effective teacher professional development.* Palo Alto, CA: Learning Policy Institute. Accessed at https://learningpolicy institute.org/media/476/download?inline&file=Effective_Teacher_Professional_Development _REPORT.pdf on June 21, 2024.

Day, C., Sammons, P., & Gorgen, K. (2020). *Successful school leadership.* Reading, Berkshire, England: Education Development Trust. Accessed at https://eric.ed.gov/?id=ED614324 on November 4, 2024.

de Lima, J. A. (2003). Trained for isolation: The impact of departmental cultures on student teachers' views and practices of collaboration. *Journal of Education for Teaching, 29*(3), 197–217. https://doi.org/10.1080/0260747032000120105

Deno, S. L. (1985). Curriculum-based measurement: The emerging alternative. *Exceptional Children, 52*(3), 219–232.

Desimone, L. M., & Garet, M. S. (2015). Best practices in teachers' professional development in the United States. *Psychology, Society and Education, 7*(3), 252–263.

Dewalt, D. A., Berkman, N. D., Sheridan, S., Lohr, K. N., & Pignone, M. P. (2004). Literacy and health outcomes: A systematic review of the literature. *Journal of General Internal Medicine, 19*(12), 1228–1239. https://doi.org/10.1111/j.1525-1497.2004.40153.x

Dickinson, D. K., Nesbitt, K. T., Collins, M. F., Hadley, E. B., Newman, K., Rivera, B. L., et al. (2019). Teaching for breadth and depth of vocabulary knowledge: Learning from explicit and implicit instruction and the storybook texts. *Early Childhood Research Quarterly, 47*, 341–356. https://doi.org/10.1016/j.ecresq.2018.07.012

Didion, L., Toste, J. R., & Filderman, M. J. (2020). Teacher professional development and student reading achievement: A meta-analytic review of the effects. *Journal of Research on Educational Effectiveness, 13*(1), 29–66. https://doi.org/10.1080/19345747.2019.1670884

Dilakshini, V., & Kumar, S. (2020). Cognitive dissonance: A psychological unrest. *Current Journal of Applied Science and Technology, 39(30),* 54–60. https://doi.org/10.9734/cjast/2020/v39i3030970

Doran, G. T. (1981). There's a SMART way to write management's goals and objectives. *Management Review, 70*(11), 35–36.

Dresser, R. (2012). The impact of scripted literacy instruction on teachers and students. *Issues in Teacher Education, 21*, 71–87.

DuFour, R., DuFour, R., Eaker, R., & Many, T. (2006). *Learning by doing: A handbook for Professional Learning Communities at Work* (1st ed.). Bloomington, IN: Solution Tree Press.

DuFour, R., DuFour, R., Eaker, R., Many, T. W., & Mattos, M. (2016). *Learning by doing: A handbook for Professional Learning Communities at Work* (3rd ed.). Bloomington, IN: Solution Tree Press.

DuFour, R., DuFour, R., Eaker, R., Many, T. W., & Mattos, M. (2020). *Learning by doing: A handbook for Professional Learning Communities at Work* (3rd ed., Canadian version). Bloomington, IN: Solution Tree Press.

DuFour, R., DuFour, R., Eaker, R., Many, T. W., Mattos, M., & Muhammad, A. (2024). *Learning by doing: A handbook for Professional Learning Communities at Work* (4th ed.). Bloomington, IN: Solution Tree Press.

DuFour, R., DuFour, R., Eaker, R., Mattos, M., & Muhammad, A. (2021). *Revisiting Professional Learning Communities at Work: Proven insights for sustained, substantive school improvement* (2nd ed.). Bloomington, IN: Solution Tree Press.

DuFour, R., & Marzano, R. J. (2011). *Leaders of learning: How district, school, and classroom leaders improve student achievement.* Bloomington, IN: Solution Tree Press.

Duke, N. K., Pearson, P. D., Strachan, S. L., & Billman, A. K. (2011). Essential elements of fostering and teaching reading comprehension. In S. J. Samuels & A. E. Farstrup (Eds.), *What research has to say about reading instruction* (4th ed., pp. 51–93). Newark, DE: International Reading Association.

Dulay, K. M., Law, S. Y., McBride, C., & Ho, C. S. H. (2021). Reciprocal effects of morphological awareness, vocabulary knowledge, and word reading: A cross-lagged panel analysis in Chinese. *Journal of Experimental Child Psychology, 206,* 105100. https://doi.org/10.1016/j.jecp.2021.105100

Dunn, D. M. (2018). *Peabody Picture Vocabulary Test* (PPVT-5; 5th ed.) [Measurement instrument]. San Antonio, TX: Pearson Assessments.

Edmonds, M. S., Vaughn, S., Wexler, J., Reutebuch, C., Cable, A., Tackett, K. K., et al. (2009). A synthesis of reading interventions and effects on reading comprehension outcomes for older struggling readers. *Review of Educational Research, 79*(1), 262–300. https://doi.org/10.3102/0034654308325998

Ehri, L. C. (1997). Learning to read and learning to spell are one and the same, almost. In C. A. Perfetti, L. Rieben, & M. Fayol (Eds), *Learning to spell: Research, theory, and practice across languages* (pp. 237–269). Mahwah, NJ: Lawrence Erlbaum Associates.

Ehri, L. C., Nunes, S. R., Stahl, S. A., & Willows, D. M. (2001). Systematic phonics instruction helps students learn to read: Evidence from the National Reading Panel's meta-analysis. *Review of Educational Research, 71*(3), 393–447.

Ellis, C., Holston, S., Drake, G., Putman, H., Swisher, A., & Peske, H. (2023). *Teacher prep review: Strengthening elementary reading instruction.* Washington, DC: National Council on Teacher Quality.

Erbeli, F., Rice, M., Xu, Y., Bishop, M. E., & Goodrich, J. M. (2024). A meta-analysis on the optimal cumulative dosage of early phonemic awareness instruction. *Scientific Studies of Reading, 28*(4), 345–370. https://doi.org/10.1080/10888438.2024.2309386

Ergül, C., Kudret, Z. B., Ökcün-Akçamuş, M. Ç., Akoğlu, G., Demir, E., & Tülü, B. K. (2022). How do phonological awareness and rapid naming predict reading? Findings from a highly transparent orthography. *Literacy Research and Instruction, 61*(1), 41–60. https://doi.org/10.1080/19388071.2021.2008557

Fadlun, F., & Fatmawati, E. (2023). The effect of teacher performance on academic achievement of elementary school. *An-Nidzam: Jurnal Manajemen Pendidikan dan Studi Islam, 10*(1), 39–49. https://doi.org/10.33507/an-nidzam.v10i1.1128

Fielding-Barnsley, R. (2010). Australian pre-service teachers' knowledge of phonemic awareness and phonics in the process of learning to read. *Australian Journal of Learning Difficulties, 15,* 99–110. https://doi.org/10.1080/19404150903524606

Fisher, D., & Frey, N. (2021). *Better learning through structured teaching: A framework for the gradual release of responsibility* (3rd ed.). Alexandria, VA: Association for Supervision and Curriculum Development.

Filderman, M. J., Austin, C. R., Boucher, A. N., O'Donnell, K., & Swanson, E. A. (2022). A meta-analysis of the effects of reading comprehension interventions on the reading comprehension outcomes of struggling readers in third through 12th grades. *Exceptional Children, 88*(2), 163–184. https://doi.org/10.1177/00144029211050860

Fishco, V. V. (2019). *Nelson-Denny Reading Test forms I and J: Examiner's manual*. Rolling Meadows, IL: Riverside.

Fletcher, J. M., & Vaughn, S. (2009). Response to intervention: Preventing and remediating academic difficulties. *Child Development Perspectives, 3*, 30–37. https://doi.org/10.1111/j.1750-8606.2008.00072.x

Foorman, B., Beyler, N., Borradaile, K., Coyne, M., Denton, C. A., Dimino, J., et al. (2016). *Foundational skills to support reading for understanding in kindergarten through 3rd grade* (NCEE 2016–4008). Washington, DC: National Center for Education Evaluation and Regional Assistance, Institute of Education Sciences, U.S. Department of Education. Accessed at https://ies.ed.gov/ncee/WWC/Docs/PracticeGuide/wwc_foundationalreading_040717.pdf on June 20, 2024.

Foorman, B. R., Petscher, Y., & Herrera, S. (2018). Unique and common effects of decoding and language factors in predicting reading comprehension in grades 1–10. *Learning and Individual Differences, 63*, 12–23. https://doi.org/10.1016/j.lindif.2018.02.011

Frey, N., & Fisher, D. (2009). Using common formative assessments as a source of professional development in an urban American elementary school. *Teaching and Teacher Education, 25*, 674–680. https://doi.org/10.1016/j.tate.2008.11.006

Frey, N., & Fisher, D. (2013). *Gradual release of responsibility instructional framework*. Alexandria, VA: Association for Supervision and Curriculum Development. Accessed at https://pdo.ascd.org/lms courses/pd13oc005/media/formativeassessmentandccswithelaliteracymod_3-reading3.pdf on November 17, 2024.

Fry, E. B. (1999). *The vocabulary teacher's book of lists* (1st ed.). San Francisco: Jossey-Bass.

Fuchs, L. S. (2017). *Project PROACT MAZE reading passages, grade 6*. Nashville, TN: Vanderbilt University.

Fuchs, L. S., & Fuchs, D. (1992). Identifying a measure for monitoring student reading progress. *School Psychology Review, 21*(1), 45–58.

Fullan, M. (2005). *Leadership and sustainability: System thinkers in action*. Thousand Oaks, CA: Corwin Press.

Furnes, B., & Samuelsson, S. (2011). Phonological awareness and rapid automatized naming predicting early development in reading and spelling: Results from a cross-linguistic longitudinal study. *Learning and Individual Differences, 21*(1), 85–95. https://doi.org/10.1016/j.lindif.2010.10.005

Gabor, A. (2018). *After the education wars: How smart schools upend the business of reform*. New York: The New Press.

Galdames-Calderón, M. (2023). Distributed leadership: School principals' practices to promote teachers' professional development for school improvement. *Education Sciences, 13*(7), Article 715. https://doi.org/10.3390/educsci13070715

Galuschka, K., Ise, E., Krick, K., & Schulte-Körne, G. (2014). Effectiveness of treatment approaches for students and adolescents with reading disabilities: A meta-analysis of randomized controlled trials. *PLOS One, 9*(2), Article e89900. https://doi.org/10.1371/journal.pone.0089900

Gardner, D., & Davies, M. (2014). A new academic vocabulary list. *Applied Linguistics, 35*(3), 305–327. https://doi.org/10.1093/applin/amt015

Georgiou, G., Aro, M., Liao, C.-H., & Parrila, R. (2016). Modeling the relationship between rapid automatized naming and literacy skills across languages varying in orthographic consistency. *Journal of Experimental Child Psychology, 143*, 48–64.

Georgiou, G. K., & Das, J. P. (2015). University students with poor reading comprehension: The hidden cognitive processing deficit. *Journal of Learning Disabilities*, *48*(5), 535–545. https://doi .org/10.1177/0022219413513924

Georgiou, G., & Dunn, K. (2023). *The phonics companion: 120 lessons for teachers*. North York, Ontario: Pearson Canada.

Georgiou, G., Inoue, T., & Parrila, R. (2021). Developmental relations between home literacy environment, reading interest, and reading skills: Evidence from a 3-year longitudinal study. *Child Development*, *92*(5), 2053–2068.

Georgiou, G., Kushnir, G., & Parrila, R. (2020). Moving the needle on literacy: Lessons learned from a school where literacy rates have improved over time. *Alberta Journal of Educational Research*, *66*(3), 347–359. https://doi.org/10.55016/ojs/ajer.v66i3.56988

Georgiou, G. K., Parrila, R., & Papadopoulos, T. C. (2008). Predictors of word decoding and reading fluency across languages varying in orthographic consistency. *Journal of Educational Psychology*, *100*(3), 566–580. https://doi.org/10.1037/0022-0663.100.3.566

Germuth, A. A. (2018). Professional development that changes teaching and improves learning. *Journal of Interdisciplinary Teacher Leadership (JoITL)*, *2*(1), 77–90. https://doi.org/10.46767 /kfp.2016-0025

Gilkerson, J., Richards, J. A., Warren, S. F., Montgomery, J. K., Greenwood, C. R., Kimbrough Oller, D., et al. (2017). Mapping the early language environment using all-day recordings and automated analysis. *American Journal of Speech-Language Pathology*, *26*(2), 248–265. https://doi.org/10.1044/2016_AJSLP-15-0169

Goodman, K. S. (1967). Reading: A psycholinguistic guessing game. *Journal of the Reading Specialist*, *6*(4), 126–135. https://doi.org/10.1080/19388076709556976

Gore, J., Lloyd, A., Smith, M., Bowe, J., Ellis, H., & Lubans, D. (2017). Effects of professional development on the quality of teaching: Results from a randomized controlled trial of Quality Teaching Rounds. *Teaching and Teacher Education*, *68*, 99–113. https://doi-org.login.ezproxy .library.ualberta.ca/10.1016/j.tate.2017.08.007

Gough, P. B., & Tunmer, W. E. (1986). Decoding, reading, and reading disability. *Remedial and Special Education*, *7*(1), 6–10. https://doi.org/10.1177/074193258600700104

Graham, S., & Harris, K. R. (1993). Self-regulated strategy development: Helping students with learning problems develop as writers. *The Elementary School Journal*, *94*(2), 169–181. https://doi.org/10.1086/461758

Grande, G., Diamanti, V., Protopapas, A., Melby-Lervåg, M., & Lervåg, A. (2024). The developmental of morphological awareness and vocabulary: What influences what? *Applied Psycholinguistics*, *45*(4), 745–765. https://doi.org/10.1017/S0142716424000213

Graves, M. F. (2000). A vocabulary program to complement and bolster a middle-grade comprehension program. In B. M. Taylor, M. F. Graves, & P. van den Broek (Eds.), *Reading for meaning: Fostering comprehension in the middle grades* (pp. 116–135). New York: Teachers College Press.

Graves, M. F. (2006). *The vocabulary book: Learning and instruction*. New York: Teachers College Press.

Graves, M. F., Schneider, S., & Ringstaff, C. (2018). Empowering students with word-learning strategies: Teach a child to fish. *The Reading Teacher*, *71*(5), 533–543. https://doi.org/10.10 02/trtr.1644

Graves, M. F., & Watts-Taffe, S. M. (2002). The place of word consciousness in a research-based vocabulary program. In A. E. Farstrup & S. J. Samuels (Eds.), *What research has to say about reading instruction* (3rd ed., pp. 140–165). Newark, DE: International Reading Association.

Hall, B. (2022). *Powerful guiding coalitions: How to build and sustain the leadership team in your PLC at Work.* Bloomington, IN: Solution Tree Press.

Hall, C., Dahl-Leonard, K., Cho, E., Solari, E. J., Capin, P., Conner, C. L., et al. (2023). Forty years of reading intervention research for elementary students with or at risk for dyslexia: A systematic review and meta-analysis. *Reading Research Quarterly, 58*(2), 285–312. https://doi.org/10.1002/rrq.477

Hall, C., Dahl-Leonard, K., Denton, C. A., Stevens, E. A., & Capin, P. (2021). Fostering independence while teaching students with or at risk for reading disabilities. *Teaching Exceptional Children, 54*(2), 89–98.

Hallinger, P., & Heck, R. H. (2010). Collaborative leadership and school improvement: Understanding the impact on school capacity and student learning. *School Leadership and Management, 30*(2), 95–110. https://doi.org/10.1080/13632431003663214

Hamzah, M. I. M., & Jamil, M. F. (2019). The relationship of distributed leadership and professional learning community. *Creative Education, 10*(12), 2730–2741. https://doi .org/10.4236/ce.2019.1012199

Hanover Research. (2016, November). *Early skills and predictors of academic success.* Accessed at https://portal.ct.gov/-/media/sde/essa-evidence-guides/early_skills_and_predictors_of_academic _success on January 21, 2025.

Harris, K. R., & Graham, S. (2017). Self-regulated strategy development: Theoretical bases, critical instructional elements, and future research. In R. F. Redondo, K. Harris, & M. Braaksma (Eds.), *Design principles for teaching effective writing* (Vol. 34, pp. 119–151). Boston: Brill.

Hart, B., & Risley, T. R. (1995). *Meaningful differences in the everyday experience of young American children.* Baltimore: Brookes.

Hasbrouck, J., & Hougen, M. C. (2020). Fluency instruction. In M. C. Hougen & S. M. Smartt (Eds.), *Fundamentals of literacy instruction and assessment, pre-K–6* (2nd ed., pp. 183–201). Baltimore: Brookes.

Hasbrouck, J., & Tindal, G. (2006). Oral reading fluency norms: A valuable assessment tool for reading teachers. *The Reading Teacher, 59*(7), 636–644. https://doi.org/10.1598/RT.59.7.3

Hasbrouck, J., & Tindal, G. (2017). *An update to compiled ORF norms* (Technical Report No. 1702). Eugene: Behavioral Research and Teaching, University of Oregon. Accessed at https://files.eric.ed.gov/fulltext/ED594994.pdf on June 20, 2024.

Hatcher, P. J., Hulme, C., & Snowling, M. J. (2004). Explicit phoneme training combined with phonic reading instruction helps young children at risk of reading failure. *Journal of Child Psychology and Psychiatry, 45*, 338–358. https://doi.org/10.1111/j.1469-7610.2004.00225.x

Hattie, J. (2009). *Visible learning: A synthesis of over 800 meta-analyses relating to achievement.* London: Routledge.

Hattie, J. (2023). *Visible learning: The sequel: A synthesis of over 2,100 meta-analyses relating to achievement.* London: Routledge.

Heggerty. (2022). *Phonemic awareness* [Literacy resources]. Oak Park, IL: Author.

Hernandez, D. J. (2011, April). *Double jeopardy: How third-grade reading skills and poverty influence high school graduation.* Baltimore: The Annie E. Casey Foundation. Accessed at https://files.eric.ed.gov/fulltext/ED518818.pdf on June 20, 2024.

Hess, K. (2014). *The Hess cognitive rigor matrixes (CRMs) integrating DOK and Bloom.* Accessed at https://www.karin-hess.com/free-resources on November 4, 2024.]]

Hudson, R. F., Pullen, P. C., Lane, H. B., & Torgesen, J. K. (2009). The complex nature of reading fluency: A multidimensional view. *Reading and Writing Quarterly, 25*(1), 4–32.

Hudson, R. F., Torgesen, J. K., Lane, H. B., & Turner, S. J. (2012). Relations among reading skills and sub-skills and text-level reading proficiency in developing readers. *Reading and Writing, 25*(2), 483–507. https://doi.org/10.1007/s11145-010-9283-6

Hughson, T. (2022, August 5). *Literacy: Why it matters.* Accessed at https://theeducationhub.org.nz/literacy-why-it-matters-2 on January 21, 2025.

Hulme, C., Goetz, K., Gooch, D., Adams, J., & Snowling, M. J. (2007). Paired-associate learning, phoneme awareness, and learning to read. *Journal of Experimental Child Psychology, 96*(2), 150–166. https://doi.org/10.1016/j.jecp.2006.09.002

Hulme, C., & Snowling, M. J. (2011). Children's reading comprehension difficulties: Nature, causes, and treatments. *Current Directions in Psychological Science, 20*(3), 139–142. https://doi.org/10.1177/0963721411408673

Hulme, C., & Snowling, M. J. (2014). The interface between spoken and written language: Developmental disorders. *Philosophical Transactions of the Royal Society of London. Series B, Biological Sciences, 369,* Article 20120395. http://dx.doi.org/10.1098/rstb.2012.0395

Inoue, T., Manolitsis, G., de Jong, P. F., Landerl, K., Parrila, R., & Georgiou, G. (2020). Home literacy environment and early literacy development across languages varying in orthographic consistency. *Frontiers in Psychology, 11,* Article 1923. https://doi.org/10.3389/fpsyg.2020.01923

International Literacy Association. (2018). *Reading fluency does not mean reading fast.* Newark, DE: Author.

Johansson, S., Strietholt, R., Rosén, M., & Myrberg, E. (2014). Valid inferences of teachers' judgements of pupils' reading literacy: Does formal teacher competence matter? *School Effectiveness and School Improvement, 25*(3), 394–407. https://doi.org/10.1080/09243453.2013.809774

Johnson, E. S., Pool, J. L., & Carter, D. R. (2011). Validity evidence for the Test of Silent Reading Efficiency and Comprehension (TOSREC). *Assessment for Effective Intervention, 37*(1), 50–57. https://doi-org.login.ezproxy.library.ualberta.ca/10.1177/1534508411395556

Jones, C. D., & Reutzel, D. R. (2012). Enhanced alphabet knowledge instruction: Exploring a change of frequency, focus, and distributed cycles of review. *Reading Psychology, 33*(5), 448–464. https://doi.org/10.1080/02702711.2010.545260

Joshi, R. M., Binks, E., Hougen, M., Dahlgren, M. E., Ocker-Dean, E., & Smith, D. L. (2009). Why elementary teachers might be inadequately prepared to teach reading. *Journal of Learning Disabilities, 42*(5), 392–402. https://doi.org/10.1177/0022219409338736

Karlgaard, R., & Malone, M. S. (2015). *Team genius: The new science of high-performing organizations.* New York: Harper Business.

Kearns, D. (n.d.). Word list for 137 grapheme-phoneme correspondences (up to 100 words each) ordered by frequency. Accessed at https://curriculum.learnalberta.ca/cdn/resources/boards/public/implsupport/120%20Most.Grd.2.pdf on December 3rd, 2024.

Keenan, J. M., & Betjemann, R. S. (2006). Comprehending the Gray Oral Reading Test without reading it: Why comprehension tests should not include passage-independent items. *Scientific Studies of Reading, 10*(4), 363–380. https://doi.org/10.1207/s1532799xssr1004_2

Keenan, J. M., Betjemann, R. S., & Olson, R. K. (2008). Reading comprehension tests vary in the skills they assess: Differential dependence on decoding and oral comprehension. *Scientific Studies of Reading, 12*(3), 281–300. http://dx.doi.org/10.1080/10888430802132279

Keenan, J. M., & Meenan, C. E. (2014). Test differences in diagnosing reading comprehension deficits. *Journal of Learning Disabilities, 47*(2), 125–135. https://doi.org/10.1177/0022219412439326

Kern, M. L., & Friedman, H. S. (2008). Early educational milestones as predictors of lifelong academic achievement, midlife adjustment, and longevity. *Journal of Applied Developmental Psychology, 30*(4), 419–430.

Kierstead, M., Georgiou, G., Mack, E., & Poth, C. (2023). Effective school literacy culture and learning outcomes: The multifaceted leadership role of the principal. *Alberta Journal of Educational Research, 69*, 551–567. https://doi.org/10.55016/ojs/ajer.v69i4.77510

Kilpatrick, D. A. (2015). *Essentials of assessing, preventing, and overcoming reading difficulties.* Hoboken, NJ: Wiley.

Kim, J. S. (2008). Research and the reading wars. *The Phi Delta Kappan, 89*(5), 372–375.

Kim, Y.-S. G. (2015). Developmental, component-based model of reading fluency: An investigation of predictors of word-reading fluency, text-reading fluency, and reading comprehension. *Reading Research Quarterly, 50*(4), 459–481. https://doi.org/10.1002/rrq.107

Kirby, J. R., & Bowers, P. N. (2017). Morphological instruction and literacy. In K. Cain, D. L. Compton, & R. K. Parrila (Eds.), *Theories of reading development* (pp. 437–462). Amsterdam, Netherlands: Benjamins.

Kirby, J. R., Deacon, S. H., Bowers, P. N., Izenberg, L., Wade-Woolley, L., & Parrila, R. (2012). Children's morphological awareness and reading ability. *Reading and Writing, 25*(2), 389–410. https://doi.org/10.1007/s11145-010-9276-5

Kirby, J. R., Parrila, R. K., & Pfeiffer, S. L. (2003). Naming speed and phonological awareness as predictors of reading development. *Journal of Educational Psychology, 95*(3), 453–464. https://doi.org/10.1037/0022-0663.95.3.453

Klingner, J. K., Vaughn, S., Argüelles, M. E., Hughes, M. T., & Ahwee Leftwich, S. (2004). Collaborative strategic reading: "Real world" lessons from classroom teachers. *Remedial and Special Education, 25*(5), 291–302. https://doi.org/10.1177/07419325040250050301

Klingner, J. K., Vaughn, S., Boardman, A., & Swanson, E. (2012). *Now we get it! Boosting comprehension with collaborative strategic reading.* San Francisco: Jossey-Bass.

Kramer, S. V., & Schuhl, S. (2017). *School improvement for all: A how-to guide for doing the right work.* Bloomington, IN: Solution Tree Press.

Kuhn, M. R., & Stahl, S. A. (2003). Fluency: A review of developmental and remedial practices. *Journal of Educational Psychology, 95*(1), 3–21. https://doi.org/10.1037/0022-0663.95.1.3

LaBerge, D., & Samuels, S. J. (1974). Toward a theory of automatic information processing in reading. *Cognitive Psychology, 6*(2), 293–323.

Landerl, K., Castles, A., & Parrila, R. (2022). Cognitive precursors of reading: A cross-linguistic perspective. *Scientific Studies of Reading, 26*(2), 111–124. https://doi.org/10.1080/10888438.2021.1983820

Larsen, L., Schauber, S. K., Kohnen, S., Nickels, L., & McArthur, G. (2020). Children's knowledge of single- and multiple-letter grapheme-phoneme correspondences: An exploratory study. *Early Childhood Research Quarterly, 51*, 379–391. https://doi.org/10.1016/j.ecresq.2019.12.001

Lee, J., & Yoon, S. Y. (2017). The effects of repeated reading on reading fluency for students with reading disabilities: A meta-analysis. *Journal of Learning Disabilities, 50*(2), 213–224. https://doi.org/10.1177/0022219415605194

Lesnick, J., Goerge, R., Smithgall, C., & Gwynne, J. (2010). *Reading on grade level in third grade: How is it related to high school performance and college enrollment?* Illinois: Chapin Hall at the University of Chicago.

Lexia. (2022, July 18). *What is the science of reading? How the human brain learns to read* [Blog post]. Accessed at https://www.lexialearning.com/blog/what-is-the-science-of-reading-how-the -human-brain-learns-to-read on June 20, 2024.

Lin, N., & Cheng, H. (2010). Effects of gradual release of responsibility model on language learning. *Procedia—Social and Behavioral Sciences, 2,* 1866–1870. https://doi.org/10.1016/J .SBSPRO.2010.03.1000

Ling, X., Bai, Y. J., Li, B. B., & Yang, Z. (2023). The application of distributed leadership in middle school classrooms. *Frontiers in Education, 8.* https://doi.org/10.3389/feduc.2023 .1200792

Little, J., Gearhart, M., Curry, M., & Kafka, J. (2003). Looking at student work for teacher learning, teacher community, and school reform. *Phi Delta Kappan Magazine, 85,* 184–192. https://doi.org/10.1177/003172170308500305

Lonigan, C. J., & Burgess, S. R. (2017). Dimensionality of reading skills with elementary-school-age children. *Scientific Studies of Reading, 21*(3), 239–253. https://doi.org/10.1080/10888 438.2017.1285918

Lonigan, C. J., Burgess, S. R., & Schatschneider, C. (2018). Examining the simple view of reading with elementary school children: Still simple after all these years. *Remedial and Special Education, 39*(5), 260–273. https://doi.org/10.1177/0741932518764833

Lonigan, C. J., Wagner, R. K., Torgesen, J. K., & Rashotte, C. A. (2007). *Test of Preschool Early Literacy* (TOPEL) [Measurement instrument]. Austin, TX: Pro-Ed.

Lortie, D. C. (2002). *Schoolteacher* (2nd ed.). Illinois: University of Chicago Press.

Luo, Y. C., Chen, X., & Geva, E. (2014). Concurrent and longitudinal cross-linguistic transfer of phonological awareness and morphological awareness in Chinese-English bilingual children. *Written Language and Literacy, 17*(1), 89–115. https://doi.org/10.1075/wll.17.1.05luo

Lutfia, A., Sa'ud, U., Nurdin, D., & Meirawan, D. (2022). Effectiveness of professional learning community programmes to improve school quality. *Cypriot Journal of Educational Sciences, 17(12),* 4570–4582. https://doi.org/10.18844/cjes.v17i12.8073

Lyon, G. R. (1998, April 28). *Overview of reading and literacy initiatives* [Statement given to the Committee on Labor and Human Resources, Room 430, Senate Dirkson Building, Washington, DC]. Bethesda, MD: National Institute of Child Health and Human Development. Accessed at https://files.eric.ed.gov/fulltext/ED444128.pdf on June 20, 2024.

Lyster, S.-A. H., Snowling, M. J., Hulme, C., & Lervåg, A. O. (2021). Preschool phonological, morphological and semantic skills explain it all: Following reading development through a 9-year period. *Journal of Research in Reading, 44*(1), 175–188. https://doi.org/10.1111/1467 -9817.12312

MacGinitie, W., MacGinitie, R., Maria, K., & Dreyer, L. G. (2000). *Gates-MacGinitie Reading Tests* (GMRT; 4th ed.) [Measurement instrument]. Itasca, IL: Riverside Insights.

Manolitsis, G., Georgiou, G. K., Inoue, T., & Parrila, R. (2019). Are morphological awareness and literacy skills reciprocally related? Evidence from a cross-linguistic study. *Journal of Educational Psychology, 111*(8), 1362–1381. https://doi.org/10.1037/edu0000354

Martin, N. A., & Brownell, R. (2011). *Expressive One-Word Picture Vocabulary Test* (EOWPVT-4; 4th ed.) [Measurement instrument]. San Antonio, TX: Pearson Assessments.

Marzano, R. J. (2003). *What works in schools: Translating research into action.* Arlington, VA: ASCD.

Marzano, R. J., Waters, T., & McNulty, B. A. (2005). *School leadership that works: From research to results.* Arlington, VA: ASCD.

Mason, L. H. (2004). Explicit self-regulated strategy development versus reciprocal questioning: Effects on expository reading comprehension among struggling readers. *Journal of Educational Psychology, 96*(2), 283–296. https://doi.org/10.1037/0022-0663.96.2.283

Mason, L. H. (2013). Teaching students who struggle with learning to think before, while, and after reading: Effects of self-regulated strategy development instruction. *Reading and Writing Quarterly, 29*(2), 124–144. https://doi.org/10.1080/10573569.2013.758561

Mather, N., Hammill, D. D., Allen, E. A., & Roberts, R. (2014). *Test of Silent Word Reading Fluency* (TOSWRF-2; 2nd ed.) [Measurement instrument]. Austin, TX: Pro-Ed.

Mattos, M., Buffum, A., Malone, J., Cruz, L. F., Dimich, N., & Schuhl, S. (2025). *Taking action: A handbook for RTI at Work* (2nd ed.). Bloomington, IN: Solution Tree Press.

Mattos, M., DuFour, R., DuFour, R., Eaker, R., & Many, T. W. (2016). *Concise answers to frequently asked questions about Professional Learning Communities at Work.* Bloomington, IN: Solution Tree Press.

Maximini, D. (2015). *The scrum culture: Introducing agile methods in organizations.* Cham, Switzerland: Springer.

McNamara, D. S. (2007). *Reading comprehension strategies: Theories, interventions, and technologies.* Mahwah, NJ: Lawrence Erlbaum Associates.

McNamara, J. K., Scissons, M., & Gutknecth, N. (2011). A longitudinal study of kindergarten children at risk for reading disabilities: The poor really are getting poorer. *Journal of Learning Disabilities, 44*(5), 421–430. https://doi.org/10.1177/0022219411410040

McNeil, E. (2015, October 29). *Survey explores why people go into teaching in the first place.* Accessed at https://www.edweek.org/teaching-learning/survey-explores-why-people-go-into-teaching-in-the-first-place/2015/10 on June 21, 2024.

Meeks, L., Madelaine, A., & Stephenson, J. (2020). New teachers talk about their preparation to teach early literacy. *Australian Journal of Learning Difficulties, 25*, 161–181. https://doi.org/10.1080/19404158.2020.1792520

Melby-Lervåg, M., & Hulme, C. (2013). Is working memory training effective? A meta-analytic review. *Developmental Psychology, 49*(2), 270–291. https://doi.org/10.1037/a0028228

Melby-Lervåg, M., Redick, T. S., & Hulme, C. (2016). Working memory training does not improve performance on measures of intelligence or other measures of "far transfer": Evidence from a meta-analytic review. *Perspectives on Psychological Science, 11*(4), 512–534. https://doi.org/10.1177/1745691616635612

Meyer, M. S., & Felton, R. H. (1999). Repeated reading to enhance fluency: Old approaches and new directions. *Annals of Dyslexia, 49*, 283–306.

Miyagawa, S., Berwick, R. C., & Okanoya, K. (2013). The emergence of hierarchical structure in human language. *Frontiers in Psychology, 4*, Article 71. https://doi.org/10.3389/fpsyg.2013.00071

Moats, L. (1994). The missing foundation in teacher education: Knowledge of the structure of spoken and written language. *Annals of Dyslexia, 44*, 81–102. https://doi.org/10.1007/BF02648156

Moats, L. C. (2000, October). *Whole language lives on: The illusion of "balanced" reading instruction.* Washington, DC: Thomas B. Fordham Foundation. Accessed at https://files.eric.ed.gov/fulltext/ED449465.pdf on June 21, 2024.

Moats, L. C. (2020a). *Speech to print: Language essentials for teachers* (3rd ed.). Baltimore: Brookes.

Moats, L. C. (2020b). Teaching reading "Is" rocket science: What expert teachers of reading should know and be able to do. *American Educator, 44*(2), 4–9, 39.

Moats, L. C., & Lyon, G. R. (1996). Wanted: Teachers with knowledge of language. *Topics in Language Disorders, 16*, 73–81. https://doi.org/10.1097/00011363-199602000-00007

Moats, L., & Tolman, C. (2017). *Language Essentials for Teaching Reading and Spelling* (LETRS; 3rd ed.). Dallas, TX: Voyager Sopris Learning.

Morrisroe, J. (2014, September). *Literacy changes lives 2014: A new perspective on health, employment and crime.* London: National Literacy Trust. Accessed at https://files.eric.ed.gov/fulltext/ED560667.pdf on June 21, 2024.

Muhammad, A., & Hollie, S. (2012). *The will to lead, the skill to teach: Transforming schools at every level.* Bloomington, IN: Solution Tree Press.

Mulcahy, E., Bernardes, E., & Baars, S. (2016). *The relationship between reading age, education and life outcomes.* London: Centre for Education and Youth. Accessed at cfey.org/reports/2016/12/the-relationship-between-reading-age-education-and-life-outcomes on October 23, 2024.

Murre, J., & Dros, J. (2015). Replication and analysis of Ebbinghaus' forgetting curve. *PLoS ONE, 10*(7), Article e0120644. https://doi.org/10.1371/journal.pone.0120644

Muter, V., Hulme, C., Snowling, M. J., & Stevenson, J. (2004). Phonemes, rimes, vocabulary, and grammatical skills as foundations of early reading development: Evidence from a longitudinal study. *Developmental Psychology, 40*(5), 665–681. https://doi.org/10.1037/0012-1649.40.5.665

Nation, K., Adams, J. W., Bowyer-Crane, C. A., & Snowling, M. J. (1999). Working memory deficits in poor comprehenders reflect underlying language impairments. *Journal of Experimental Child Psychology, 73*, 139–158. https://doi.org/10.1006/jecp.1999.2498

National Center for Education Statistics. (n.d.a). *Dropout rates.* Accessed at https://nces.ed.gov/fastfacts/display.asp?id=16 on June 21, 2024.

National Center for Education Statistics. (n.d.b). *Expenditures.* Accessed at https://nces.ed.gov/fastfacts/display.asp?id=66 on June 21, 2024.

National Governors Association Center for Best Practices & Council of Chief State School Officers. (2010). *English language arts standards: Common Core State Standards Initiative.* Accessed at https://www.thecorestandards.org/ELA-Literacy/ on November 17, 2024.

National Reading Panel. (2000). *Teaching children to read: An evidence-based assessment of the scientific research literature on reading and its implications for reading instruction: Reports of the subgroups* (NIH Publication No. 00–4754). Bethesda, MD: National Institute of Child Health and Human Development. Accessed at https://www.nichd.nih.gov/sites/default/files/publications/pubs/nrp/Documents/report.pdf on June 21, 2024.

Nation's Report Card. (n.d.a). *Data tools.* Accessed at https://www.nationsreportcard.gov/ndecore/xplore/NDE on June 21, 2024.

Nation's Report Card. (n.d.b). *NAEP report card: Reading.* Accessed at https://www.nationsreportcard.gov/reading/nation/scores/?grade=4 on June 21, 2024.

Oakhill, J., & Cain, K. (2012). The precursors of reading comprehension and word reading in young readers: Evidence from a four-year longitudinal study. *Scientific Studies of Reading, 16*, 91–121. https://doi.org/10.1080/10888438.2010.529219

Oakhill, J. V., Hartt, J., & Samols, D. (2005). Levels of comprehension monitoring and working memory in good and poor comprehenders. *Reading and Writing, 18*(79), 657–686. https://doi.org/10.1007/s11145-005-3355-z

Obadara, O. E. (2013). Relationship between distributed leadership and sustainable school improvement. *International Journal of Education Sciences, 5*(1), 69–74.

OECD (2023). *PISA 2022 results (volume I): The state of learning and equity in education*, PISA, OECD. https://doi.org/10.1787/53f23881-en.

Ohayon, A., & Albulescu, I. (2023). Influence of teachers' participation in professional learning community on their teaching skills. In I. Albulescu & C. Stan (Eds.), Education, Reflection, Development (ERD 2022, vol. 6). *The European Proceedings of Educational Sciences* (pp. 445–451). London: European Publisher. https://doi.org/10.15405/epes.23056.40

Okkinga, M., Steensel, R., Gelderen, A., & Sleegers, P. (2018). Effects of reciprocal teaching on reading comprehension of low-achieving adolescents. The importance of specific teacher skills. *Journal of Research in Reading, 41*, 20–41. https://doi.org/10.1111/1467-9817.12082

107th Congress. (2001, March 8). *Measuring success: Using assessments and accountability to raise student achievement* [Hearing before the Subcommittee on Education Reform of the Committee on Education and the Workforce, House of Representatives, One Hundred Seventh Congress, First Session]. Washington, DC: U.S. Government Publishing Office. Accessed at https://archive.org/details/ERIC_ED465820/page/n117/mode/2up on June 20, 2024.

Ontario Human Rights Commission. (2022). *Right to read: Public inquiry into human rights issues affecting students with reading disabilities* [Executive summary]. Toronto, Ontario, Canada: Author. Accessed at https://www.ohrc.on.ca/sites/default/files/Right%20to%20Read%20Executive%20Summary_OHRC%20English_0.pdf on June 21, 2024.

Ostovar-Nameghi, S., & Sheikhahmadi, M. (2016). From teacher isolation to teacher collaboration: Theoretical perspectives and empirical findings. *English Language Teaching, 9*(5), 197–205. http://dx.doi.org/10.5539/elt.v9n5p197

Ouellette, G. P. (2006). What's meaning got to do with it: The role of vocabulary in word reading and reading comprehension. *Journal of Educational Psychology, 98*(3), 554–566. https://doi.org/10.1037/0022-0663.98.3.554

Padeliadu, S., & Giazitzidou, S. (2018). A synthesis of research on reading fluency development: Study of eight meta-analyses. *European Journal of Special Education Research, 3*(4), 232–256. https://doi.org/10.5281/zenodo.1477124

Päivinen, M., Eklund, K., Hirvonen, R., Ahonen, T., & Kiuru, N. (2019). The role of reading difficulties in the associations between task values, efficacy beliefs, and achievement emotions. *Reading and Writing, 32*(7), 1723–1746. https://doi.org/10.1007/s11145-018-9922-x

Parrila, R., Inoue, T., Dunn, K., Savage, R., & Georgiou, G. (2024). Connecting teachers' language knowledge, perceived ability and instructional practices to students' literacy outcomes. *Reading and Writing: An Interdisciplinary Journal, 37*, 1153–1181. https://doi.org/10.1007/s11145-023-10432-4

Parrila, R., Kirby, J. R., & McQuarrie, L. (2004). Articulation rate, naming speed, verbal short-term memory, and phonological awareness: Longitudinal predictors of early reading development? *Scientific Studies of Reading, 8*(1), 3–26. https://doi.org/10.1207/s1532799xssr0801_2

Peak, C. (2022, November 10). Heinemann's billion-dollar sales have nationwide reach. *APM Reports*. Accessed at https://www.apmreports.org/story/2022/11/10/heinemann-sales-by-school-district on June 21, 2024.

Pearson, P. D. (2004). The reading wars. *Educational Policy, 18*(1), 216-252. https://doi.org/10.1177/0895904803260041

Pearson, P. D., McVee, M. B. & Shanahan, L. E. (2019). In the beginning: The historical and conceptual genesis of the gradual release of responsibility. In M. B. McVee, E. Ortlieb, J. S. Reichenberg, & P. D. Pearson (Eds.), *The gradual release of responsibility in literacy research and practice* (*Literacy Research, Practice and Evaluation*, Vol. 10, pp. 1–21). Leeds, England: Emerald Publishing. https://doi.org/10.1108/S2048-045820190000010001

Pellegrino, J. W., & Hilton, M. L. (Eds.). (2012). *Education for life and work: Developing transferable knowledge and skills in the 21st century.* Washington, DC: National Academies Press.

Peng, P., Wang, W., Filderman, M. J., Zhang, W., & Lin, L. (2024). The active ingredient in reading comprehension strategy intervention for struggling readers: A Bayesian network meta-analysis. *Review of Educational Research, 94*(2), 228–267. https://doi.org/10.3102/00346543231171345

Phillips, B. M., Clancy-Menchetti, J., & Lonigan, C. J. (2008). Successful phonological awareness instruction with preschool children: Lessons from the classroom. *Topics in Early Childhood Special Education, 28*(1), 3–17. https://doi.org/10.1177/027112140731381

Phillips, L. M., Hayward, D. V., & Norris, S. P. (2016). *Test of Early Language and Literacy (TELL).* Toronto, ON: Nelson Education.

Piasta, S. B., Connor, C. M., Fishman, B. J., & Morrison, F. J. (2009). Teachers' knowledge of literacy concepts, classroom practices, and student reading growth. *Scientific Studies of Reading, 13*(3), 224–248. https://doi.org/10.1080/10888430902851364

Piasta, S. B., Ramirez, P. S., Farley, K. S., Justice, L. M., & Park, S. (2020). Exploring the nature of associations between educators' knowledge and their emergent literacy classroom practices. *Reading and Writing, 33*(6), 1399–1422. https://doi.org/10.1007/s11145019-10013-4

Pikulski, J. J., & Chard, D. J. (2005). Fluency: Bridge between decoding and reading comprehension. *The Reading Teacher, 58*(6), 510–519. https://doi.org/10.1598/RT.58.6.2

Pinnell, G. S., Pikulski, J. J., Wixson, K. K., Campbell, J. R., Gough, P. B., & Beatty, A. S. (1995). *Listening to children read aloud: Oral fluency.* Washington, DC: U.S. Department of Education, National Center for Education Statistics. Accessed at http://nces.ed.gov/pubs95/web/ 95762.asp on January 31, 2025.

Podhajski, B., Mather, N., Nathan, J., & Sammons, J. (2009). Professional development in scientifically based reading instruction: Teacher knowledge and reading outcomes. *Journal of Learning Disabilities, 42*(5), 403–417. https://doi.org/10.1177/0022219409338737

Powell, D., & Atkinson, L. (2021). Unraveling the links between rapid automatized naming (RAN), phonological awareness, and reading. *Journal of Educational Psychology, 113*(4), 706–718. https://doi.org/10.1037/edu0000625

Ramirez, G., Chen, X., Geva, E., & Kiefer, H. (2010). Morphological awareness in Spanish-speaking English language learners: Within and cross-language effects on word reading. *Reading and Writing, 23*(3–4), 337–358. https://doi.org/10.1007/s11145-009-9203-9

Rasinski, T. (n.d.). *The art and science of teaching reading fluency* [Blog post]. Accessed at https://www.learninga-z.com/site/resources/breakroom-blog/dr-rasinski-art-and-science-of-fluency on October 14, 2023.

Rasinski, T. V. (2012). Why reading fluency should be hot! *The Reading Teacher, 65*(8), 516–522.

Rasinski, T. V., Reutzel, D. R., Chard, D., & Linan-Thompson, S. (2011). Reading fluency. In M. L. Kamil, P. D. Pearson, E. B. Moje, & P. P. Afflerbach (Eds.), *Handbook of reading research* (Vol. 4, pp. 286–319). London: Routledge.

Razali, F. (2020). Teacher understanding in implementing curriculum change in Indonesia. *International Journal of Scientific Research and Management (IJSRM), 8*(3), 1263–1267. https://doi.org/10.18535/ijsrm/v8i03.el04

Reading League. (2022). *Science of reading: Defining guide.* Syracuse, NY: Author. Accessed at https://www.thereadingleague.org/wp-content/uploads/2022/03/Science-of-Reading -eBook-2022.pdf on November 17, 2024.

Reeves, D. B. (2006). *The learning leader: How to focus school improvement for better results.* Arlington, VA: ASCD.

Reynolds, S. A., Andersen, C., Behrman, J., Singh, A., Stein, A. D., Benny, L., et al. (2017). Disparities in children's vocabulary and height in relation to household wealth and parental schooling: A longitudinal study in four low- and middle-income countries. *SSM: Population Health, 3,* 767–786. https://doi.org/10.1016/j.ssmph.2017.08.008

Rigelman, N., & Ruben, B. (2012). Creating foundations for collaboration in schools: Utilizing Professional Learning Communities to support teacher candidate learning and visions of teaching. *Teaching and Teacher Education, 28,* 979–989. https://doi.org/10.1016/J .TATE.2012.05.004

Rose, J. (2006, March). *Independent review of the teaching of early reading* [Final report]. Annesley, Nottingham, England: Department for Education and Skills. Accessed at https://dera.ioe .ac.uk/5551/2/report.pdf on November 18, 2023.

Ryan, R. M., & Deci, E. L. (2017). *Self-determination theory: Basic psychological needs in motivation, development, and wellness.* New York: Guilford Press.

Ryan, H., & Goodman, D. (2016). Whole language and the fight for public education in the US. *English in Education, 50*(1), 60–71. https://doi.org/10.1111/eie.12096

Sanders, S. (2020). Using the self-regulated strategy development framework to teach reading comprehension strategies to elementary students with disabilities. *Education and Treatment of Children, 43*(1), 57–70. https://doi.org/10.1007/s43494-020-00009-z

Sarıçoban, A., & Mengü, G. (2008). Motivational characteristics of foreign language teachers. *Çankaya University Journal of Arts and Sciences, 9,* 65–74.

Saskatchewan Human Rights Commission. (2023, September). *Equitable education for students with reading disabilities* [Report]. Saskatoon, Saskatchewan, Canada: Author. Accessed at https://saskatchewanhumanrights.ca/wp-content/uploads/2024/03/SHRC-Reading -Disabilities-Report-Sept-2023.pdf on June 20, 2024.

Savage, R., & Cloutier, E. (2017). Early reading interventions: The state of the practice, and some new directions in building causal theoretical models. In K. Cain, D. L. Compton, & R. K. Parrila (Eds.), *Theories of reading development* (pp. 409–436). Amsterdam, Netherlands: Benjamins.

Savage, R., Georgiou, G., Parrila, R., Maiorino, K., Dunn, K., & Burgos, G. (2020). The effects of teaching complex grapheme-phoneme correspondences: Evidence from a dual site cluster trial with at-risk grade 2 students. *Scientific Studies of Reading, 24*(4), 321–337. https://doi.org /10.1080/10888438.2019.1669607

Scanlon, D. M., Vellutino, F. R., Small, S. G., Fanuele, D. P., & Sweeney, J. M. (2005). Severe reading difficulties: can they be prevented? A comparison of prevention and intervention approaches. *Exceptionality, 13*(4), 209–227. https://doi.org/10.1207/s15327035ex1304_3

Scarparolo, G. E., & Hammond, L. S. (2018). The effect of a professional development model on early childhood educators' direct teaching of beginning reading. *Professional Development in Education, 44*(4), 492–506. https://doi.org/10.1080/19415257.2017.1372303

Schrank, F. A., McGrew, K. S., Mather, N., Wendling, B. J., & Dailey, D. (2014). *Woodcock-Johnson IV* (4th ed.) [Measurement instrument]. Itasca, IL: Riverside Insights.

Schumacher, K. (2013). *Alphabet stew and chocolate too: Songs for developing phonological awareness, literacy, and communication skills.* [Figure]. Kathy Schumacher, MT-BC. Accessed at https://tunefulteaching.com/phonological-awareness-developmental-continuum/ on December 3, 2024.

Scott, J. A., Jamieson-Noel, D., & Asselin, M. (2003). Vocabulary instruction throughout the day in twenty-three Canadian upper-elementary classrooms. *The Elementary School Journal, 103*(3), 269–286. https://doi.org/10.1086/499726

Seleznyov, S. (2018). Lesson study: An exploration of its translation beyond Japan. *International Journal for Lesson and Learning Studies, 7*(3), 217–229. https://doi.org/10.1108/IJLLS-04-2018-0020

Shanahan, T. (2023). *Knowledge or comprehension strategies? What should we teach?* Accessed at https://www.shanahanonliteracy.com/blog/knowledge-or-comprehension-strategies-what -should-we-teach on October 3, 2024.

Shapiro, L. R., & Solity, J. (2008). Delivering phonological and phonics training within whole class teaching. *British Journal of Educational Psychology, 78*(4), 597–620. https://doi .org/10.1348/ 000709908X293850

Share, D. L. (1995). Phonological recoding and self-teaching: *Sine qua non* of reading acquisition. *Cognition, 55*(2), 151–218.

Shrestha, P. (2017, November 17). *Ebbinghaus forgetting curve.* Accessed at https://www.psyche study.com/cognitive/memory/ebbinghaus-forgetting-curve on June 21, 2024.

Sieck, W. (2021, September 20). *What is cognitive task analysis?* Accessed at https://www.global cognition.org/cognitive-task-analysis/ on June 21, 2024.

Sigurðardóttir, A. (2010). Professional learning community in relation to school effectiveness. *Scandinavian Journal of Educational Research, 54*(5), 395–412. https://doi.org/10.1080/003138 31.2010.508904

Snowling, M. J., Stothard, S. E., Clarke, P., Bowyer-Crane, C., Harrington, A., Truelove, E., et al. (2012). *York Assessment of Reading for Comprehension* (YARC) [Measurement instrument]. London: GL Assessment.

Solity, J., & Vousden, J. (2009). Real books vs reading schemes: A new perspective from instructional psychology. *Educational Psychology, 29*(4), 469–511. https://doi.org/10.1080/01443410903103657

Sparapani, N., Connor, C. M., McLean, L., Wood, T., Toste, J., & Day, S. (2018). Direct and reciprocal effects among social skills, vocabulary, and reading comprehension in first grade. *Contemporary Educational Psychology, 53*, 159–167. https://doi.org/10.1016/j.cedpsych.2018.03.003

Speer, S. R., & Ito, K. (2009). Prosody in first language acquisition: Acquiring intonation as a tool to organize information in conversation. *Language and Linguistics Compass, 3*(1), 90–110. https://doi.org/10.1111/j.1749-818X.2008.00103.x

Spencer, M., Fuchs, L. S., & Fuchs, D. (2020). Language-related longitudinal predictors of arithmetic word problem solving: A structural equation modeling approach. *Contemporary Educational Psychology, 60*, Article 101825. https://doi.org/10.1016/j.cedpsych.2019.101825

Spicer, C., & Robinson, D. (2021). Alone in the gym: A review of literature related to physical education teachers and isolation. *Kinesiology Review, 10*, 66–77. https://doi.org/10.1123 /kr.2020-0024

Steacy, L. M., Wade-Woolley, L., Rueckl, J. G., Pugh, K. R., Elliot, J. D., & Compton, D. L. (2019). The role of set for variability in irregular word reading: Word and child predictors in typically developing readers and students at-risk for reading disabilities. *Scientific Studies of Reading, 23*(6), 523–532. https://doi.org/10.1080/10888438.2019.1620749

Stevens, E. A., Walker, M. A., & Vaughn, S. (2017). The effects of reading fluency interventions on the reading fluency and reading comprehension performance of elementary students with learning disabilities: A synthesis of the research from 2001 to 2014. *Journal of Learning Disabilities, 50*(5), 576–590. https://doi.org/10.1177/0022219416638028

Stiggins, R., & DuFour, R. (2009). Maximizing the power of formative assessments. *Phi Delta Kappan, 90*(9), 640–644. https://doi.org/10.1177/003172170909000907

Swanson, H. L., Trainin, G., Necoechea, D. M., & Hammill, D. D. (2003). Rapid naming, phonological awareness, and reading: A meta-analysis of the correlation evidence. *Review of Educational Research, 73*(4), 407–440. https://doi.org/10.3102/00346543073004407

Taylor, J. S. H., Davis, M. H., & Rastle, K. (2017). Comparing and validating methods of reading instruction using behavioural and neural findings in an artificial orthography. *Journal of Experimental Psychology: General, 146*(6), 826–858. https://doi.org/10.1037/xge0000301

Therrien, W. J. (2004). Fluency and comprehension gains as a result of repeated reading: A meta-analysis. *Remedial and Special Education, 25*(4), 252–261.

Thompson, E. (2022, March 21). *Reading through the lines: The correlation between literacy and incarceration.* Accessed at www.northcarolinahealthnews.org/2022/03/21/reading-through-the-lines-the-correlation-between-literacy-and-incarceration on January 21, 2025.

Torgesen, J. K. (2004). Avoiding the devastating downward spiral: The evidence that early intervention prevents reading failure. *American Educator, 28*(3), 6–47.

Torgesen, J. K., & Bryant, B. R. (2004). *Test of Phonological Awareness* (TOPA-2+; 2nd ed., Plus) [Measurement instrument]. Austin, TX: Pro-Ed.

Torgesen, J. K., Wagner, R. K., & Rashotte, C. A. (2012). *Test of Word Reading Efficiency* (TOWRE-2; 2nd ed.) [Measurement instrument]. Avila Beach, CA: Gander Publishing.

Torgesen, J. K., Wagner, R. K., Rashotte, C. A., Burgess, S., & Hecht, S. (1997). Contributions of phonological awareness and rapid automatized naming ability to the growth of word-reading skills in second- to fifth-grade children. *Scientific Studies of Reading, 1*(2), 161–185. https://doi.org/10.1207/s1532799xssr0102_4

Torppa, M., Niemi, P., Vasalampi, K., Lerkkanen, M.-K., Tolvanen, A., & Poikkeus, A.-M. (2020). Leisure reading (but not any kind) and reading comprehension support each other: A longitudinal study across grades 1 and 9. *Child Development, 91*(3), 876–900. https://doi.org/10.1111/cdev.13241

Toste, J., & Lindström, E. (2022). science of reading in special education teacher preparation. *Intervention in School and Clinic, 59,* 5–8. https://doi.org/10.1177/10534512221130064

University of Oregon. (2021). *Dynamic Indicators of Basic Early Literacy Skills* (DIBELS®). Eugene: Author.

Vadasy, P. F., & Sanders, E. A. (2021). Introducing grapheme-phoneme correspondences (GPCs): Exploring rate and complexity in phonics instruction for kindergarteners with limited literacy skills. *Reading and Writing, 34*(1), 109–138. https://doi.org/10.1007/s11145-020-10064-y

van Bergen, E., Hart, S. A., Latvala, A., Vuoksimaa, E., Tolvanen, A., & Torppa, M. (2023). Literacy skills seem to fuel literacy enjoyment, rather than vice versa. *Developmental Science, 26*(3), Article e13325. https://doi.org/10.1111/desc.13325

Vaughn, M. (2019). Adaptive teaching during reading instruction: A multi-case study. *Reading Psychology, 40*, 1–33. https://doi.org/10.1080/02702711.2018.1481478.

Vaughn, M., Parsons, S., Gallagher, M., & Branen, J. (2016). Teachers' adaptive instruction supporting students' literacy learning. *The Reading Teacher, 69*, 539–547. https://doi.org/10.1002/TRTR.1426

Vaughn, S., Klingner, J. K., Swanson, E. A., Boardman, A. G., Roberts, G., Mohammed, S. S., et al. (2011). Efficacy of collaborative strategic reading with middle school students. *American Educational Research Journal, 48*(4), 938–964. https://doi.org/10.3102/0002831211410305

Venezky, R. L. (1967). English orthography: Its graphical structure and its relation to sound. *Reading Research Quarterly, 2*(3), 75–105.

Verhoeven, L., & van Leeuwe, J. (2008). Prediction of the development of reading comprehension: A longitudinal study. *Applied Cognitive Psychology, 22*(3), 407–423. https://doi.org/10.1002/acp.1414

Vescio, V., Ross, D., & Adams, A. (2008). A review of research on the impact of professional learning communities on teaching practice and student learning. *Teaching and Teacher Education, 24*(1), 80–91. https://doi.org/10.1016/j.tate.2007.01.004

Voelkel, R. H., & Chrispeels, J. H. (2017). Understanding the link between professional learning communities and teacher collective efficacy. *School Effectiveness and School Improvement, 28*(4), 505–526. https://doi.org/10.1080/09243453.2017.1299015

Vousden, J. I., Ellefson, M. R., Solity, J., & Chater, N. (2011). Simplifying reading: Applying the simplicity principle to reading. *Cognitive Science, 35*(1), 34–78. https://doi.org/10.1111/j.1551-6709.2010.01134.x

Voyager Sopris Learning, & Hasbrouck, J. (2023, August 15). The power of early literacy: *Building strong foundations for lifelong learning* [Blog post]. Accessed at www.voyagersopris.com/vsl/blog/the-power-of-early-literacy on January 21, 2025.

Wagner, R. K., Torgesen, J. K., Rashotte, C. A., & Pearson, N. A. (2010). *Test of Silent Reading Efficiency and Comprehension* (TOSREC) [Measurement instrument]. Austin, TX: Pro-Ed.

Wagner, R. K., Torgesen, J. K., Rashotte, C., A., & Pearson, N. A. (2013). *Comprehensive Test of Phonological Processing* (CTOPP-2; 2nd ed.) [Measurement instrument]. Austin, TX: Pro-Ed.

Washburn, E. K., Binks-Cantrell, E. S., Joshi, R. M., Martin-Chang, S., & Arrow, A. (2016). Preservice teacher knowledge of basic language constructs in Canada, England, New Zealand, and the USA. *Annals of Dyslexia, 66*(1), 7–26. https://doi.org/10.1007/s11881-015-0115-x

Webb, N. L. (1997). *Criteria for alignment of expectations and assessments in mathematics and science education.* Washington, DC: Council of Chief State School Officers.

Webb, N. L. (2002). *Alignment study in language arts, mathematics, science, and social studies of state standards and assessments for four states.* Washington, DC: Council of Chief State School Officers.

Webber, C., Patel, H., Cunningham, A., Fox, A., Vousden, J., Castles, A., et al. (2024). An experimental comparison of additional training in phoneme awareness, letter-sound knowledge and decoding for struggling beginner readers. *British Journal of Educational Psychology, 94*(1), 282–305. https://doi.org/10.1111/bjep.12641

Wechsler, D. (2009). *Wechsler Individual Achievement Test* (WIAT-III; 3rd ed.) [Measurement instrument]. San Antonio, TX: Pearson Assessments.

Wechsler, D. (2014). *Wechsler Intelligence Scale for Students* (WISC-V; 5th ed.) [Measurement instrument]. San Antonio, TX: Pearson Assessments.

Weddle, H., Lockton, M., & Datnow, A. (2020). Teacher collaboration in school improvement. *Education.* https://doi.org/10.1093/obo/9780199756810-0248

Wiederholt, J. L., & Bryant, B. R. (2012). *Gray Oral Reading Test* (GORT-5; 5th ed.) [Measurement instrument]. San Antonio, TX: Pearson Clinical.

Wilkinson, G. S., & Robertson, G. J. (2017). *Wide Range Achievement Test* (WRAT-5; 5th ed.) [Measurement instrument]. San Antonio, TX: Pearson Assessments.

Williams, K. T. (2001). *Group Reading Assessment and Diagnostic Evaluation: Teacher's scoring and interpretive manual.* Circle Pines, MN: American Guidance Service.

Wolf, M., & Bowers, P. G. (1999). The double-deficit hypothesis for the developmental dyslexias. *Journal of Educational Psychology, 91*(3), 415–438. https://doi.org/10.1037/0022-0663.91.3.415

Wolf, M., & Denckla, M. B. (2005). *Rapid Automatized Naming and Rapid Alternating Stimulus Tests* (RAN/RAS) [Measurement instrument]. Austin, TX: Pro-Ed.

Wolf, M., & Katzir-Cohen, T. (2001). Reading fluency and its intervention. *Scientific Studies of Reading, 5*(3), 211–239. https://doi.org/10.1207/S1532799XSSR0503_2

Woodcock, R. W., McGrew, K. S., & Mather, N. (2001). *Woodcock-Johnson III* (WJ-III) [Measurement instrument]. Itasca, IL: Riverside Publishing.

Woolliscroft, J. O. (2020). *Implementing biomedical innovations into health, education, and practice: Preparing tomorrow's physicians.* London: Academic Press.

Wormeli, R. (2018). *Fair isn't always equal: Assessment and grading in the differentiated classroom* (2nd ed.). Columbus, OH: Stenhouse.

Wren, S., & Watts, J. (2002). *The Abecedarian Reading Assessment* [Measurement instrument]. Chapel Hill, NC: Sharpen/Abcedarian Company.

Wright, T. S., & Neuman, S. B. (2014). Paucity and disparity in kindergarten oral vocabulary instruction. *Journal of Literacy Research, 46*(3), 330–357. https://doi.org/10.1177/1086296X14551474

Xavier, T. (2022). Bridging the gap in decoding instruction: From research to explicit teacher training. *Canadian Journal for New Scholars in Education, 13*(2). Accessed at https://journalhosting.ucalgary.ca/index.php/cjnse/article/view/75846 on November 17, 2024.

Yan, Z., & Chiu, M. (2023). The relationship between formative assessment and reading achievement: A multilevel analysis of students in 19 countries/regions. *British Educational Research Journal, 49*(1), 186–208. https://doi.org/10.1002/berj.3837

Yoon, K. S., Duncan, T., Lee, S. W.-Y., Scarloss, B., & Shapley, K. L. (2007). *Reviewing the evidence on how teacher professional development affects student achievement: Issues & answers* (REL 2007-No. 033). Washington, DC: U.S. Department of Education, Institute of Education Sciences, National Center for Education Evaluation and Regional Assistance, Regional Educational Laboratory Southwest (NJ1).

Young, N. (2016). *Secret code actions: A resource to support learning to read and spell the English language.* Author.

Zhang, S.-Z., Inoue, T., Cao, G., Li, L., & Georgiou, G. K. (2023). Unpacking the effects of parents on their children's emergent literacy skills and word reading: Evidence from urban and rural settings in China. *Scientific Studies of Reading, 27*(4), 355–374. https://doi.org/10.1080/10888438.2023.2169147

Zheng, X., Yin, H., & Liu, Y. (2019). The relationship between distributed leadership and teacher efficacy in China: The mediation of satisfaction and trust. *The Asia-Pacific Education Researcher, 28*(6), 509–518. https://doi.org/10.1007/s40299-019-00451-7

Zucker, T. A., Cabell, S. Q., & Pico, D. L. (2021). Going nuts for words: Recommendations for teaching young students academic vocabulary. *The Reading Teacher, 74*(5), 581–594. https://doi.org/10.1002/trtr.1967

Zutell, J., & Rasinski, T. V. (1991). Training teachers to attend to their students' oral reading fluency. *Theory Into Practice, 30*(3), 211–217.

# INDEX

## A

accountability
  reciprocal accountability, 17, 53–54
  teacher and team accountability, 18
active learning, 42, 253. *See also* professional development
adaptive instruction, 25–26, 253. *See also* instruction
adult learning theory, 42
alphabetic principle, 93, 95, 253
art and science of teaching, 57, 253
assessments. *See also* formal assessments; informal assessments; *specific assessments*
  assessing fluency, 121–127
  assessing phonics, 107–111
  assessing phonological awareness, 96–98
  assessing reading comprehension, 152–158
  assessing vocabulary, 138–141
  assessment data, 47–51, 77
  instruction, planning units of, 81
  R.E.A.L. criteria and, 60
  science of reading and, 14
  types of, 71–72
  writing common assessments, 72–74
assisted reading, 128
autonomy, 26

## B

background knowledge, 161–162, 163. *See also* prior knowledge
balanced literacy approach, 12, 253
Barth, R., 44

## C

case for change
  about, 9–11
  conclusion, 19
  key readings and resources for, 20
  motivation for change, 26–27
  Reading Wars, 11–12
  school-based solutions, 16–19
  science of reading, 13–15
CBM-Maze, 153–155
checks for understanding, 71–72. *See also* assessments
Cheung, W., 46
choral reading, 129
cognitive dissonance, 39
cognitive task analysis (CTA), 68–70
collaboration
  guiding coalitions and, 41
  lesson study process and, 46
  professional development and, 43
  professional learning communities and, 31–32
collaborative practice, 84
collaborative strategic reading (CSR), 164–165
collaborative teams. *See* teams
collective commitments, 29–30
collective efficacy, 30–31
Collins, J., 41
common assessments, writing, 72–74. *See also* assessments
competence, 26
comprehension. *See also* reading comprehension
  comprehension monitoring, 162
  comprehension strategy summaries, 159
  how to teach comprehension, 162–165
  language comprehension, 158–159, 160–161
Comprehensive Test of Phonological Processing, Second Edition (CTOPP-2), 97
continuous improvement, 40
critical question four, 80. *See also* professional learning communities (PLCs)
critical question one. *See also* professional learning communities (PLCs)
  about, 58–59
  and cognitive task analysis, 68–70
  and creating a reading year plan, 67–68
  and essential reading standards, aligning, 64–67
  and essential reading standards, selecting, 60–64

283

critical question three. *See also* professional learning communities (PLCs)
about, 75
and data, 75, 77
interventions, making plans for, 78–80
critical question two, 70–74. *See also* professional learning communities (PLCs)
cumulative instruction, 14. *See also* instruction
curriculum-based measurements (CBM), 121, 153–155
cycles of instruction, 46

## D

data
adaptive instruction and, 25
assessment data, using, 47–51
discussing the data, 75, 77
instruction, planning units of, 81
school-based solutions and, 17
decoding
alphabetic principle and, 93
fluency and, 117, 118, 119, 120–121, 131
Phonemic Decoding Efficiency (PDE), 108, 111, 124
phonics and, 94, 106, 115
phonological awareness and, 96, 102
reading comprehension and, 152, 158, 159, 160–161
reading goals and, 34
Reading Wars and, 11
vocabulary and, 134
Depth of Knowledge (DOK), 69
Diagnostic Placement Test (Scholastic), 155
DIBELS-8 Oral Reading Fluency Test, 123
Dilakshini, V., 39
dropping out/drop outs, 9
dyslexia, 94, 160. *See also* reading difficulties and disabilities

## E

echo reading, 129
end-of-unit assessments, 72. *See also* assessments
enrichments, 80
essential standards
aligning, 64, 66–67
critical question one and, 59
example essential standards proficiency scale, 73
examples of, 65–66, 70
reading year plans and, 67–68
selecting, 60–64
evidence-based reading practices, system for transitioning to
about, 39–40
assessment data, using, 47–51
conclusion, 54–55
guiding coalitions, forming, 40–41
interventions and, 51–53
job-embedded professional development and, 42–47
key readings and resources for, 56
reciprocal accountability and, 53–54
exit tickets, 72

explicit instruction. *See also* instruction
explicit vocabulary instruction, 142–143
phonological awareness and, 91, 95
reading comprehension and, 158
science of reading and, 14
Expressive One-Word Picture Vocabulary Test, Fourth Edition (EOWPVT-4), 140
expressive vocabulary, 134, 140–141. *See also* vocabulary
extensions, 80

## F

fluency
about, 117
assessing, 121–127
conclusion, 131
fluency growth chart, 130
key readings and resources for, 132
lesson plans, reproducibles for, 222–238
lesson plans, sample of, 131
meaning of, 118–119
nonsense word fluency assessment, 110
norms by grade, 122
prerequisite skills for, 120–121
science of reading and, 14
teaching, how to teach, 127–131
teaching, why we should teach, 119–120
focused instruction, 84. *See also* instruction
forgetting curve, 23, 28
formal assessments. *See also* assessments; *specific assessments*
fluency and, 123–127
phonics and, 108, 111
phonological awareness and, 97–98
reading comprehension and, 155–158
vocabulary and, 139–141
Fullan, M., 71

## G

Gates MacGinitie Reading Test, Fourth Edition (GMRT-4), 157–158
glossary of terms, 253–259
goals. *See also* SMART goals
meaningful and attainable reading goals, 33–36
reading goal formula, 35
student growth goals, 50–51
Goodman, K., 11
gradual release of responsibility (GRR), 83–84
Graves, M., 147
Gray Oral Reading Test, Fifth Edition (GORT-5), 125
Group Reading Assessment and Diagnostic Evaluation (GRADE), 141
guaranteed and viable curriculum, 59, 60
guided instruction, 84. *See also* instruction
guiding coalitions
essential reading standards and, 60
forming, 40–41
multitiered system of supports and, 52
professional development and, 42–47

## H

Hamzah, M., 40

## I

independent practice, 84
independent reading, 83, 120, 142
informal assessments. *See also* assessments; *specific assessments*
  fluency and, 121–123
  phonics and, 107–108
  phonological awareness and, 96
  reading comprehension and, 153–155
  vocabulary and, 138–139
instruction. *See also* explicit instruction
  cycles of, 46
  glossary of terms, 253
  literacy instruction at the leadership and teams level, 7–8
  morphology lesson using an instructional framework, 85–87
  phonics and, 111
  phonological awareness and, 91, 95
  planning units of, 80–81
  reading comprehension and, 158
  science of reading and, 13–14
  science of reading in lesson design, using, 81–84
  scripted versus adaptive instruction, 24–26
interventions
  intensive interventions, 52–53
  intervention group planning chart, 79
  making an intervention plan, 78, 80
  phonics and, 107
  phonological awareness and, 95
  reading comprehension and, 158, 159
  sample of a multiple-round intervention schedule, 78
intrinsic motivation, 26
introduction
  about this book, 3–5
  how we came together, 2
  purpose of this book, 2–3
irregular words, 105, 134
isolated words, reading first, 131
isolation, 22–23, 27–28

## J

Jamil, M., 40

## K

Kumar, S., 39

## L

language comprehension, 158–159, 160–161. *See also* comprehension
language experiences and vocabulary, 141–142. *See also* vocabulary
leadership

  classroom implementation using the science of reading, 90
  literacy instruction at the leadership and teams level, 7–8
learning targets
  assessments and, 72, 73, 74
  cognitive task analysis and, 68–69
  example learning target proficiency charts, 76
  identifying student learning needs by target, 75
  units of instruction, planning, 81
lesson design
  morphology lesson using an instructional framework, 85–87
  using the science of reading in, 81, 83–84
lesson study process, 46
letter knowledge, 94, 114
letter-sound correspondences
  continuum of phonological awareness, 93
  phonics and, 105, 106, 107, 111, 113–114
  Reading Wars and, 11
  test of, 109
literacy instruction. *See* instruction
literacy skills
  as a basic human right, 9
  impact of, xi, 9–10
  reading proficiency and, 1
Lortie, D., 22

## M

Marzano, R., 16
McNulty, B., 16
Mispronunciation Correction strategy, 134
mission and professional learning communities, 28–29
mistakes, 77
morphology. *See also* vocabulary
  about, 143
  morphology lesson using an instructional framework, 85–87
  morphology terms educators should know, 143–144
  reproducibles for, 244–245
  scope and sequence in, 145–147
  why we should teach, 144–145
Multidimensional Fluency Scale, 126
multilinguistic content, 14
multimodal instruction, 14. *See also* instruction
multitiered system of supports (MTSS), 51–52. *See also* interventions

## N

National Assessment of Educational Progress (NAEP) prosody scale, 126
Nelson-Denny Reading Test, 125–126, 141, 158
nonsense words, 108, 110
norms
  characteristics of quality screeners, 48
  using schoolwide norm-referenced assessment data, 47–51

286 | BETTER TOGETHER

## O

one-size-fits-all instruction, 13, 24. *See also* instruction
oral language
  development of, 13
  formal assessments and, 98, 141
  problem solving and, 136
  promoting, 142
  reading comprehension and, 158, 160–161
  whole language approach and, 12
oral reading fluency (ORF) assessment, 121–123
orthographic mapping, 95
outside expertise, 46

## P

partner reading, 129
Peabody Picture Vocabulary Test, Fifth Edition (PPVT-5), 139–140
peers
  peer-assisted reading, 128
  school-based solutions and, 17
Peter Effect, 15
phonemes. *See also* phonics; phonological awareness
  of English, 107
  and fluency, 120
  and phonics instruction, 14, 106, 114
  and phonological and phonemic awareness, meaning of, 92–93
  and Reading Wars, 12
  and Structured Word Inquiry, 146–147
  word-to-phoneme breakdown, 94
Phonemic Decoding Efficiency (PDE), 108, 111, 124
phonics
  about, 105–106
  assessing, 107–111
  conclusion, 115
  instruction by grade, 113–114
  key readings and resources for, 116
  lesson plans, reproducibles for, 206–219
  lesson plans, sample of, 114–115
  meaning of, 106
  phonological awareness and, 94, 95
  prerequisite skills for, 114
  Reading Wars and, 12
  science of reading and, 14
  scope and sequence in, 111–113
  teaching, how to teach, 111, 113–115
  teaching, why we should teach, 106–107
phonograms, 120–121
phonological awareness
  about, 91–92
  assessing, 96–98
  conclusion, 102
  continuum of, 93
  difficulty level of a phonological awareness activity, 99, 101
  key readings and resources for, 103–104
  lesson plans, reproducibles for, 172–203
  lesson plans, sample of, 101–102

meaning of phonological and phonemic awareness, 92–93
  morphology and, 145
  phonics and, 106, 114
  science of reading and, 14
  scope and sequence in, 99, 100
  teaching, how to teach, 98–102
  teaching, why we should teach, 93–96
phonological processing, 92
post-lesson discussions, 46
preassessments, 71. *See also* assessments
prelistening to the text, 129–130
prior knowledge, 71, 139, 159, 164
professional development
  example of, 43–44
  facilitating job-embedded, 42–47
  guiding coalitions and, 40
  instructional framework, advantages of using, 83
  planning template for, 45
  professional learning communities and, 28
  school-based solutions and, 16–19
  teacher isolation and learning loss and, 23
  teaching reading and, 15
professional learning communities (PLCs)
  actions steps in the process for, 170
  becoming a PLC, 27–28
  big ideas of, 31–33
  foundation of, 28–31
  four critical questions of, xii, 58. *See also specific critical questions of a PLC*
  guiding coalitions and, 40
  school-based solutions and, 18–19
proficiency scales, 73, 76, 81
prosody
  fluency and, 118, 119
  prosody assessments, 126–127

## R

rapid automatized naming (RAN), 127, 128
reader's theater, 129
reading comprehension
  about, 151–152
  assessing, 152–158
  conclusion, 165
  fluency and, 117
  key readings and resources for, 166–167
  lesson plans, reproducibles for, 247–252
  lesson plans, sample of, 165
  meaning of, 152
  morphology and, 145
  prerequisite skills for, 160–162
  Reading Wars and, 11, 12
  science of reading and, 15
  teaching, how to teach comprehension, 162–165
  teaching, how to teach reading comprehension, 158–162
  teaching, why we should teach, 152
  vocabulary and, 134
reading difficulties and disabilities

and decoding and oral language skills, 160
and phonological awareness, 91, 94
and RAN, 127
and reading as a human right, 9
and reading comprehension, 158, 162
Reading Fluency tasks, 125
reading screeners, 48, 49. *See also specific screeners*
Reading Wars, 11–12
reading year plans, 67–68
R.E.A.L. criteria, 60
receptive vocabulary, 134, 139–141. *See also* vocabulary
Reeves, D., 41
relatedness, 26
repeated reading, 129–131
reproducibles for fluency lesson plans
  emphasize it! 233–234
  onset and rime, 222–227
  punctuation practice, 235–238
  sentence fluency, 228–232
reproducibles for phonics lesson plans
  sorting words, 206–213
  tap, map, blend, 214–219
reproducibles for phonological awareness lesson plans
  blend it! 185–189
  onset and rime time, 173–176
  say the sound, 181–184
  sound count, 194–199
  sound switch, 200–203
  syllable clap, 172
  take away, 190–193
  where's the sound? 177–180
reproducibles for reading comprehension lesson plans
  making the "clunk" click, 250–252
  summarizing text, 248–249
reproducibles for vocabulary lesson plans
  building vocabulary, 240–241
  name the word family, 242–243
  understanding morphemes, 244–245
results orientation. *See* professional learning communities (PLCs)
rigor/cognitive rigor, 69
Rose report, 16

## S

school culture and professional learning communities, 28
*Schoolteacher* (Lortie), 22
science of reading, 13–15
science of reading, implementing
  about, 21
  classroom implementation using the science of reading, 89–90
  conclusion, 36
  key readings and resources for, 37
  meaningful and attainable reading goals, 33–36
  motivation for change, 26–27
  professional learning communities, 27–33
  science of reading in lesson design, using the, 81–84
  scripted versus adaptive instruction, 24–26

teacher isolation and learning loss, 22–23
scope and sequences
  morphology, 145–147
  phonics, 111–113
  phonological awareness, 99, 100
scripted instruction, 24–25. *See also* instruction
self-regulated strategy development (SRSD), 162–164
Sentence Comprehension, 155–156
Sentence Comprehension and Passage Comprehension, 157
sentence-level fluency assessments, 125. *See also* fluency
Sieck, W., 68
Sight Word Efficiency (SWE), 124
sight words, 105, 120, 121, 124
simple view of reading theory, 158, 160
SMART goals, 30–31, 35–36, 81
spelling
  morphology and, 143, 145, 146
  phonics and, 106, 107
  phonological awareness and, 91, 92, 94
standard scores. *See also specific assessments*
  about, 48, 49
  decoding and oral language skills and, 160
  interventions and, 52–53
  student growth goals and, 50
structured literacy, 2, 14
Structured Word Inquiry (SWI), 146–147
student learning needs, 34
successful schoolwide implementation of the science of reading. *See* science of reading, implementing
system for transitioning schools to evidence-based reading practices. *See* evidence-based reading practices, system for transitioning to
systematic teaching, 14

## T

teacher-assisted reading, 128
teachers
  apprenticeship of observations, 22
  classroom implementation using the science of reading, 89–90
  literacy instruction at the leadership and teams level, 8
  teacher isolation and learning loss, 22–23
teams
  about work of teacher teams, 57–58
  conclusion, 84, 87
  critical question four, answering, 80
  critical question one, answering, 58–70
  critical question three, answering, 75–80
  critical question two, answering, 70–74
  guiding coalitions and, 40
  key readings and resources for, 88
  literacy instruction at the leadership and teams level, 7–8
  professional learning communities and, 27–28
  school-based solutions and, 17
  science of reading in lesson design, using the, 81, 83–84
  teacher and team accountability, 18

units of instruction, planning, 80–81

Test of Early Language and Literacy (TELL), 98, 140–141

Test of Phonological Awareness, Second Edition: Plus (TOPA-2+), 97

Test of Preschool Early Literacy (TOPEL), 97

Test of Reading Comprehension, Fourth Edition (TORC-4), 156

Test of Silent Reading Efficiency and Comprehension (TOSREC), 49, 125, 157

Test of Silent Word Reading Fluency (TOSWRF), 49, 124

Test of Word Reading Efficiency (TOWRE), 49, 108, 111, 120, 124

text-level fluency assessments, 125–126. *See also* fluency

Tier 1

multitiered system of supports and, 51, 52

vocabulary, 137

Tier 2

multitiered system of supports and, 51, 52

vocabulary, 137

Tier 3

multitiered system of supports and, 51, 52–53

vocabulary, 137

top-down leadership, 21, 33–34

## V

Vaughn, M., 25

vision, 29. *See also* professional learning communities (PLCs)

vocabulary

about, 133

assessing, 138–141

conclusion, 148

explicit vocabulary instruction, 142–143

expressive vocabulary, 134, 140–141

fluency and, 120

instructional framework, advantages of using, 83

key readings and resources for, 149–150

lesson plans, reproducibles for, 240–245

lesson plans, sample of, 147–148

meaning of, 133–134

morphology and, 145

receptive vocabulary, 134, 139–141

science of reading and, 14

teaching, how to teach, 141–148

teaching, why we should teach, 134–138

vocabulary gap, 135–136, 142

vocabulary knowledge scale, 138

## W

Waters, T., 16

Wechsler Individual Achievement Test, Third Edition, 108

Wechsler Intelligence Scale for Children, Fifth Edition (WISC-V), 140

whisper reading, 129

whole language approach, 12

Wong, W., 46

Woodcock-Johnson IV Tests of Achievement, 108, 156

word consciousness, 147

word lists, 136–137, 137–138

word matrix, 146, 147

word recognition

about, 105

fluency and, 118

vocabulary and, 134

word recognition scale, 139

word-learning strategies, 143–147. *See also* vocabulary

word-level fluency assessments, 124. *See also* fluency

words correct per minute (WCPM), 122, 129

work of teacher teams. *See* teams

working memory, 99, 160, 161

written text, development of, 13

## Y

York Assessment of Reading for Comprehension (YARC), 98, 156–157

### Literacy in a PLC
*Paula Maeker and Jacqueline Heller*
Rely on this essential guide to provide equitable literacy outcomes for every student. Learn practical strategies for utilizing data as collaborative teams to answer the four critical questions of learning, and access templates and protocols to improve literacy for all.
**BKG046**

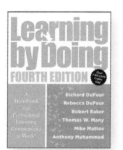

### Learning by Doing, Fourth Edition
*Richard DuFour, Rebecca DuFour, Robert Eaker, Thomas W. Many, Mike Mattos, and Anthony Muhammad*
In this fourth edition of the bestseller Learning by Doing, the authors use updated research and time-tested knowledge to address current education challenges, from learning gaps exacerbated by the
**BKG169**

### Power of Effective Reading Instruction
*Karen Gazith*
Through research-supported tools and strategies, this book explores how children learn to read and how neuroscience should inform reading practices in schools. K–12 educators will find resources and reproducible tools to effectively implement reading instruction and interventions, no matter the subject taught.
**BKG104**

### Taking Action, Second Edition
*Mike Mattos, Austin Buffum, Janet Malone, Luis F. Cruz, Nicole Dimich, and Sarah Schuhl*
The second edition of the bestseller Taking Action delves deeper into the essential actions needed to create a highly effective multitiered system of supports. New recommendations and tools are included to better target assessments, engage students, and proactively address resistance.
**BKG136**

### It's Possible
*Pati Montgomery and Angela Hanlin*
Based on research regarding how to improve outcomes for students and highly effective schools, leaders, including principals, now have a reliable guide to ensure universal literacy instruction while supporting their teachers and increasing reading proficiency for all students.
**BKG161**

## Solution Tree | Press

Visit SolutionTree.com or call 800.733.6786 to order.

# Quality team learning **from authors you trust**

Global PD Teams is the first-ever **online professional development resource designed to support your entire faculty on your learning journey.** This convenient tool offers daily access to videos, mini-courses, eBooks, articles, and more packed with insights and research-backed strategies you can use immediately.

 **GET STARTED**
SolutionTree.com/**GlobalPDTeams**
800.733.6786